WHAT EARLY READERS ARE SAYING

ABOUT *EAST*

"I loved your book."

–Paula Swenson
Greenfield, Massachusetts

"In *East: A Woman on the Road to Kathmandu,* author Shelley Buck recounts her adventures on the overland trail to Asia. She captures a bygone time and place when young people took to the road, crossing the Bosphorus and then the steppes and deserts of the Middle East, to the Indus Valley and the Himalayan foothills beyond, often by public transport. Buck's unique vantage point as a female traveler who refused to be deterred by those who said she couldn't or shouldn't travel on her own across lands now long-closed by war, makes for riveting reading."

–Judith Pierce Rosenberg, author of
A Swedish Kitchen: Recipes and Reminiscences

"A compelling read, sensitively written, by an informed and courageous woman, on the trip of a lifetime. I felt that I was taken along, tucked inside her backpack."

–Nancy Pringle
Eureka, California

EAST

ALSO BY SHELLEY BUCK

MEMOIR

Floating Point

EAST

A WOMAN
ON THE ROAD
TO KATHMANDU

Shelley Buck

WriteWords Press
Pinole, California

East

A Woman
on the Road
to Kathmandu

Copyright © 2013 by Shelley Buck

WriteWords Press
Pinole, California
writewordspress@gmail.com

First Print Edition
Published by WriteWords Press, 2013
ISBN-13: 978-0-9793573-7-4 (pbk)

eBook Edition by ePícaro Press
ISBN-13: 978-0-9829233-8-2 (epub)

Library of Congress Control Number: 2013945905

Printed in the United States of America
Cover photograph by Shelley Buck

For my writing group:
Margaret, Daniel, Nancy, and Shirley

PREFACE

IN THE YEAR 2012, a strange thing happened. After finishing writing my first book and duly marching *Floating Point* to a series of readings and events, I turned to another I had meant to write for 40 years—an account of a distant past in which I confronted my terror of traveling alone and set forth on a journey I hoped would take me to India and Nepal, using mostly public transit.

As I assembled my own notes, photographs, and intense memories, I also hunted, as I had done many times earlier, for the guidebook I bought on Telegraph Avenue so long ago that had inspired me to launch that journey. Once again, I learned that *Overland to India* was out of print and expensive. But this time I found something else as well: A rough used copy was being offered for $9.95.

I bought it.

My purchase, when it arrived, was truly in less than perfect shape. The cream cover was travel-stained and pen-marked; the spine was cracked. Inside, I could see arrows marking up the margins of the pages. Some text passages were underlined. A web address was scribbled in another margin in purple ink. On the cover, somebody had scrawled a hasty message: "THIS IS AN INTERESTING BOOK BUT DON'T PAY ATTENTION TO ANY FACTS IN IT, OR HIS OPINIONS even so . . . IT IS NEAT."

Ironically, I had paid attention. *Overland to India*, published the year before I set out, had contained a great deal of valuable and hard-to-come-by information. The author's hints for cost-cutting were sometimes dodgy, and some of the information already needed updating by 1972. However, for the most part, the advice about trains, buses, visas, and cheap hotels had been sound. There had been few other guidebooks available at the time.

Forty years later, I held a copy of it again. I looked more closely at the words written across the cover. Who would violate a book that way? The printing was a strange mixture of lower case and capital letters and ellipsis marks—the kind of hurried inscription some person might jot down when casually giving a book away—someone whose cursive writing was illegible. I knew this because my own handwriting is awful.

Suddenly, I stared hard. This printing looked familiar. On the pages inside the book, the odd arrows in the margins, pointing to bits of text, looked familiar too. They were made the way I draw them.

I felt sick. I don't like coincidences. And then I felt a whooping excitement. This was my own book! I emailed the seller and she emailed back, equally excited. She put me in touch with the person she had gotten the book from, a fellow of the Royal Geographical Society. A second journey was beginning. Maybe that, too, will someday become a book.

The adventure chronicled here, however, is of my initial journey. The facts are as I recollect them. It began in Oakland during the Vietnam War era—a messy and unstable period in American history. I set off alone amid the slow rising of the second wave of American feminism, at a time when women increasingly were probing the relationship between the personal and the political. As I traveled, the adventure evolved into a quest to discover both the world and myself. I know now that all journeys can unfold this way, if we let them. This too is an understanding I would come to along the way.

As I set out in 1972, the journey seemed to me an impossible one for a woman to undertake at all. By 2013, the overland route has become impossible to most Western travelers—male or female. Wars, insurgencies and altered governments have rendered some countries along the way either dangerous or unreachable. I could not forsee that what seemed like a closed door to me as a woman traveler in 1972 should appear in retrospect as such a rare and open one. I traveled at a brief and special time when the young and daring could pass through much-disputed lands in relative peace.

This book celebrates that open door. It celebrates my friends in farflung places, my companions of the road, and well-meaning adventurers everywhere. I have changed some names and occasionally personal details. In certain unstable countries, such as Afghanistan, being identified by name might pose a hazard to the person I have written about. Other individuals who figure in the narrative might not now welcome the jolt of being asked, without warning, "What did you do on the road to India, Grandpa?" In yet other cases, I do not possess full names to enter into a Google search. But I have not forgotten any of you and the story is a true one. Not everyone is brought up brave, but some of us, by following a dream, and exceeding the boundaries set for us, may become bolder.

Shelley Buck
Ben Lomond, California, 2013

THE GLOBE

"I DON'T WANT TO TRAVEL with a woman," explained the beefy American from San Diego, turning me down. "You get hassled." We stood in the narrow lobby of Istanbul's Hotel Güngör, in the city's ancient Sultan Ahmet District. Timeworn and jammed with longhaired backpackers, the Güngör served as a kind of Council Bluffs for the overland traffic to India—a place to scrutinize ticket prices, plot out routes, and forge alliances before setting off across Asia.

The Güngör fronted on a street close by the Topkapi Palace, now a museum. At the former palace, the hand of John the Baptist was said to be preserved. Certainly somebody's hand was. Touring the display, I eyed the relic in its glass case. The hand was wizened, brown, and smaller than my own, its fingers curled. The palace also held the Peacock Throne of India—or said it did.

In the covered bazaar, a few blocks off, I bargained for a coin bearing the face of Alexander the Great, dressed up as a god. Probably Alexander also got told he couldn't go east, as he staged his Macedonian fighters before crossing the Hellespont into Asia. But unlike Alexander, I lacked an army to deal with hassles. It was 1972, and I hated being told "no."

Europe had been pretty safe, but the prospect of traveling beyond Istanbul all alone frightened me. And yet I wanted badly to go. To make this trip to India was to keep a promise made in childhood. As far back

1

as my memory stretches, the antique globe in my parents' living room entranced me with its mysterious names and hues. By today's standards, this globe was odd. On it, Oklahoma was marked "Indian Territory." The Russian Empire stretched from the Arctic Ocean to Cape Bering. There was a Dalmatia, but no Finland or Poland. Dotted lines traced the routes of submarine telegraph cables. On *my* globe, as I secretly called it, oceans were not sky-blue, but milky green, like the shallow waters in a tropical harbor. Land was the creamy yellow of old parchment treasure maps.

In the living room, the entire family sat each evening—parents reading, children quarreling. At the furthest border of the gray wool nubby carpet, the globe poised on its ornate brass feet like a Jules Verne rocket on a Victorian launch pad. It glowed, as a moon might, with reflected light from the reading lamps. I reached for my globe, as if drawn by an irresistible lure. With a finger, I nudged it. Creakily, the sphere started to swivel on its canted axis. I pushed again, harder. The globe began to rotate more quickly.

Half-hidden in the corner, out of my sister's pestering reach and perhaps forgotten by my parents, I spun my private wheel of fortune. One hand braced the thimble-shaped nut at the globe's top, keeping it stable. With the other, I urged the sphere faster and faster, just as Superman in the comic book might whip the planet around in an effort to speed up time.

Soon the globe was hurtling round and round on its own without any further help from me at all. My fingertips rode its lacquered surface like a carousel, rising gently as each longitudinal seam slid under them. The raised yellow ribbon that marked the International Dateline glided by, a bigger bump.

But merely gliding became too passive. With a forefinger, I stabbed at sea and land on the little world that I had set in motion. *There*, I promised, *I'll go there and there and there.* And with a final thump, my finger came down hard on the largest yellow landmass, halting the globe's erratic whirl entirely.

I looked at the spot where my finger had landed. Asia! The matter was settled. I would go East.

FLEAS

*P*OTHOS IS A GREEK WORD MEANING "irresistible urge." The term comes up a lot in discussions of Alexander's eastward yearnings. In his view, he just had to go. As I grew, any *pothos* I had about travel was well-cut with envy. Back in high school, I envied Kristina, a classmate who had lived in India with her diplomat parents. Kristina told of a holiday visit to a village where residents flung cow pats at people in a gesture of festivity. Unfortunately, Kristina had left the car's window open. A moist cowpat struck her squarely in the face. It sounded gross, but Kristina just laughed about it.

I got a job at the dime store where Kristina worked, so I could hear more of her tales. Maybe some of the aura of adventure would rub off. Leaning over the jewelry counter, which displayed false pearls, plastic bead necklaces, and dangly earrings whose ear wires were neither gold nor sterling, Kristina told of dating a prince from a small Himalayan country. The prince had been a classmate at her high school during her father's Foreign Service posting to Delhi. Where she went on the date didn't matter. She had actually dated a prince! I was hooked.

At university, I envied Barton, a fellow Berkeley student, who had just returned from India and played the *tabla*. Getting the tank filled up on my ancient humpbacked Volvo, I envied Jim, who wore a wooly watch cap and pumped gas at the service station at the corner of Oxford and Hearst. Jim told me he was leaving soon to crew a sailboat in Samoa. From there, he would sail on to Asia, and then journey by land to Kathmandu in Nepal. One day he was no longer at the station checking oil.

Then Don and Twilight quietly left their Mendocino commune, sloughing off their country life like an outgrown skin. Jettisoning the dome, the abalone shells, the organic garden, and the goats, they departed. "For India," they said. They didn't come back.

Still later, my housemate Theo, who had served in Nepal with the Peace Corps, sat on the porch of the 1908 Craftsman bungalow that five of us rented in East Oakland. A bunch of us had hauled out old rockers and other pre-World War I wooden furniture that came with the rental. We lounged on the porch in the sepia light like figures out of a western movie.

It was a time of hair. Tall and lean, my boyfriend Joe sat folded in a mission oak Morris chair, his thick blond moustache drooping like a 19th century bandit's. Stephanie and I wore our hair long and brown and parted primly in the middle. Theo's shot out in a frizz around his face, so that he looked like a redheaded Einstein after a powerful electric shock. Perry, the landlord's son, snagged his in a neat pony-tail. Of the men, only Edgar, who had a fulltime job, was clean-shaven.

It was flea season, and the porch provided respite from the leaping creatures in the wooden-floored living room. A debate was still raging over how we should get rid of them.

"Walk a hairy dog through," advised Perry, who lived over the garage next door. "All the fleas will hop on it and leave." I lifted the hem of my ankle-length skirt to examine the bites on my legs. East Oakland fleas, I had discovered, could jump a foot or more to get to a juicy bite of human calf. I didn't think they would abandon this nice available diet for a taste of dog hair.

"Let's use a flea bomb," urged Edgar, our most silent roommate, the one who usually closed his door and spoke to no one. Having spoken, he stood up stiffly, opened the screen door, and marched back to his room. I could hear his door lock click.

We had cats, which might be hurt by flea poisons, and were still undecided about what to do.

The sun's last light flashing off the gilded steeples of the Mormon Temple in the Oakland Hills distracted us from the discussion. By now the flatlands where we sat had grown dim. In the near distance, headlights jittered and flickered on the city streets and freeway. Overhead, a patrolling police helicopter circled busily, its searchlight seeking out evildoers in the flatland neighborhood surrounding us.

"It looks like the Monkey Temple," Theo said thoughtfully.

"The what?" I had been drifting for a moment, watching the searchlights.

"It reminds me of the Monkey Temple in Kathmandu," Theo repeated, more distinctly. Theo kept a leopard skin, acquired during his Peace Corps travels, on the *tatami*-covered floor of his room, an old closed-in sun porch at the back of the house. The leopard's stuffed head stood up in a startling fashion, its teeth bared. Sometimes Theo talked about the skulls hung under the longhouses where he had stayed in Borneo. Keeping eaten enemies' craniums dangling there made them part of the family after a while, Theo said.

Usually, I was proud of Theo and thought he lent our household *panache*. He was a poet who had dedicated a volume to Laurence Ferlinghetti. He had seen the world, and he had discovered this rental house in this Oakland backwater, with its creaking Morris chair, lace curtains, upright piano, and wide front porch. Theo was good at leading parties of residents to Fenton's on Piedmont Avenue to indulge noisily in towering ice cream concoctions, or to the movie theater on MacArthur, where twin roly-poly security guards, like Tweedle-Dee and Tweedle-Dum, shouted unsuccessfully at the raucous audience to behave themselves, while on the screen, Clint Eastwood stalked silently across an endless desert in a war-torn land.

Theo linked us all to a tradition both bohemian and beat. He had traveled widely and could tell of it. He had found the *there* in Oakland and was taking us traveling in it. I was glad to be included, but sometimes I envied him bitterly. Theo had had adventures, and I had not.

On a summer weekend, we all played Monopoly with Theo's cousin who was up visiting from Azusa. Woodie, the visiting cousin, looked on in palpable distress as we snapped up the properties we landed on and then socialized the best ones, declaring them to be "People's Parks."

That wasn't in the rules, Woodie protested. But we were making our own.

It was fun, but it was not enough. Sometimes, as I left for work at the hospital in San Pablo where I typed pathology reports for a living, I just hated Theo for having led a richer life. There were few jobs in the Bay Area for an English major, and the hospital paid union scale. Each day the pathology reports came in recorded on the dictation machine. I typed them out: "This is the body of a well-nourished woman...." They were never other than well-nourished, despite being dead. I typed on, making profitable use of all that Latin I had studied in high school.

I knew I was not well-nourished, but life in California seemed to be running by Woodie's rules, not my own.

My travel choices after work were limited to routes back to Oakland from San Pablo. The options were two freeways or a country road. Often I took a long time getting home, dawdling far eastward on the country road. I explored byways that petered out in the grassy hills. I discovered a seedy ghost town at the river's edge where a drowned side-wheeler left over from Mark Twain's time still lay rotting in the shallow waters of the Sacramento River. My restlessness grew. On Saturday excursions, I drove out to the Sacramento River Delta. I photographed the new lambs at a farm beside the road in Collinsville, a decaying church at Bird's Landing.

I was fed up with a lot of things and I didn't know what to do with myself next. I'd tried teaching, encounter groups, settling into the commune with Joe. I'd tried cooking and wandering under the redwoods with my camera. I'd tried everything, I thought. Joe made better coffee than me. He also fixed my car, took better photographs, and built a sailboat. We'd shared our love of nature and our money, but lately had not had much to say to one another. Joe seemed satisfied. I began to be not all there.

The lab in the hospital where I worked analyzed tissue samples as well as dead bodies. One day, a severed breast from Surgery sailed by on a tray, its nipple still erect as a temple's steeple. It looked biblical, somehow, or like a cutting snipped from a mutilated saint, or perhaps a sliced pear with a cherry on top—the kind that comes in a can with heavy syrup. Dispassionately watching the breast go by, I realized suddenly I was going to have to type up the pathologist's report on what was wrong with it. I gagged. I knew I could not hang onto this job much longer.

And then I was saved by a book. At Cody's on Telegraph Avenue where Theo sold his stapled-together poetry book, I discovered a small paperback, titled *Overland to India*. The author argued that one could make this journey cheaply. He described the buses and trains and pitfalls. He made the dangerous sound ordinary. I wasn't going to India. I couldn't. Nevertheless, I bought the book.

Knowing such a journey was impossible, I read the book anyway. I had to go somewhere. Maybe I would get as far as Greece.

One day I came home to find no fleas. Edgar, our silent housemate, had set off a flea bomb in the living room, without any further community discussion. He was not around. His door was still locked. My cat seemed to be all right, but I wasn't.

PASS OVER THE NEXT FEW MONTHS. I saved. I scrimped. I begged. I sold my furniture at the flea market. I pleaded. I talked my boyfriend into a promise to sell the Volvo and send me the money. He promised to care for our cat. I found a cheap student ticket to London at the student travel office on the Berkeley campus. I packed sturdy sandals with chunky heels and tee shirts. I packed the *Overland to India* book.

A friend who had traveled in Africa gave me a miniature length of clothesline and four tiny plastic clothespins. "Use them to hang up your underwear after you wash it out in a youth hostel sink," she said. I bought a youth hostel card. I packed a needle and thread into the pack's front pocket, and a plastic rain poncho into its depths. I wore my best jeans. My hiking boots would not fit in the pack. I wore them too, and a navy peacoat from the army surplus store.

The jeans were dark red. Dressed for departure, in my gray camping socks, the maroon jeans and the peacoat, I must have looked like an American flag, but muted. It didn't matter. I was frightened and ecstatic. I was going traveling.

ICARUS

ENVY TURNED TO ACTION on a fine April day. After consigning the backpack to the airplane's hold, I walked aboard a charter flight for Europe, holding on tightly to a purse containing traveler's checks and my boarding pass.

The plane out of Los Angeles was packed with returning Scottish tourists. We were all bound for tiny Stansted Airport, outside London.

I nestled into my seat and fastened my seatbelt. The upholstery felt scratchy, but that was OK. I was on my way. I tried to talk to my middle-aged seatmate, but it was difficult. Although we both spoke English, we could not understand one another. I gathered generally that she had been to visit her grandchildren in Los Angeles and was now going home to Scotland. The remaining details were harder to make out.

We took off, and the plane swooped around in a half circle, gaining altitude. As it banked steeply, I peered over my seatmate, looking at the coastal hills beneath us, still green with winter's rain. I thought, "I'm going to miss a California summer." The plane righted again, and forged eastwards. We sped on. I played with my seat. The seat reclined when I pressed a button. I tried out my tray table. It worked, too.

Somewhere above upstate New York, a passenger arose stiff and robot-like, lurched up the aisle, and attempted to pry open the door to the pilot's cabin. The man's face was gray and puffy, like a zombie's. Led firmly back to his assigned seat by the flight steward, a broad-shouldered Scot, the zombie refused to sit. He launched himself anew in the direction of the cockpit.

"Won't somebody help me with this guy? I can't lay a finger on him," cried the steward. A bulky red-faced man, who turned out to be a professional wrestler from Los Angeles, speedily obliged. He ferociously muscled the zombie back to his seat and pinned him there.

"Goddamn it," the wrestler sputtered, his face growing even redder, "I waited all year for this vacation and you're not going to spoil it for me."

I cringed in my seat. A row in front of me, a psychologist from Los Angeles took all this in calmly. "Wasn't that wonderful how he restrained him with just the right combination of force and gentleness," the therapist said to his seatmate. My own seatmate said nothing at all. Most of the passengers said nothing. I couldn't believe it. I wanted to jabber and was amazed at their silence.

WE MADE AN UNSCHEDULED LANDING in Bangor, Maine. Rotating red lights flashed from police cars waiting on the runway. The crew handed the zombie over. Snow fell vigorously as we took off again. Once we were aloft, the flight attendant opened a bottle of expensive liqueur and walked the aisle, bending solicitously over passengers in each row. "Drambuie?" she queried in an urgent tone, offering to slosh out a cupful.

Drambuie, for Scots, is a freighted drink. Charles Edward Louis Philip Casimir Stuart—known to the English as "the Pretender" and to the Scots as Bonnie Prince Charlie—brought Drambuie to Scottish shores along with his claims to the throne. Once there, Charles earned Scottish reverence forever by raising Jacobites and Highlanders in a rebellion that wrenched Scotland from English control.

Overconfident, Charles had then hurled an attack against England itself. That attack failed. Scottish hopes for permanent autonomy met horrible and crushing defeat at the battle of Culloden in 1746. His forces defeated, the would-be monarch was forced to flee disguised in women's clothes to the Isle of Skye. There the royal fugitive hid out in a cave until a French ship could ferry him back to the continent. In the wake of the debacle, once-insurgent Scots learned to cultivate their yearnings for the good old days in ballads. The royal revolutionary, meanwhile, dragged out his final years wandering the European continent. Still in exile, Charles died in 1788, the year before the start of the French Revolution.

At some point in his sojourn in Scotland—perhaps while pacing the cave awaiting sight of a rescuing ship to bear him to Europe—the prince found time to share the recipe for his favorite booze with a Mr. MacKinnon, of Skye. MacKinnon subsequently began making it for everybody else. The name, Drambuie, is said to be Gaelic for "the drink that satisfies." Or so the bottle label maintains.

Now, barely out of Bangor, and still shaky from what might have been a hijacking, I was being offered the golden solace of the House of Stuart. I begged for an aspirin, too, and while most of the UK passengers aboard opted for tea, I swallowed my painkiller, washing it down like a communion wafer with the sweet liqueur of the dead aspiring monarch. Wincing at the Drambuie's syrupy sweetness, I gazed benignly down like a dispassionate conqueror at the frozen gray vastness of Greenland, thirty-five thousand feet below.

A hazy time ensued. Muzzily awakening somewhat later from the half-sleep of transit, I realized the dry aircraft air was no longer searing my throat. In fact, the air now felt quite moist. Throughout the passenger cabin, water was gathering on plastic undersides of the storage bins above the seats.

Glancing upward, I perceived a cluster of shining globules clinging to the plastic surface above my head. These glinted like a fairy crown in the reflected beam of my reading light and swung slightly from side to side as the airplane gently rocked.

As I watched, the ceiling began dripping softly. It was as if the craft were transforming itself under the influence of water into some older, more primitive structure—a cave, say, with a minute spring, or perhaps some vacant hut whose haystack roof was seeping under April drizzle. Droplets plunged down gently at uneven intervals on Scots and English and me. I smelled wet wool.

Have we sprung a leak? I wondered sleepily. But that seemed unthinkable. The line of thought led all too swiftly to ruptured hulls, passengers sucked through windows, and the silver aircraft tumbling end over end like a lethal spindle to join the Titanic in the icy deeps, below.

I pondered also that early air traveler, Icarus son of Daedalus, who had dared ascend the skies on wings of waxed-on plumes, and later hurtled toward earth amid a shroud of loosened feathers, once the sun had warmed his waxy wings. The Greek word *hubris*—that headlong overconfidence which precedes a nasty thwacking from the gods—came forcefully to mind. Was I also presuming too much by fleeing Oakland, leaving cat and aging Volvo to the care of housemates? Would I get waxed myself and then tumble like some stricken fighter pilot into the shivering surges of the North Atlantic, and have to endure the ultimate immersion in the company of such dour cabin mates? Would anybody even speak on the way down?

I shuddered away from the notion. Dividing like a threatened amoeba, I forcibly imposed reasonableness upon my squalling inner self. *Surely the ominous dripping must be due to condensation*, I told myself. *Maybe the air conditioning's kaput. Or perhaps the plane's insides are steaming up the way a car does on a frosty morning.* Across the aisle, one white-haired lady stoically unfurled her umbrella to shield against the precipitation, which by now was pouring down more steadily. Her smile melded embarrassment with a peculiar smirking satisfaction I couldn't understand.

The flight attendant heaved herself up the aisle again, still proffering the Drambuie bottle, but I spoke no word. I wasn't going to ask her for anything more. I was resigned. My plastic cup still held a few drops of Drambuie. Raising the cup to my lips, I downed them gravely.

AND THEN I MUST HAVE SLEPT again, for not much later, the plane was sprinting down a runway in a gray dawn. And not long after that, I stretched legs grown cramped and unfamiliar from disuse one-by-one, rose clumsily, and stumbled down the aisle toward England.

On earth in a misty English landscape, I looked on as baggage handlers flung my backpack from the hold, wondering hazily if my precious camera were being smashed. Then I staggered with the other passengers to a shuttle bus.

"It's so beautiful here," exclaimed my seatmate on the bus, a woman in her thirties from the Middle East. After a dozen hours in the air (not counting the emergency stop in Bangor) she still had perfect hair and makeup. "How I love the English countryside! Look, look, how beautiful it is!" she exulted, nudging me. I peered out the window, expecting a magical landscape. Instead, I saw trees, fog, fields, a thatched roof, more fields—nothing large or dramatic like a California redwood or Transylvanian castle. The landscape looked like the ordinary New England terrain that we call "back East" back home. I couldn't figure out what she was talking about.

Stansted Airport lay far out in the country. It took us many miles on the bus to get to London. Brick buildings replaced the fields. "There, that was where the bomb fell in World War II," the elderly driver informed us cheerfully as the bus rolled down a block with a gap in it. I saw a hole among the tenements, with more bricks flung around helter-skelter on an empty lot. It looked like an urban renewal site.

We arrived eventually at Victoria Station. Still dazed from the flight and alcohol, I climbed out of the bus and eyed my pack, now lying on the pavement where the shuttle driver in his turn had plopped it. The bulging green frame pack looked somehow bigger and strange. I tried to decide whether the pack had become an unfamiliar possession from which I had become detached or had turned into some kind of numinous object like the Holy Grail, fraught with significance about the journey of life. Perhaps both. I couldn't cope with meaning and jetlag at the same time.

It was very early. A taste of rain was in the April air, which felt chillier than California's. The pack lay like an obedient but expectant dog to whom one owes an obligation—a dog that intends to collect on the debt.

Whaddo I do now? I wondered. Sitting down on the sidewalk, groggily, I thrust my arms into the pack's padded shoulder straps. Even if I didn't know exactly where I was going, my home for the next months was now at least attached to my own back.

But I still had to get up. However, like an overturned beetle, I could neither rise nor right myself. I heard a voice and looked up. The Scottish seatmate from my flight stood before me. She clucked sympathetically as I thrashed on the ground. Again, I couldn't understand a word. Finally, extending her hands and grasping mine, she simply tugged. With both of us working at it, I finally struggled upright.

LOW COUNTRY ROADS

"I T'LL BE EASY, MY FELLOW hosteler said, unfolding a large map on the youth hostel table. Albert was an American from New Jersey who seemed to know his way around. His finger traced a bright network of roads I still persisted in calling *freeways,* leading south to France.

I was in a hostel by a canal in Amsterdam, where I had found a bunk and the company of other travelers. Making my way this far hadn't been difficult. From London, I had hitchhiked to Dover where I found a ferryboat to take me across the North Sea to Ostend. After that I took a bus to Ghent and another on to Brussels. I ate an Italian dinner near the train station and then caught the train to Amsterdam. It had all gone fast.

I had come on a whim, but now the decision seemed to make sense: The city was bustling with young people. With others from the hostel, I toured the Amstel Brewery and sampled Dutch beer. I visited the Anne Frank House and somberly pondered the dreadful heritage of war and loss and the heroism of those Dutch who tried to hide and save their fellow citizens from the Nazis.

At the Rijksmuseum, I stared hard and critically at a giant doll-house representing the home of a 17th- century bourgeois Dutch family, complete with spaces for servants and lots of babies. From an American perspective, it appeared more of a baby factory than a family dwelling.

I was not sure what to do next. I found the city enchanting, but the weather was chilly compared to a California April. Back at the hostel, when Albert suggested I hitchhike with him to France, I quickly agreed to go. We would hitchhike—*faire auto-stop*—together along the *autobahns* or *autostradas* or whatever these European superhighways were called. And I could see Paris.

European drivers proved unexpectedly tolerant of innocents abroad. We set out from Amsterdam, easily catching rides southwards through the damp low-country spring. Albert carried a flask of licorice-flavored *Pernod* and bars of Swiss chocolate as survival supplies. I wore my winter peacoat and carried my heavy pack.

A morning of swift successive rides brought us easily across the flat countryside of Holland. Midway through Belgium, though, the spring rain began pouring down in torrents. Nobody stopped. We polished off the chocolate, standing wet and disconsolate by the roadside. Then we nipped at Albert's flask to stave off the chill and waited for someone— anyone—to stop.

I was irritated that Albert hadn't checked a weather report. I hadn't known about the rain, either, but Albert had presented himself as experienced at hitching. *He should have warned me*, I thought unfairly. We stood side-by-side, with nothing to say to each other.

Finally, a Belgian businessman slowed, stopped, and gallantly took our soaking selves and baggage into his dry sedan. Speeding up again, he stretched his right arm behind him into the back seat, holding out a cigarette packet. I didn't smoke, but I was wet and cold and hungry. Like the Drambuie on the plane, the cigarette seemed a kind of comfort, proffered in hospitality. I took one. Clicking the driver's lighter and feeling a bit like a movie character in a *noir* film, I lit up. Then, holding the cigarette gingerly so as not to get burned, I tried to smoke it.

Rain streaked the car windows. The water-soaked road ahead glittered like a mirror. The car seat was warm. When the driver offered another cigarette, I accepted it too. This time, I inhaled. The car hummed on, taking us southwards, towards France.

On foot again, after crossing into France, the American and I bivouacked on a green hillside overlooking the city of Lille. Rolling out our sleeping bags, we covered them with ponchos. Throughout the night, spring rain drizzled down.

WE WOKE UP COLD AND SOPPING to the yammer of dogs from a cluster of gypsy wagons in a hollow below. We were hungry and thirsty. The chocolate was all eaten up and the last drops of the *Pernod* had been swallowed on the road. Yet the raindrops clinging to the tall grasses around us glimmered and shone even in this dismal daybreak. And the gypsies down the hill, with their hoop-topped wagons, barking dogs, and smoking cooking-fires, seemed sprung out of some Victorian fairytale.

Neither my hitching buddy nor I had thought to change any money at the border. Without French francs, we could not buy breakfast. We waited hungrily in the cold dawn for the bank to open.

Finally, the town came to life. Lights came on. Doors opened. We limped down into Lille with our wet packs, changed traveler's checks for francs, and raced to buy croissants and coffee. Then we pushed on for Paris.

We wound up at a suburban youth hostel located in a modern building. It was miles from the Paris city center. The price was right, but not the location. We could as easily have been in New Jersey as Paris.

It was time for a talk. Albert wanted to head further south, hoping for warmer weather, but I was fed up with hitchhiking. There was little promise that the south of France would be much warmer in April, anyway. We weren't a couple, so it wasn't like breaking up. I wished him well and stayed on to see Paris.

AN EYEFUL OF PARIS

ESCAPING THE distant suburb and moving into the real Paris turned out not to be difficult. I teamed up with a pair of southern California women from the women's dormitory at the hostel. Together, we easily found a *pension* room on the Left Bank. The room had French windows that opened on a petite balcony. Naomi and Susan were taking on the Continent after a junior year abroad studying in England. In a few days they would be going home to Los Angeles.

The two spoke strange English, telling stories about friends without using the past tense or the word "said." Flopped on her narrow bed, with her suitcase open at its foot, Naomi related: "And then he goes, 'You've got to stop that.'" "And then she goes. 'Well...'"

Susan answered in kind. Their LA *patois* was a little hard to follow. It made my head buzz. I longed for cultured discourse on Sartre or Camus. Below, traffic clattered on the narrow street.

Susan was determined to get back to California with a Paris haircut. We three picked out a beauty parlor near our *pension*, only to find the hairdresser spoke almost no English. Susan's knowledge of French was equally scanty. Mine was better. Diligently, I translated Susan's requests into French.

The hairdresser nodded politely, and then began snipping away. We all agreed the result was *tres chic*. Susan boarded her plane home a happy woman, capped with shining hair and giving off an aura of Paris *couture*.

Only later on did I figure out I had accidentally asked the beautician to clip Susan's *horses,* not her hair. Perhaps the hairdresser spoke more English than she let on, or perhaps she simply knew how to deliver a great haircut, no matter what the customer babbled.

I subsequently became more hesitant about speaking French. This hesitancy was to change the course of my journey. Although my ultimate destination lay further east, the City of Light was far more than just a way station on my travels. I felt Paris held the key to understanding how the adventure should unfold. I already understood that I intended to become a writer.

Back in East Oakland, inside a window seat, in the house that I had shared with Theo and Stephanie and Edgar and Joe, along with my unreadable master's papers, lay notebooks filled with poetry and recounted dreams.

Paris meant literature. Paris had been the spawning ground for romantic and revolutionary writers, as well as for playwrights, poets, and novelists. Diarist Anaïs Nin had lived here. So had Ernest Hemingway, Laurence Durrell, and F. Scott Fitzgerald. James Joyce had worked on *Ulysses* in Paris. Even Oakland's Gertrude Stein—who had scornfully written, "There is no *there* there," about her California hometown—had discovered a spiritual home in Paris.

The thought of all these accomplished people meeting and talking and hanging out together in the cafes inflamed me with a desire to connect to this place. Why not me, too?

I was good with words. If I had been less shy about speaking, I might have somehow found my way into the nearest literary conversation, and my life would have turned out quite differently. But not having a voice forced me into becoming better at observing. I was already interested in photography. In the East Oakland window seat, photo prints of the Alameda flea market, small towns on the Sacramento River Delta, and Rocky Mountain mining towns, were piled along with the manuscripts. Just before leaving, I took a photography course at the University of California Extension. And by chance, my teacher there, a Czech exile, had lived awhile in Paris, himself.

I had studied some art history in college, so I already knew Paris was a magnet for artists as well as writers. Romantics and Impressionists and Surrealists and Existentialists, and Abstract Expressionists had lived and worked in Paris. So had ballet dancers and modern dancers and filmmakers. Sculptors, too. Even photographers.

Sometimes major decisions are made quite casually in unfamiliar surroundings. It didn't seem such a major decision on that spring day in Paris when I chose art over literature, and went off to the Louvre to see some. But the Louvre was a surprise. I walked through galleries full of massive nudes and battle scenes, coming away with a general sense of chopped-up snorting horses and Greece—or maybe it was a militant *Marianne* (or some other plus-sized allegorical lady—even *France* herself, perhaps)—expiring in a cloud of boiling dust amid vibrant splashes of red, and with one or more breasts bared like an Amazon. Surely *National Geographic* must have derived its wildly successful strategy of illustrating destinations with images of naked and half-naked primitive women from this cultural font!

I wasn't impressed.

But this was the opinion of a thin American woman with long hair parted in the middle and wearing maroon jeans eyeing the generous volumes of embattled, eternal truths, incarnated naked and female. *So what makes you the expert?* I asked myself derisively?

I was a barbarian from Oakland, after all, so who should care if the heroic scenes reminded me of cartoon animals fighting on Saturday morning television? From a spinning circle of activity, a head sticks out here, then a tail, there, details rendered indeterminate by furious motion: *Bam, pow, zowie*! For France, add epaulettes.

But it was disappointing.

Had I stayed longer at the museum and delved deeper into its collections, I might have come away with other impressions, but I didn't. I went outside, seeking daylight. I was standing on the broad pavement in front of the Louvre, undecided what to do next, when a man approached me. He was young—early twenties, good looking, well dressed in a sports jacket. He looked like the sort of person I might have gone out with while in college. The man was short by California standards where so many of the men tend to be as lofty as redwoods, but this did not prejudice me against him. Actually, it was a novelty to look a guy in the eye without getting a crook in the neck.

Go with him? Perhaps I should tag along, have a coffee, and find out more about this city and this young man. The invitation seemed innocent enough. In Mexico City, a few years back, my friends and I had met local guys this way. We had visited clubs, learned what the exciting scenes were, and wound up sedately shaking hands at the door of our hotel at the evening's end. Everything then was up and up and proper, in fact, full court 19th-century Catholic formal. France was Catholic, too, so maybe things here worked the same way.

But why was this presentable young man speaking to me in this *sing-songy* way? Did he think I was an idiot?

Language didn't make the difference here. The man's words were the usual ones, about where I was going and could he take me somewhere. But I had just come out of the museum, and I was not just listening to what was being said so much as actually *looking* at what was going on. What I saw didn't match what I heard. This man looked unfriendly, insistent. And why was he being so damned pushy?

He grasped my arm. I shook it off. At home, construction workers in hard hats whistled, hooted, or shouted comments when young women passed by, but they had never grabbed at me. I had never seen any well-dressed stranger behave this way. Was he trying to score in some private power game?

It was impossible to feel frightened of someone no bigger than myself in broad daylight on a public square. But clearly the territory in front of the museum was claimed. As a woman on her own, I was apparently a claim jumper not to be allowed to wander about unescorted. I stalked away, feeling diminished and angry.

I calmed down strolling along the edge of the Seine, thinking vaguely how the developed river's edge reminded me of some of the more extreme flood-control projects executed by the Army Corps of Engineers back in California. The sidewalk ended at a kind of cement seawall that formed an abrupt edge to the historic river. Booksellers offered their wares on stands along the steel railings marking the drop-off at the edge of the waterway. In the river itself, the massive buttresses of the Cathedral of Notre Dame seemed to rise directly from the water. The building was a stone island—a fortress. Carved gargoyles leered from the cathedral's heights.

MY MOTHER, WHO WENT TO PARIS in 1939, had brought back plaster casts of these carved demons to use as bookends. She had also purchased Van Gogh prints of the Bridge at Arles, probably from the fathers of these same riverside venders whose wares were now spread out on tables by the steel railings above the Seine.

The prints my mother bought depict the mechanism of the drawbridge, like a giant balance scale, against a southern sky. Compared to the turbulent flux of Van Gogh's other work, they look like mechanical drawings.

As a child, I was fascinated by the gargoyles and Van Gogh prints. Mementos of my mother's own youthful European travels, they suggested an earlier, more adventurous life she had led before I was born. But I was always puzzled about her knack for picking out such ugly things as souvenirs.

Now I understood. What were her choices? To stock up on reproductions of the belligerent nudes? In a snapshot from her trip, my mother is sitting at an outdoor cafe, swinging a foot in a saddle shoe. She looks beautiful, as always, but she also looks extremely pissed off. Perhaps she, too, had needed to fend off unwanted male attentions, even though she was traveling with her husband.

Gazing up at the stone demons on the stone cathedral dominating the bottled up and over-engineered river, I had a sudden further insight: What I was observing along the banks of the Seine was that in Paris, nature, the expressive, the river, and even the temporarily solo female, got wrestled into well-controlled mathematically-correct situations. *No danger of flooding by this river,* I thought, and felt oppressed. No wonder French philosophers had dreamed of Noble Savages galloping across wide open spaces in the New World! This place was locked up.

In the near distance loomed the mathematical precision of the Eiffel Tower. The tower reminded me of a huge banking pyramid which was going up on the site of San Francisco's old bohemian Monkey

Block neighborhood—former home to three generations of West Coast artists and poets. Like the San Francisco pyramid, this older metal tower appeared to me as awe-striking, but impersonal, out of human scale. The Eiffel tower reminded me too of the war in Vietnam from which I was withholding my tax money by going abroad and not earning anything: The tower was another steely juggernaut, like the war. And come to think of it, hadn't we inherited that war from the French?

I was in a bad mood.

Like tourists from a thousand U.S. provincial towns, I had come humbly to Paris expecting to gape at and appreciate the works of civilized man. Well, they were certainly *men's* works! After a morning's eyeful of oversized canvases glorifying war and monuments to technological megalomania, I had to wonder: What was this civilization about? Big stuff? Pushy guys?

I was, after all, a tourist. I still dutifully tried to photograph the Eiffel Tower, but could not wrestle the looming iron icon into a picture. Its magnitude defied my viewfinder, as if I were trying to do a portrait of a giant but could only get his toes in focus.

In my childhood, my father periodically marched the family outside for dreaded photo sessions. Lining us up before him, he used to shout out orders to open our eyes and look straight into the sun behind his shoulder. The pictures which resulted are a studies in squints and scowls of resentment as we complied, blinding ourselves in the process like unwilling *yogis*.

If I was shifting from verbalizing to looking, I certainly didn't mean that kind. I was not going to become a photo bully. Besides, you cannot order a model to be happy or compel a metal landmark to hunch down to fit a 35-mm format. It was a problem of perspective. I gave up.

I WENT BACK TO THE *PENSION* to lie on my bed. Naomi and Susan were surely by now back in California, enjoying sunny weather. I was on my own, my eyes and mind so full that they ached. But I went on looking. I glanced out through the French windows to the tiny balcony extending off the second floor room. No one lounged in the sun on this balcony.

There was no space to safely stand outside without tumbling over purely decorative wrought iron railing into the street below. Beyond the useless railing, I could see a similar building, trimmed with useless balconies, and above it, an overcast morning. It was cloudy out, though not cold.

I fussed with my pack. I spread its contents out. There were too many things: those high-heeled sandals the clerk at the shoe store on Shattuck Avenue had persuaded me would be wonderful for walking, the bulky peacoat with its oversized sailor buttons, make-up, sweaters, the *Overland to India* book

Some things must go. I put the sewing kit, the tiny clothesline and clothespins, shampoo, and toothpaste in a pile to repack and thought about the morning's experiences. Perhaps these mechanical achievements in steel and stone bred their own antitheses as humans struggled to comprehend them.

VILIM KRIZ, MY PHOTO TEACHER in San Francisco, had lived in Paris after the Second World War. Kriz, a Czech expatriate, had climbed the Cathedral of Notre Dame, lugging his large-format camera up to a dangerous perch in order to capture the view from on high. In his postwar picture, a solarized stone bird and a gargoyle brood bleakly over a nightmare city.

My teacher's slim paper-covered catalog of a recent show was not among the heap of things on the bed in the *pension*, but it had traveled with me, nonetheless.

Kriz told our class about how he cleaned attics to earn money for photography. In one of these Paris attics, he discovered and photographed a pair of dolls. In his photograph, the carton containing the dolls sits beneath a rack of dresses. The dress hems of a vanished age dangle obliquely across the top of the photograph, like a slanting swag over a proscenium arch, giving a theatrical air to the scene. One doll lies stiffly back, inanimate, staring blindly upwards. The other doll, wearing a turban like a doll pasha, stares enigmatically straight out of the picture. Its unfaltering glass-eyed gaze is like that of the tabby cats imprinted on American Colonial pillows, whose eyes seem to stare directly back at the onlooker, no matter where she stands.

Caught in the doll's blind stare, I realized Kriz had simultaneously evoked grandeur, theatricality, and decay. Here was a complex and implausible mystery: a regal, Oriental turbaned presence in a moldering paper box, gazing implacably back at the viewer. And yet, at the same time, the abandoned dolls called to mind the post-war refugee children of Europe, wandering in disarray and finding shelter where they could.

To my teacher, the photographic moment was everything. It must be seized. To get proper light to photograph the dolls, Kriz told our class, he had lighted a fire using old newspapers he found in the attic. He had held his camera shutter open for hours as the papers burned, illuminating the dolls' painted faces with tongues of flame. In the photograph, the faces of the dolls—and the shabby cardboard carton which holds them—are luminous against a background dark with the lustrous black of oxydized silver. There are no hard-edged shadows.

Studying my teacher's photograph as it appeared in my mind's eye, I realized I had absorbed Paris before the fact. It was Kriz's vision that had traveled within me: I already carried the sure knowledge that an image can be both itself and metaphor, that an era of horror, human courage and endurance can be evoked through an photograph of an inanimate thing, and that a child's toy and a flame-lit object of veneration might be identical.

I had learned from Kriz that to those fleeing repression elsewhere, Paris could be a doorway to liberation. But this wasn't something that simply appeared when you got off the train. You had to make it. In Paris, Kriz had created a way to live free amid hard-edged realities. I liked his city better than the one I had just seen.

I replaced the things in my pack, gently wrapping the *Overland to India* book in a tee shirt and stowing it behind the underwear, where it would not get crushed. I laid the peacoat and un-sensible shoes out on the bed, to be mailed home. Kriz's catalog in its fading green cover needed no such special care. The physical catalog was still resting snug and safe in the window seat back in East Oakland. Kriz's haunting images now took up space only in my mind and weighed nothing at all. When I retrieved the catalog after my travels, I would discover it included a glowing introduction to Kriz's work by Jean Cocteau.

But it was I, not my teacher, who was in Paris now. And through the French window of my room in the 16th *arondissement*, I could glimpse an earthly street and hear its rattle. The street drew me out. Meekly, once more looping the camera strap around my neck, I went out to look at it. Like Vilem Kriz, in the days of the Surrealists, I had become determined to stake a claim. Since I had not found freedom ready-made, I could at least try to create some through a personal vision.

CONTACT

S TRANGE AMERICAN, onlookers must have thought, seeing me nosing about—head bent like a penitent—directing the camera lens at the ground by my feet. "Is she studying the pee stains on the pavement or watching for dog *merdes?*" they must have wondered. Having given up on efforts to capture the Eiffel Tower on film, I was wandering about, photographing the decorative iron grillwork in the ground surrounding the trees. I shot an entire precious roll of film on grilles.

But it was not really so odd. At home in those days, people were painting ordinary things—cereal boxes and soup cans. Back in East Oakland, I had a whole collection of barn doors, windows, and fences from towns with names like Collinsville, Telluride, and Birds Landing, all lovingly printed in the darkroom and stowed in the window seat alongside Kriz's book. Paris had few barns, so instead, I was photographing other icons—the city's decorative ironwork—its round, flat tree grilles, and manhole covers. It felt good, connected, to record the dynamic textures of those ornate iron circles amid the broad squares of concrete sidewalk pavement.

I wondered about the tree grilles. They reminded me of the cattle guards on California country roads where I frequently went photographing. In ranching country, lengths of metal pipe are laid parallel in the ground at the entrances to ranches where the livestock rove unfenced. Animals that try to cross these barriers find their hoofs get trapped in the gaps between the pipes. Once cattle are programmed to expect such difficulties, it is easy to restrain their wanderings by merely *painting* parallel stripes on the ground. Then there is no need to install a costly gate.

Did the grilles function on a similar principle? Were they more than purely ornamental? Had they been placed to protect the trees against depredations by dogs or to prevent the trees' roots from growing outwards? Or were they meant to keep people away from trees? *Do the paintings in the Louvre establish boundaries too?* I wondered suddenly.

I am myopic, and so was my camera. Both photography classes and English classes had trained me to zero in on the small picture, to explore what detailed examination of something close at hand reveals about the greater world. The Paris grilles were wrought iron and ornate, beautiful actually, but even under this close scrutiny, they also reminded me of the bars on the windows in Gold Rush-era jails. I had learned from my teacher. I had fled California, not thinking clearly. Now I was seeing what was truly on my mind only as the camera shutter clicked—a pile of analogies, superimposed on one another.

When I think of Paris, even now, not vast buildings, heroic paintings, *Folies Bergère* or larger-than-life writers or performers like Collette or Josephine Baker come foremost to mind. Not even Peter Sellers as Inspector Clouseau! I see instead the near foreground, the sandwich in my hand, Kriz's dolls and gargoyles, and the sidewalks under my nose.

A day later, I was at an outdoor market near my *pension*, focusing through the lens of my Pentax on a bin of vegetables shimmering in the rain, when my left contact lens popped out. The lens landed with a click and rolled along the cobbles.

I had dropped contact lenses before and knew what to do. In its minor way, the hunt for a runaway contact lens is like any other quest—say, the pursuit of a beautiful deer or unicorn. It involves patience and stalking skills:

> *Still the inner excitement; watch out of the corners of the eyes for the telltale glitter of sunlight reflected from the lens surface. Track that tiny glint to its source. Pounce.*

Shoppers, merchants, and passers-by were at first curious and then grew concerned about the young American woman stooping and squinting at the street, but after I explained the problem with gestures, they too joined in the search. Meat cutters and fruit sellers and ladies with shopping bags on their arms circled ever wider, their eyes also on the pavement. In their rubber boots, they milled along with me in the drizzle, and peered downward, as I did, at the ground beneath their feet.

But locating a skittering lens in a wet Paris April is not as easy as stalking one in a steamy East Oakland bathroom, even if the lens catches the light. The beautiful cobbles all glimmered in the rain. Everything shone. Plus with everyone stomping around, the elusive lens stood the same chance against the heavy boots as an acorn on an aboriginal grinding stone. Not even a fragment turned up. We all were out of luck.Due to the lost lens, my photography session had caused even Parisians to view their surroundings differently; however, this time there was not even a picture to show for it.

BACK AT THE *PENSION*, I wrote in my journal: "Lost a contact lens today. Mixed feelings. Fifteen people in heavy boots help me search in the street. What consideration! What devastating attention. Naturally the lens was *not* found. Now I can't (don't have to be) pretty anymore."

In retrospect, I believe I changed that day from considering myself as a being to be *looked at* to asserting in some half-conscious way that I would be the one doing the looking. The accident with the contact lens had put that shift in focus. I pulled out my back-up glasses, put them on, and then closed my eyes to think.

My growing commitment to the camera was a good thing, I decided. That outward-looking eye of the lens on my Pentax was sharp enough to record what I saw and show me the truth of my vision. But the eye behind the lens still had a problem. Fresh out of California and an atrophied relationship, it was this "I" that was out of focus. Although I had found the tool to capture the change, I could only blurrily see who I was becoming. But perhaps that blur was because, even here in Paris, at the very beginning of my journey East—and as yet uncertain whether I would even attempt that journey—I was already growing at warp speed.

CHEMIN DE FER

ALTHOUGH I WAS getting a lot out of being in Paris, my timing was off. I was a generation late. I had arrived with some fantasy of myself like a Roaring Twenties-era expatriate sitting at an outdoor cafe–say the *Deux Magots*–being served by a cool and condescending waiter in a black tie and pencil mustache with a towel over his arm. Conversation would be international, intense, and involve the arts. I would be saying and hearing things I had only read in books.

But the Bohemian life in the garret had evaporated. The *Deux Magots* was still there, but to my shock, I could not afford to eat or drink anything at that or any other cafe. Either there had been a lot of inflation, or the expats had gotten hefty checks from home. Or maybe some of them had lied a little, while diddling with the exchange rates to keep afloat.

This lively Paris of expatriates, students and artists had mostly disappeared. Where were the *Apache* dancers in striped tee-shirts, the *absinthe* drinkers staring sullenly into tumblers of liquor spiked with wormword? Nobody was singing in the rain.

In the Paris of 1972, those little outdoor iron tables at cafes where Anaïs Nin used to sit scribbling in her diaries about shocking love affairs, were filled instead with chatting well-dressed customers. The outdoor tables seemed to be—and often even actually were—on the other side of glass walls.

It cost too much to go up the Eiffel Tower. It cost to get into the Louvre. It cost to buy film. It cost to buy those books on the pleasant outdoor stands along the Seine. Even the plaster gargoyles like those my mother brought home at the end of the Great Depression were beyond my fiscal reach. I couldn't even afford to replace the contact lens. Paris in April, 1972, was simply too expensive for an underemployed American English major.

I did not go hungry, but the search for cheap food became a priority. I learned where to buy Algerian sandwiches at five francs from a stand down an alley. These were large and filling, and were pretty much like American submarine sandwiches, only the bun, instead of being oblong, was round as a small wagon wheel.

At night in the *pension*, I dreamed of birds. In my dream, the world ended. Not exactly the world, but humanity. What emerged instead, shrieking and cooing in the cloudy morning of the dream, was a race of strange white birds. *Well, if humanity is done for and this is what's next,* I said to myself, *it's OK. What can you say to the inevitable when it's so beautiful?*

In the morning, I noticed pigeons crowding in the stony niches of the buildings. These cooed, too, but were not beautiful. Their shit streaked the buildings, and no rain washed it away.

The rain had stopped. The weather was getting warmer. Travel looked less chilly and less daunting. To lighten my pack, I wrapped up my high-heeled shoes, took a trip to the post office, and mailed them back to East Oakland. The far-from-new peajacket turned out to be too expensive to mail. I abandoned it on a garbage can, fleeing quickly. After the contact lens episode, I was afraid anyone who saw me leave the jacket behind would race after me trying to return it.

I made plans to leave. I stuffed my remaining belongings in the pack. I planted my steel-framed granny glasses firmly on my nose. I discovered there was a night train to Italy. I decided to take it.

The *Gare de Lyon* with its clock tower and iron superstructure was enormous and daunting. I did not know how to find the right track for the train to Milan. A well-dressed Frenchwoman, sensing my inability to comprehend instructions, grasped my hand and raced with me down the length of a train. Then she stopped and urgently gestured that I must climb aboard a car indistinguishable in the twilight from any of the others.

Tottering under the backpack, which rocked as I ascended the steep steps, I pulled myself onto the train. It was the correct train! And I had boarded at the ultimate moment. Before I even reached a seat, the train began pulling out of the station.

Thus I set off for Florence without a ticket.

As the train whirled away from Paris into the night, I began rehearsing an explanation about what had happened. I was nearly ready by the time a uniformed conductor came by to take tickets. Tight-jawed with nervousness, I delivered it in halting French to this smartly-clad official: "...*la femme...le chemin de fer...le dernier minute*...the unbought ticket...*Je voudrais acheter un billette,*" I concluded lamely.

Pas de probleme! Graciously, the uniformed official scribbled out a ticket for me on the spot. There was a sizable penalty added to the amount due, as a punishment for the unauthorized boarding. I pulled the money out of my wallet and counted it out regretfully. The surcharge for the infraction of boarding without a ticket would have kept me in Algerian sandwiches for days.

Then I relapsed into the seat. The train rolled onwards through the night. The compartment was warm. The neighbors were generous. People brought out food; they shared; they chatted. I dozed.

And we passed over the Alps—or at least I think we did. I missed it all, for I was asleep. When I awoke, we were in Italy.

FISHING WITH DYNAMITE

I FOUND MY WAY to a youth hostel outside Florence. The hostel was a once-grand mansion replete with plaster angels and cloud-borne *puttos.* Half-naked ladies sculpted with enormous bosoms bent precariously from the painted and domed ceiling over the structure's principal stairwell. These figures, which seemed about to tumble out of their flimsy drapes, were no doubt virtues or vices personified in female form, but I lacked cultural context to discover which was goddess, which was virtue, and which was merely Italy incarnate.

I hadn't cared much for French heroic painting and had turned my nose up at the Louvre's too, too fleshy heroines. Now Italy was providing its own overblown allegorical dames, ponderous creatures gesturing in a crowded mythic landscape, beneath which we burdened backpackers must trudge ant-like up the marble stairs like some of Dante's pilgrims toiling their way up the Mount of Purgatory.

Our own more plebian destinations, however, were not some Dantean paradise, but rather either of the twin communal dormitories on the second floor—boys' and girls'. Both versions were as chaste and Spartan as a military barracks or some monkish roost.

Coming from earthquake country in California, I was preoccupied with the threat of these heavily-stuccoed creatures overhead. A king might be brave enough to drowse beneath a dangling sword, but the idea of being clobbered by a plaster virtue from the ceiling during a temblor struck me as a particularly cheesy way to make an exit. I had heard Italy had earthquakes. Volcanoes, too. Wasn't Mt. Vesuvius around somewhere?

There was something repellant about the contrast between the worlds of ceiling and staircase that primed my thoughts for contemplation of unpleasant extremes. This hostel, I was sure, had stood witness to plenty of them.

The hostel, a bus ride out of Florence—or *Firenze*—as I was learning to call it, had come down in the world. Although it now housed itinerant students and other wanderers journeying from America, Canada, and Northern Europe to gawk excitedly at Michelangelo's *David* and the Botticelli *Venus*, the building was itself the former country hideaway of Mussolini's mistress. The estate's descent from love nest to communal kitchen and bunks for wandering youth seemed a final insult to the unknown departed courtesan who had unwisely chosen *Il Duce* for a lover. Or perhaps, once Mussolini fell astern, the lady, as courtesans sometimes do, had jumped ship and allowed herself to be rescued by some new-arriving Allied general.

I realized I would need to study up on a little more history.

Pacing the grounds outside, with the shadow of war on my mind, I paused to light a cigarette on the grand steps out in front of the august decaying dwelling. I had been smoking for over a week now, ever since that rainy ride through Belgium. I felt I could now grasp the cigarette securely with a greater nonchalance. I paused on a broad entry step and passed time in conversation with an Israeli backpacker. Moshe said he was freshly released from his mandatory military service, so naturally I asked him about war.

But you don't always get what you ask for. Moshe told me, not of the alarms and uproar of the Seven Days' War—not long past—but rather of his adventures catching fish with dynamite, a skill he mastered while serving in the Israeli Army. His English grew better as he narrated the sequence: the flinging of the lit sticks into the river, the pause to watch the ensuing explosions erupt in watery fountains. He told with satisfaction of the appearance of gasping stunned creatures as they floated to the surface for harvesting.

Once he was certain I was suitably shocked, Moshe shifted personas disconcertingly. He began to lecture me on the art of travel. "Always, always, pick up the free literature at places like this," he advised. The maps on the free handouts would save me the cost of buying expensive city street maps, he said. I nodded, a bit overwhelmed.

Having related this advice, Moshe ground out his cigarette with his heel on Mussolini's mistress's front steps and retreated inside to climb back up the marble staircase beneath the frolicking deities and cupids.

I was so struck by the irony of an Israeli warrior so literally treading in the footsteps of *Il Duce* that he might as well have clobbered me with a stunned trout. Carefully, I stubbed out my own cigarette. Once again I had forgotten to inhale. Then I too marched up the grand staircase, taking note of the acorn-sized genitals on the *puttos*. *If Mussolini had been into comparing sizes, these must have offered some comfort*, I thought, rather nastily, for I had no use for dictators.

After reaching the spartan women's dormitory, I unrolled my sleeping bag, reflexively reminding myself that I must make sure to grab the free literature whenever it was offered. Such frugality made sense for someone on a budget as tight as mine. It was good advice, and I was still learning how to travel.

Somewhere along this bouncing line of reasoning, the mistress, and *IL Duce's* ghost escaped out the back. Years later, in the age of Google, I would set out to track them down, but I had no luck. Predictably, however, I still follow Moshe's suggestion and pick up any literature offered for free at tourist bureaus, museums, and galleries.

In Firenze, I viewed the gigantic statue of David in a circular room shaped remarkably like a condom. At the Uffizi Gallery, I gazed on Botticelli's painting of Venus rising from the sea. This Venus—riding her seashell like a well-balanced boogie board—was not some fleshy giantess. Unlike the oversized female personages of the youth hostel, Venus was proportioned more on the scale of a real, living woman. She was skinnier. *Good for her!* I thought. I noticed the entire painting was only an inch or two taller than I was.

Did I eat a hot tripe sandwich from a stand, after paying entry fees and buying bread and cheese to take back to the hostel for my dinner?

The truth is that I don't remember. What sticks instead is my vivid memory of peering at my wallet and realizing its contents had shriveled. Regretfully, I passed by venders' stalls offering bookmarks stamped with rich golden filigree patterns. There was not enough money for souvenirs. As I climbed on the bus back to the hostel, I realized I must go somewhere cheaper still, and quickly.

Greece!

THE ROAD SOUTH

KIMMY FROM NEW HAVEN, a neighbor in the women's dormitory, also wanted to go to Greece. We set forth the next morning, hitchhiking southwards on the *autostrada*. Our plan was to go first to Naples, on the shin of the boot-shaped Italian peninsula; from there, we could cross over to to Brindisi, perched on the peninsula's stiletto heel. From Brindisi, a ferry crossed the Adriatic Sea to Greece.

The road trip went fast. We had no trouble getting rides. Kimmy's waist-length Pre-Raphaelite red hair stopped traffic everywhere. She was traveling while considering whether to divorce her husband. There had been a sexual tangle and mutual adulteries, Kimmy explained. She told me she loved going to health clubs: "You can be there with other people, but be alone."

The thought resonated. Perhaps that was what all those ceiling sculptures in the hostel had been for—to provide *Il Duce* and his sweetie with the comfort of not being alone without creating any need to talk. The buxom statues wouldn't have disagreed with him, as living fellow-residents might have. They wouldn't have spoken up to caution the Italian dictator against making any chummy deals with that Hitler guy. Sometimes you need friends to warn you if you are about to make a big mistake. I wondered if Mussolini, when they were taking him out to hang him, had finally realized that keeping company with uncritical statues was a bad idea. They had certainly been in awful taste.

I realized, too, that I was accomplishing being alone in a crowd by traveling. Unlike Mussolini, I didn't need any statues to create the illusion.

But traveling with Kimmy that day wasn't contributing to solitude. Her flaming hair attracted attention everywhere. The rides came swiftly, and the drivers were invariably courteous. We learned it is possible to stuff more passengers and their packs into a Fiat 500 when four Italian naval officers already occupying the tiny vehicle stopped for us.

As we struggled to talk in the tiny car, I shared the only Italian I knew beyond phrasebook fare, a passage from Dante. *"Nel mezzo del cammin di nostra vita mi ritrovai per una selva oscura..."* I began reciting. ("In the middle of the road of my life, I found myself on an unknown path...") Recognizing at once the opening lines of the *Inferno*, the officers cried out with appreciation. I had stunned these men by quoting Dante. Suddenly I was glad I had taken that college class on the Classics in Translation. While I was surely not the first wanderer to recite Dante in Italy, the words had cut through the surface differences to a shared reality. Italian and American, we agreed on the big issues, clearly.

The overloaded little Fiat bobbled harmoniously along the sun-bright *autostrada*, heading southwards into warmer weather. The only shadows on our moods occurred with occasional sightings of *carabinieri*, members of the dark-uniformed national police, who carried long guns and cultivated a menacing attitude. They seemed holdovers from Italy's Fascist past. After only a few days in the country, I was already learning to fear and despise these men—an attitude picked up almost by osmosis from the moods of people around me. This was another, less poetic, commonality.

The young officers dropped us off in Naples, at a crowded intersection, where we might catch a bus going past the youth hostel. A bus stood at the stand, but as Kimmy and I squeezed ourselves out of the little Fiat, the bus began pulling away. Snatching up our packs, we raced after the moving bus through a cloud of diesel exhaust.

The driver heard our frantic shouts, or perhaps Kimmy's hair again worked its magic, for with a screech of brakes, the bus driver gallantly ground to a halt. As we dragged our packs up the steps and into the vehicle's shadowed interior, I was thinking, "Italy sure is gracious." This was not like riding an elevator at a temp job, jammed together with silent people trying to shrink away. Once again, we were crushed in with humanity that gave back. I was charmed.

But neither Kimmy nor I could hang around Naples. Both of us needed to get to Greece. The next morning we caught a bus to Brindisi. Somewhere along the way, the bus passed strange cone-shaped houses. *Trulli,* someone called them. The stone dwellings baking in the sunlight looked a little like the geodesic domes people were putting up at the old farm in Mendocino where Don and Twilight had kept goats before departing on their journey to India. But while the California domes had been new structures built in an effort to get back to the earth, these pointy-topped buildings seemed genuinely primordial. They looked Neolithic.

Somewhere deep within, I sensed my grip on time loosening. That peasants and shepherds and frolicking sheep might also appear under my nose as living things rather than book illustrations became plausible. Why not? The thought was disorienting, but not unpleasantly so. While Kimmy scribbled out postcards on the aisle side of the seat, I pressed my face to the window, hoping to see more strangeness—as if the window were a television screen and the vista just outside a set for the *Twilight Zone.* I couldn't really absorb this change, but I didn't want to miss a bit.

THE GREEK FERRY

I N THE AFTERNOON, the bus reached Brindisi on the Adriatic coast. We were suddenly back in modern times—up to the 18th century at least. We walked along the waterfront looking for the ferry. Kimmy found stamps somewhere and stuffed her postcards in a mail slot. We bought boat tickets to Greece from a broker.

The boat was to leave in two hours. We killed time eating thin pizza at a stand. It had only tomato sauce on it. "This is what pizza really is," I thought—not the topping-loaded stuff on puffy crust I usually devoured at home, which came billed as "the real thing" from New York. Brindisi's pizza, if not as tasty, was at least authentic.

Then we boarded the ferry for the first leg of the journey that would take us across the Adriatic to the Greek island of Corfu—*Kerkyra*. After walking all over the big old boat, and looking over its cafe, its bursar's office, and its series of decks, I selected a bench inside by the coffee bar and dumped my pack beside it. It had been a tiring scramble to reach Brindisi. Now, as the engines grumbled and the big boat swung out into the Adriatic Sea, I curled up, letting, the vessel's gentle motion rock me in this hard nest. In no time, I was asleep.

Later, as the dawn brightened on the water, I went out on deck. A high green island appeared to one side. We had come around the island in the night and were now running along a strait between the island's eastern coast and the mainland. The island was Corfu.

On the mainland shore just to the east, lay forbidden Albania, closed off from Europe by a radical communist government. I had never seen a communist country before: It looked grey and grim in the dawn, and uninteresting. I turned my eyes back westward, to Corfu. We were approaching port.

As the ferry from Brindisi angled heavily towards the dock, I wrestled my pack again onto my back. The pack was lighter now without the dressy shoes and winter coat. Shrugging the straps higher on my shoulders and tightening the special patented belt, which was supposed to protect me from back injuries according to the salesman at the Berkeley Co-op where I bought it, I walked off the ferry into the Greek morning.

A short bus ride away, the island's youth hostel perched in the highlands by a flowering meadow. Warm weather had arrived; or rather I had traveled to meet it. That evening fireflies as big as damselflies lit up the dusk, swooping like the fairies in the Max Reinhardt movie version of *Midsummer Night's Dream*. California had no fireflies, but I could remember them from when I was growing up on the East Coast. I was grown up now and I had no jar to catch lightning bugs with, but I ran through the field by the hostel anyway, stretching out my arms and flapping them joyously among the darting lights.

In the morning, I was grateful for this brief regression into childhood, but by light of day this leafy paradise seemed too familiar. It was not foreign enough. I was looking for an island stark with Cubist villages, white as bones, surrounded by the strange turquoise waters I had heard about. While Kimmy stayed behind to drink in Corfu, I left by boat and bus for Athens, on my way east to the Aegean. Perhaps, after all the richness and chumminess of Italy, I was really craving a desert island.

WITH ATHENS YOU GET SOUVLAKI

UT BEFORE THAT, I would have to deal with Athens. I left Corfu by ferryboat again, but not for long. At Patras, a westernmost port of the Peloponnesian Peninsula, the boat unloaded its load of Greeks and tourists and travelers. Most hustled aboard a waiting bus for the run to Athens.

In Athens, after climbing wearily off the bus, we non-Greeks retrieved our packs from the luggage bins and hoisted them again onto our backs. Then we stood, mystified and groggy, on the narrow cement sidewalk.

What next? Nobody knew.

All of us were befuddled. A throng of babbling English speakers with backpacks on our shoulders, we milled indecisively as downtown traffic whizzed by only inches away.

We needed a youth hostel. We needed showers. We needed clean toilets. But although we were certainly downtown in a busy city, we were just as certainly lost. Modern Athens, bustling with jolting, smoke-breathing buses, motorcycles, sedans, and delivery trucks, bore street signs like any other European capital; however, these looked more like interesting equations than usable information, for the street signs all were written in the Greek alphabet. Like most Americans, I had studied Latin in high school. Greek was not offered. I could read the Greek letters used by American college fraternities, but this was not much help.

We had no basis for complaining. When in Greece, expect Greek, right? Everyone acknowledged this. What we hadn't expected was the effect on us. Without our familiar Latin alphabet, we were helpless, functionally illiterate.

A businessman in a dark suit, observing the cluster of foreigners blocking all foot traffic on the narrow sidewalk, stepped in to rescue us. He gestured directions and pointed out the bus to the youth hostel. I suspected that this experience, which was unique to us, presented a daily challenge to hurrying Athens residents whenever the bus from the ferry arrived. Helping bemused tourists was not entirely altruistic. Perhaps anyone who had to get through this street would have pitched in to get us moving.

And then we were on a city bus, plowing through the urban traffic. Once again, the hostel we sought was located a long way out of town—this time in a boring suburb. After Paris, I knew what to do. I quickly recruited fellow travelers to share a guesthouse room back in the old city near the winding hilly alleys of the Plaka neighborhood. Quickly, too, I was out the door and hunting for an older, quieter Greece.

I did not have to go far. On the hilltop above stood the Acropolis. There I saw the roofless ruined Parthenon; many of its sculptures had been lugged away generations ago to the British Museum. Nearby, on the side of the Erechtheion, I discovered the less-famous Porch of the Caryatids. There, dignified female figures acted as columns, holding up the marble-clad cornice above their heads. I wondered if these load-bearing females had been models for the many overblown and underdressed allegorical sculptures which had dogged my journey up to now. Were these even the original figures, or copies? I didn't know, but they were powerful and stately. Despite the Caryatids' body-hugging draperies, I felt I was looking for the first time at likenesses of women crafted with pride rather than prurience.

Turning from ancient art, and peering down from these once-sacred heights, I could see a teeming smoggy city below. I went down to it.

At a street stand, I bought *souvlaki*, a sandwich of lamb sliced from an upright spit, then wrapped in a thick round of pita bread and slathered with *tzatziki*, a sauce of yoghurt and cucumber. It was delicious. I paid for it in *drachmae.* There were thirty Greek *drachmae* to the dollar, and for the first time, I did not feel the need to wince as I counted out money. Athens might be ancient and smoggy and grimy, but it was also homey and affordable. I loved the place.

However, my heart was still set on a high stony island. "You will be amazed by the color of the Aegean," my friend Ellen had told me before I left California. It was like nothing she had seen before. She showed me a photo-portrait she had made on Mikonos—an old man in a seaman's cap posing before a white stucco wall, as stately and as dignified as one of the female figures on the Athens hilltop. Beside the old man, a birdcage swung from a nail pounded into the wall. I imagined a canary within it, sitting and singing. As with Paris, I had been hooked beforehand by a photograph. I must see this place!

But while Paris still looked like the Paris of my fantasies, Mikonos, where Ellen had been, was now completely changed. I heard the island had become a jet-set haven, crowded with wealthy beautiful people and their big boats. A neighboring island, Ios, remained rustic and cheap. It had the kind of snowy white village I was craving. I decided to go there, instead.

But first, I must buy film. After mailing the film I shot in Paris back to California, I had been moving too fast to purchase more. Now I bought a few rolls of black-and-white film at a small shop near Syntagma Square. They were expensive. Color film cost even more. I splurged on a single roll and tucked it away, hoping it had not been too badly damaged by baking in the shop's sunlit window. I would save it for something very special.

From Piraeus, the big port by Athens, I caught a ferry heading south into the Aegean. I staked out my place in a deep chair which looked and felt like a recliner in a better-class airline waiting room. The night was warm. As the boat's engines hummed and rumbled, I fell asleep, much as a baby does when placed next to a running vacuum cleaner. I dreamed of being cared for and nurtured.

THE CAVE

ARLY IN THE GRAY dawn, I roused from sleep washed of all thought, not knowing who or where I was

On the deck outside I met an American returning to the island. We shared his cheese with my bread and water. It was simple food. The urban luxuries of chocolate and Pernod lay far behind me in the chilly north.

Throughout the day, I watched from the high deck as the ship stopped at various islands, dropping passengers, taking on goods.

When we got to it, the harbor at Ios was too tiny for the huge ferryboat to come in to port. The big boat merely paused, its propellers holding it in place, while smaller watercraft scurried out from the tiny waterfront to take goods and passengers ashore. Following the others disembarking, I climbed down ferry's rocking side, handed my pack to the boatmen, and leaped the last foot or two into a motorized launch. This *caique* carried me me to the *paralia*–or waterfront. There, on a tiny esplanade, out in front of a small cafe, some Americans lounged in rush-seated chairs at a table covered with checkered oil cloth. Everything looked just as I thought a Greek Island should.

The cafe's customers rose and cheered as the *caiques* arrived. They hugged the returning travelers stepping out of the small boats.

I passed by these reunions, following my acquaintance from the boat. Still following Ernie, I climbed a steep stone trail to a small, whitewashed town high above the *paralia*. Here, there were no cars for the island had no real roads. Ernie pointed out the sights as we climbed through the village. Here was the post office; there the police station. The diamond-white houses were piled one upon another like Anasazi dwellings in the American Southwest. The buildings spoke of generations of living in close proximity to neighbors.

"Be very discreet with your dope," Ernie whispered. He didn't need to warn me. I knew about the military Junta which had taken over the Greek government and that the mainland had become a police state. I carried nothing illegal.

"This is the place where there will be a road next year," he said, pointing ahead. "They'll bring cars, hotels." He didn't say who *they* were and I didn't see how a hotel could be fitted in. The way through the town was barely wider than a path, which shifted into steps without warning as the land grew steeper. Even to put in a road, you would have to tear down half the houses.

We climbed up and up. The steps became a narrow street again, and then broadened a tiny plaza. Music from the Woodstock Festival spilled from the village *taverna*

"You can drop your bag here," my companion told me. "No one will steal it." There were more Americans in jeans, more hugs. Opening his own pack, Ernie passed around the treasure he had brought back from the mainland—a jar of peanut butter. I drank a soda and learned a dozen new names.

After this second reunion, we retrieved the packs, and then climbed some more up beyond the town, passing silent windmills, their sails furled. The trail grew broader as we reached the ridge top. We walked by villas, white structures facing out to sea. One of them had been a movie set, Ernie told me.

Beyond the last of the villas, the trail—now a mere donkey path—dipped down, steeply. Below us, a scattering of small white farmhouses dotted a pale green valley fronting on a small beach. I could see olive trees. We clambered downward over a series of well-worn boulders. "Be careful. It's slippery," Ernie cautioned. "Someone fell here just last week." (Much later, in an Asian city, I was to meet the boy who had fallen.)

"Are there snakes?" I asked, suddenly anxious. The day was warming. In country like this in the Sierra Nevada Mountains, rattlesnakes slither out among smooth rocks to catch the sunlight. Did these islands, like Cleopatra's Egypt, have asps? The daylight was already waning, but perhaps Greek snakes weren't too fussy.

"Yeah, two kinds of snakes." I had my hiking boots on. Earlier I had been fretting that they were growing heavy and clumsy in the summery heat. I had considered mailing them back to California. Now I was glad to have worn them.

Getting back up this hill would probably be difficult later. I did not have a flashlight. "Don't worry," Ernie's reassuring voice went on. "There's plenty of light. While the moon is out, you won't need it."

At the bottom of the rocky hillside, the path came out onto a stony beach facing a gentle, lapping sea. We followed tracks left by a herd of goats crossing from one side of the valley to the other. The beach had a small marsh on it, fading daylight reflecting on ripples in the wet patches. Ernie's rented farmhouse sat just inland. I could see a donkey and colt tethered to a pair of spindly trees. An outdoor well stood amid high grass.

It was starting to get dark. Ernie pushed open the wooden door. Inside the house were a kerosene lantern, a gasoline stove, a wooden bedstead with a sleeping bag on it, and some shoes. A plow belonging to the landlord leaned against the wall.

"There's space on the floor," Ernie said. "You can crash there if you like and find a place tomorrow." It sounded like a good idea. My host lit a mosquito coil on a tin stand. As it smoked and stank, I rolled out my mummy bag on the floor. I slept soundly until the donkey outside brayed to greet the dawn.

Milapota, this valley reached by donkey trail, had its own *taverna*. Over a small cup of thick Greek coffee there in the morning, I learned that one of the foreign travelers had gone away and that his desirable camping spot—an empty cave—was now available. I claimed it.

The cave was just steps from the *taverna*. It was not a real cavern, only a hole about a dozen feet deep, one of many that pocked the porous rock face behind the *taverna*. It had an arched entrance and a flattish floor. To reach it, I climbed the ridge behind the *taverna* until I was more or less above the opening, then worked my way a few feet down the slope. Small bushes on the hillside made good hand-holds, and the descent from the ridge to the cave opening turned out not to be as sheer as it looked from above. Getting back down from the cave to the *taverna* at the beach was not as tricky as it looked, either. I could even slide down, if I didn't mind damaging my jeans.

In no time, I learned how to scamper straight down the rock face to the *taverna* with no trouble at all. There, I tasted and liked *mavro*–the dark island wine made by the *taverna's* proprietors. This "black" wine was not really black at all, but dark red. The color started me musing. I once read that ancient people perceived colors differently. In the *Odyssey*, Homer writes about Odysseus traveling a "wine-dark sea." Did he use that same all-purpose word—*mavro?* Was this because the poet was blind? Some said that Homer was buried in a cave at the northernmost tip of Ios. Had he actually lived here drinking *mavro* at some predecessor of the present seaside *taverna?* The water by the small beach was a stunning turquoise, not wine-dark at all. Even if the poet wasn't born blind, he surely could never have seen this brightly-colored sea.

I DRANK MORE MAVRO. I ate island dishes, *pasticcio,* a ground meat and macaroni dish under a thick layer of cheesy cream sauce, *kotoupolo,* a golden half-chicken on a platter. Food money was no longer a problem. I had no rent to pay. I marveled that I could live in a cave and still go out for dinner.

I learned how to climb straight up the rock face to the cave. The climb required good visibility. I bought a flashlight, so that I could stay later talking with other travelers at the *taverna* and still make it safely up the cliff. I drank more *mavro* and grew more agile.

At the *taverna,* I learned how Greeks fix meatballs with mint. I learned to love the rice pudding from the cooler case.

I learned how Greeks extend the battery life for their cassette recorders by pulling out the batteries and setting them in the warm sunlight like little plants. New batteries were expensive. I climbed back to the high village and bought a kerosene lantern.

I learned how to cook in my cave, pulling off the lamp's glass chimney to hold canned octopus in a metal drinking cup over the tiny open flame. A handy hiking sock became a potholder. I bought fresh-made yogurt and ate it with island honey drizzled on top. I learned the trick of squatting in the wild to pee, keeping hidden as cleverly as any deer though the only woods around were sparse olive trees and brush amid stones.

Cave life suited me. I was going back in time. Back to before the crowded commute from the hospital in San Pablo, before the SATs and college sit-ins, the anti-war demos and summer typing jobs. Back to stone and sea and olive trees.

One day, after climbing back from the *taverna*, full of midday *moussaka* washed down with the *taverna's* dark-red home-brew, I encountered visitors. Two goats stood in my cave, staring at me with their strange wide set cat-eyes. A herdsman who wandered the island had brought his flock up the ridge. Goats were straying everywhere, munching on the scanty herbs and brush that grew on the rock-strewn hillsides. I shooed the goat invaders out. I hunted down pink spiders which lived on the cave walls and offered these creatures, too, a speedy exit.

AT NIGHT, SITTING IN ONE WHITEWASHED stone peasant cottage, or another, or perhaps in a neighboring cave, I traded stories with other travelers: Ray's tale of being bitten by a snake. He had survived. The bite was healing into a wide red swelling on his leg. Amanda's auto accident before traveling. Given up for dead with her liver cut in half, she had managed to battle back to health. Now she was trying to live twice as fast. A Dutch friend said little, but was always psychically present. I remember the stone pathway where we sat in happy silence. Others talked of Curtis, the Canadian who came to live here who got money from home.We thought he had an inheritance, but no one knew for sure. An American woman, back from Israel, where she had lived in the Wadi, told of the *bedu*.

I realized this community, quiet as it seemed, served as a gathering spots for travelers. We became an *ad hoc* travel forum. Americans returning from India joined the conversations, telling of their journeys, too.

These travelers were very low key, almost flat in manner. Dry-spoken and undramatic, the India travelers moved and talked like people who had been bleached of emotion. They described the routes, the trains, the buses.

The consensus among the foreigners in the valley was that travel should be simple and slow: "Go somewhere and linger. Stay a month here, a month there," Marie summarized, as she plunged the can-opener blade of her Swiss Army knife into a tin of the inky *calimari* she would soon be serving to the group of voyagers clustered in her tiny rented cottage. The original occupant, a farmer, had built himself a modern place with plumbing. Once the weather grew hotter, Marie said, her small group would catch a ferry to Marseilles, and then take another onward to the Canary Islands.

BY NOW, THE WHITE TOWN ON THE MOUNTAIN, which had once appeared so simple and quaint, seemed complicated and urban. The police, representing the Athens Junta, maintained a pair of motorcycles, the only motorized vehicles on the island.

One day in the plaza, as I came into the plaza to shop, a tourist sat in front of the small cafe, playing on his guitar. I recognized the theme from *Zorba the Greek*, a famous song by Mikis Theodorakis. We foreigners all knew it from the hit movie. To an American, this was the ultimate Greek music, its rousing beat speaking to us of passionate dancing and freedom fights. Local islanders liked it too. They stood by their small shops listening and smiling.

But the Junta's ruling colonels and their local watchdogs abhorred the music. Playing anything by Theodorakis, a perceived leftist, was forbidden. Police converged like flies. They ordered the foreign guitarist to stop.

There was a shocked silence around the tiny plaza, in which the buzzing of real flies could have been heard if there had been any. Would the tourist be arrested? He ceased playing. Satisfied, the police left. Then everything began again, but without the lively music.

The mood seemed normal but wasn't. The barber, usually a genial man, looked tightlipped and anxious. Almost too casually, he reached to put out his cigarette. All was again as if nothing had just happened, until I noticed the barber was distractedly stubbing out the still-burning cigarette on the head of a small child standing beside him. His own son. No one said a thing. The next customer probably got a very strange haircut.

Greece had exploded before. On the shore, mild rocking tides brought up bits of white pumice. These fragments came from the nearby island of Santorini where a volcano eruption had destroyed a city and decimated the earlier Minoan civilization. Some scientists had speculated that this explosion was the source of the Atlantis myth. Lightweight pebbles of pumice from this ancient cataclysm littered the narrow beach at Milapota. Picking up some smaller ones, remnants of an explosion thought to have caused the Biblical Deluge (or the parting of the Red Sea, depending on whom one listened to), I sanded travel calluses off my heels.

THE SEASON ADVANCED. The sun began to bake us all. In May, Marie and her friends moved on. I moved down from the cave and rented their farmhouse. A day after moving in, I heard noises outside and rolled out of my sleeping bag on the bedstead made of crooked boughs built into the wall. The farmer and his son were arriving with a donkey, bringing me a proper metal bed and mattress. My cave-dwelling days were truly over.

I had written my mother about living in the cave. Apparently entertained, she sent me some traveler's checks, enclosed inside a carefully-worded letter commenting on how exciting my life was growing. Had my enthusiastic letter home wooed my cautious mother into endorsing a life of adventure, or was she merely terrified on my behalf?

I didn't know. I cashed the checks. I felt flush.

Temptation grew. Maybe I could get to India. Maybe it was really only a question of practical matters such as carrying a chain to attach my pack to my bed.

What was I afraid of? I was beginning to be a seasoned traveler. After all, didn't I have my own travel tales? And now I had the money as well. The dream seemed doable. I began a plan of starts and stops in which I would visit other islands as I worked my way northwestwards, towards Turkey.

The passage would be a slow one, for the Greek Islands had a grip on me. I packed up my swimsuit and the kerosene lantern I used for cooking. I tossed a pebble of pumice from the beach into my pack. In the village, I shopped for a pair of the soft plastic sandals most Greek children wore. It was too hot now for the hiking boots. I tied the boots by their laces to the front of the pack.

I bought a padlock and chain to secure my backpack. I would need these in India.

THE THIRD HOUSE

I T'S EASY TO MAKE Greek lentils—*vacques*—as I've learned to call them. Into the pot go the rinsed-off dried legumes, like a bunch of tiny scattered coins; then in go cut-up bits of onion and garlic. In goes water, then salt. And then I seem to have company. It was at this point, when I first learned to make this soup, that Elefteria hoisted a tomato in one hand with a conspiratorial expression which said, "Why don't we, since we're flinging everything else in?" Then, with a hint of a wink, she tossed the entire tomato, uncut, into the pot.

Elefteria, whose name meant "freedom," imprisoned her thick dark hair in a scarf and wore a kind of blue pinafore to perpetually protect her dress, which I never saw except at the edges of the pinafore. She was shorter than me, and she was my landlady.

The soup pot was in her new house—a two-story dwelling, with walls of cement and slippery terrazzo floors. Her new house stood on a little hill just above an inlet forming the tiny harbor for an even tinier village on Alonissos. I had discovered this island on a map as I prepared to leave Ios, heading for Turkey. The island was a mere amoeba-shaped spot in the sea, well to the north. I was planning to make my way northward to Thessaloniki and from there, on to Istanbul. If I wanted to get to Thessaloniki by island-hopping, Alonissos lay right on my way.

Elefteria's village did not appear on my map. I only found it when I went hunting for a place to stay and discovered she had a room for rent.

The hamlet was so tiny that the village store, across the gully, was only a sitting room in someone's household. Actually the store, piled high with boxes of detergent and half-sized bottles of *retsina*—the resin-flavored light wine of the islands—took up only a corner of someone's otherwise nearly bare sitting room.

There was only one other foreigner in the village—an American man who lived on the ground floor of Elefteria's old house. This rustic older dwelling, which lacked the fancy floor and ruler-straight walls of Elefteria's new one, stood right next door.

Elefteria was fortunate to have two houses that stood so close together. A recent major earthquake had rattled and cracked the island's ancient housing stock. Afterwards, the Greek government, fearing more earthquakes, had put up new places for many of the islanders. The Junta had ordered all highland residents to move down off their hilltop into new houses nearer the water. Since Elefteria already lived by the water, she did not have to leave her village or abandon the old place. And now, with two houses, she had room to spare.

After several days of boarding with the family in the lace curtain intimacy of Elefteria's modern house, I felt a bit smothered. We arranged for me to move out and rent the top floor of her old place next door instead. This space above the American was temporarily being used for raising chickens, but Elefteria declared that she and her teenaged daughter would scrub it out, and then it could be mine.

This took a day or two. When the big room was finally cleared of feathers, I humped my pack down the new cement stairs of Elefteria's modern house and tugged it up the old steps of the place next door. I dropped the pack on the empty floor. Presto, I was at home. It might have been a bit bare, but it was far more modern than the cave on Ios.

Thus I became Elefteria's tenant, rather than her paying houseguest. I could view life from my own dwelling in a tiny village. And I still had my landlady, whom I liked, as a neighbor.

I had learned to cook Greek food because Elefteria flung the tomato with an attitude which defied all talk of cups and teaspoons. Now, trailing after Elefteria's daughter, and unwittingly acting as her chaperone, I would learn the geography of food as well.

My company was in demand, for at 15, Eleni was not allowed to go anywhere on her own. If she handed me a can and beckoned for me to follow, I would gradually figure out, as I stumbled over rocks and climbed a trail to another village, can in hand, that we were going to visit the beekeeper. The beekeeper, an older woman, dipped grainy boiled island honey into the cans we had carried with us. Later, when poured over goat milk yoghurt, the honey hardened to treacle which almost crunched when eaten.

Another day, when Eleni called out, *"Pa-me"*—"Let's go!"—I meekly followed her uphill and out of the village, confident that we would eventually find food. High on the hill we arrived at a fig tree, where we picked and ate our fill of the dangling heart-shaped fruit. Of course, we brought even more home to Elefteria.

The stony island was rimmed with blue Aegean inlets, where the water washed up softly with a swish and fishermen tethered their boats. On the hillsides, wandering with stones in my hand to drive off un-leashed dogs, I learned to gather oregano, thyme, and chamomile. Tea could be made from the chamomile. I dried the oregano and thyme leaves and saved them for cooking.

Elefteria's name was an irony. She had no freedom. She labored in the kitchen, at the cleaning and washing, the business of the house, and once a week, at the baking—for the outdoor oven in front of the family's old whitewashed stone house—now my rental—was still used to make the crusty bread I learned to relish. Each week, after Elefteria and her daughter finished baking, they left me a loaf.

As I ate my bread, dipping the crust into the olive oil purchased from the sitting-room store, I would think of the labor that went into making it: Firewood had to be brought. Then the fire was built before dawn, for it took four hours to heat up the arch-fronted outdoor oven. The mixing and preparing of the dough took place next door. I imag-ined lots of pounding and punching as the dough rose in Elefteria's new kitchen.

Finally, Elefteria and her daughter would carry out the uncooked loaves. By now, the the fire in the oven would be out and the oven hot. They would shovel the pale loaves into the oven, and afterwards, bring out the perfectly-baked bread, completed just before the heat of the day.

Eleni had to bake and clean beside her mother, but as a free adult, I could do whatever I pleased. I could hitch a ride to the island's main town, the port, by waving down a passing boat headed that way, or I could walk until a *triciclo* traveling the rutted trail over the hills picked me up.

At night I heard the fishermen coming home from revelry somewhere slightly drunk and singing. I learned to fish, but caught only small sardines.

At 15, Eleni had reached an age when a decision was called for. On the island, the tradition was that a girl would pick out the island man she would like to marry. Then her father, informed of the decision, would begin to build the couple a house.

Already a beauty, Eleni was ripe for the choice. She had light brown curly hair and a full chin like the classical Greek lady on a silver dollar. Her family owned the two buildings. But Stelios, the boy she favored, had gone to work at Athens, and building on the new marital house had not begun.

The situation was awkward.

I could not believe that Elefteria, old and squat in her blue apron, could have given birth to a child so lovely. Or that Eleni risked missing out on the spouse of her choice. But the life on the island involved lots of sun, dust, and hard labor for women. It aged them fast.

I saw Stelios around when he came back on a visit. He was long-limbed like an American high school student, and at least a foot taller than Eleni's father. He did not seem like a big city type.

Once more Elefteria and I gathered over the soup pot. Once more, with sardonic insouciance, she tossed something in at the last - this time an onion. It was just the two of us, a majority fraction of the three fates, cooking up a future. Once more the meal was a marvel.

There was a sunken village down the coast, Eleni told me, as my Greek grew better. An earthquake long ago had caused the land to slip away, leaving the village underwater.

A fisherman friend with a *caique* motored me down the coast to the site. I peered into the brown wavelets sloshing and rocking the boat, but could not see any underwater ruins. The ancient village, though still alive in local memory, had vanished.

Another day, two boys from Athens, whose father had restored a windmill on the heights, walked me over to see this vacation retreat. I climbed the narrow steps inside the tower. At the top, the father had created a bachelor pad as a love nest far away from the big city. I peered like Rapunzel out a window slit, and was bored.

Industrious as ever, Elefteria carried in dried firewood from somewhere. She baked *tiropeta*—a cheese pie encased in puff paste. She invited me over to the new house with terazzo floors to enjoy it with the family. We cracked a bottle of *retsina* and sat—Elefteria, her husband, the daughter and I—on the new balcony, overlooking the inlet, like happy tourists.

But Elefteria's husband still did not begin building Eleni's house.

Outside the wind blew over stones, dried grasses, thyme and oregano. It was summer and dry. The American neighbor living downstairs from the second floor ex-chicken house was learning Greek too. Isolated in the linguistic bubble which limited me to speaking in Greek baby talk, I felt lonely. I eyed my neighbor speculatively. There were things we could have talked about, but he was not interested in hanging out with anyone speaking English. He kept his nose in his Greek-English dictionary. I consoled myself with the thought that I was learning Greek much faster by following Eleni around the island.

Another day, walking alone, I met a Greek from the island who had emigrated to Australia. He had made a successful business in hardware and now was home, but somehow sad. Like me, he seemed adrift in the grassy hills amid the herbs and occasional stray dogs.

I began to go more often to the main town, where an Athens man with an urbane manner operated a gift gallery. I examined the clothing and handicrafts, and fingered the embroidery. I bought a small brass oil lamp, which no doubt used to dangle in some tiny whitewashed chapel. I mailed this treasure back to California.

At the waterfront—the *paralia*—I stood around watching the ferryboat tie up and the new people come off it. Back at the chicken house, by light of the trusty lantern I had brought with me from Ios, I began to study the map. I was going to India, wasn't I? There was another island just a short boat ride off. It had a bigger town, and from there, another ferry went onwards to the north.

I decided to catch that boat.

"I think I may go to Athens," Eleni told me as we said good-bye. "I have an uncle in Athens." But I never found out whether she went.

WHEN THE LENTILS ARE ALMOST DONE, the next step is to stir them in the cast iron Dutch oven where they are slowly cooking. Whenever I reach this step, I see Elefteria again in my mind's eye, with her scarf, her wrinkles, her pinafore and wit. I see her again flinging the tomato into the broth with an elegant, casual movement of her strong wrist, in a gesture expressive of utter freedom.

Then, still in my mind's eye, I watch as she adds the final seasonings—oregano and thyme—to complete the recipe. This is a recipe that has traveled with me around the world, to Stockholm, Berlin, and Berkeley. Even 40 years later, I make *vaques*—tomato and all—just as Elefteria taught me.

And always, when I sit down to eat it, I wonder what became of Eleni—whether she followed Stelios to Athens, or whether he came home to the island, after all, and her father finally was able to build the third house.

TOURISTS BEARING GIFTS

"**C**OME BACK FOR ME tomorrow...*avrio,*" I asked the driver in halting Greek, and he agreed. I lifted my pack from the back and the *triciclo* rattled away on the skinny road that circled the island. I carried it out on the deserted land spit to set up camp in the sunny midday.

On July 4th, on Elefteria's island, it had rained, and I decided that though I now knew some Greek, being cooped up in the remodeled chicken house would be unbearable. I was embarrassed to confront Elefteria with the news that I was abruptly leaving, but of course I had to. I wanted to hug her, but instead, with my belongings already stuffed back in the green pack, I hoisted it, thrust my arms once more into the padded shoulder straps, and walked to the harbor, one valley over.

And then I had caught the boat to neighboring Skopelos.

My notion was to island-hop northwards from Skopelos to Thassos and then onwards to the mainland at Thessaloniki. From Thessaloniki, a good road ran eastwards to Turkey. From Turkey, there would be ways to get to India. The plan had no exact timetable, however, and Skopelos was proving more interesting than I expected.

I had never heard of the island, except on ferryboat timetables, but it was turning out to be beautiful. The port city—also called Skopelos— seemed a genuine metropolis after Elefteria's rural hamlet. Red-roofed dwellings lined the steep hillside behind the harbor in attractive tiers.

Narrow, but modern roads ran out of town. I wondered where the roads led.

I decided to take a day or two to find out. I shopped for bread and cheese, and then found a local driver willing to take me to the country-side. He drove me to this uninhabited place on the far side of the island, where a pine-dotted peninsula stretched out into turquoise waters. And now, here I was, completely alone, on a small rise overlooking a tiny beach. I wasn't afraid. It was good to be alone after the tight coziness of village life. I had safely hitched rides all over Alonissos on triciclos and boats, and I was sure that the driver would be back as promised to pick me up. I felt safe and emboldened, ready to savor my independence.

I also wanted to think things over. I had been on the road since April and now it was summer. Did I really mean to go on to India? Was I really courageous enough to attempt the trip? Or should I instead hang out on a Greek island for the rest of my journey? Or maybe I ought to start homewards. The first two alternatives were more tempt-ing, but I realized I also missed my housemates back in East Oakland.

I decided not to try to force any decision on this bright Greek morning. I would not even think about it.

I set down my pack under a pine tree, pulled my sleeping bag out of its stuff sack, shook it to fluff up the crushed down, and spread it on the ground. I sat on it, unwrapped the *kasseri* cheese I had bought in town, and sliced off a chunk to chew on. I tore off a morsel of the fresh-baked bread and ate that, too.

Finishing this simple meal, I sat watching the water, watching ants creep in a line along the sandy soil. The setting was warm and very quiet. The air smelled of pine resin. Although India beckoned, just now I did not want to go anywhere but here. I was on my own, among the pines on Skopelos, on an overnight adventure.

I pulled out my wooden recorder from the pack's front pocket and fitted on the mouthpiece. Then—no musician—I played a song I had written back in Berkeley, while a student. It had words about adventure, about wandering monks, and headlands, which sounded in my mind as I played the melody. The woody notes quickly dissolved in the open environment, but that didn't matter. They made me a part of it, like the quiet file of ants, the lapping water on the beach of the inlet below, the breeze that very gently lifted the pine boughs.

The song contained only a short sequence of notes. Finishing these and not stopping, I began a second melody I had written a month ago while sleeping in the cave and spending mornings sunning on the beach by the *taverna* that made the *mavro* wine. This was my third island now, and each was turning out to have its own distinct mood. Merely tooting the notes didn't do justice to the mood. This song had words. I set the wooden flute down on the sleeping bag. I sang my Greek island song, as loud as I pleased, adding in a lot of bluesy attitude. Who could hear? No one but me.

I've been on this island for three weeks now, waiting for rain
And the tide between my footprints leaves a track of pumice
where the waves wash up
The pieces of what used to be Atlantis.

The sentiment, which had started out a bit bluesy, became more of a complaint. The words of loneliness and longing started sounding too whiney, and I wasn't as pleased with them. In this peaceful setting, it was hard to feel bluesy. I stopped singing. I took apart the recorder, dried it, and put the pieces back in my pack. Pine needles stirred. The sun beat down. Baby waves beat harmlessly on the shore below. There was no one to talk to.

There was no pumice on the beach below me. I was far north of Ios, where I had lived in a cave and rubbed my callused heels with feather-light pebbles from the beach. Here, on this bigger, greener island, there seemed no shadow of the ancient volcanic cataclysm which had sunk the Minoan city of Thera under the sea. While residents of Skopelos might recall the Atlantis myth, this island was too far north to have been directly affected by that ancient explosion.

It seemed more like everyday Greece, pretty, but humdrum, with no mystery or echoes of ancient disaster about it. Insects buzzed. Orderly ants followed prescribed ant roads, on some unrevealed but no doubt practical errand.

It was my second island in the Sporades group. I knew if I looked, I could probably find familiar spices—thyme and oregano—growing wild in the meadows, as I had on Alonissos. I had learned how to harvest these for cooking from Elefteria's daughter. But just now I did not choose to get up and hunt for spices. Yes, I knew how to spice my life, but I didn't feel like cooking, either. So I just sat, enjoying the peace, and growing slowly bored.

And then came an even more familiar humming. A shiny well-kept VW van was puttering along up the road that circled the island. Soon the vehicle pulled off at the shore near me. Two people in swimsuits—a man and a woman—climbed out.

Oh-no! European tourists!

From my camping spot underneath the pine tree, I could hear the pair rummaging in the back of their vehicle. Then two figures emerged, snorkels and masks dangling in their hands. They walked down to the curving beach below the land spit and kept on going, straight out into the water, adjusting the masks on their faces as they went. Soon, like seals from a more northern climate, the newcomers disappeared into the placid sea. Like seals too, they bobbed to the surface, dove, and bobbed up again, sometimes bringing pieces of things to the beach. I couldn't make out what the objects were.

I began feeling uncomfortably like a voyeur, so when they emerged from the water to rest, I stood up and waved hello. They waved back, and I walked down to the water's edge to find out what they were doing.

They were Nora and Stefan, both in their thirties, and friendly. The two came from Austria. I spoke no German. Stefan, not confident in English, only smiled, but Nora's English was very good. Both were on vacation and taking the opportunity to dive, Nora said.

The treasure they were bringing up was pottery. She gestured to the strange objects laid out on the couple's striped blanket.

Nothing was whole, and everything smelled as rank as the day's catch brought in by a boat without refrigeration. Nora handed me one of the odd-shaped pieces. It appeared to be a curving bit of clay, the broken off neck of some ancient container. "That's part of an *amphora*," she said.

Nora explained that an *amphora* was a pointy-bottomed storage vessel, which might have once held oil or wine or grain. Departing ships of long ago had customarily dropped such offerings from their cargoes into the water as they left harbors, to make sure the gods would grant them a safe voyage. In ancient times, this deserted U-shaped inlet, sheltered by the land spit, had been a harbor.

It was hard to imagine ancient stevedores jostling and wrestling with cargo, or men shouting and pushing boats off the sand at this deserted place, harder still to imagine a ship loaded with items with pointy bottoms. Didn't they tip over?

But I was holding an *amphora* - or at least a piece of what used to be an amphora - by its narrow neck. Somehow it had gotten there, under the water. And judging from Nora and Stefan's haul, there must be plenty more pieces still down there.

Not dead and white like the temples on the Acropolis, this ancient fragment was brown and clammy and viscous. The potsherd had become a base for living undersea plants. Thick, slurpy lichen-like streaks covered the ancient clay. These branching blood-red growths looked like some medical school model of the circulatory system.

Two thousand years of slime, I thought, turning the coated shard in my hands. I was not entirely happy to be in contact with it.

Nora and Stefan continued diving all afternoon, working hard to bring up more pieces. Before they left, they presented me with the fragment I had examined. Perhaps this was their own departure offering, a gift to the hermit camper inhabiting the land spit. In the sudden silence after the engine noise died off in the distance, I felt like an anchorite.

The potsherd was still wet and sticky. Somehow this seemed a sacred object, but holding it was like handling worms. I was not sure I wanted to put such a thing in my pack, either. Growing practical, I set my dubious treasure out in the sun to dry. And later, when the moisture in the slime evaporated and the brilliant blobs faded into dry fibers, I wrapped it carefully in a plastic bag and buried it deep in the green backpack, under my hiking socks. I knew I had been unexpectedly handed a precious gift. I hoped it wouldn't smell as much now that it was wrapped up.

That night, under a moon shrunk now to a sliver, the stars were bright, with no dimming competition from city lights. No skunks, deer, or other rustling creatures disturbed the silence as they might have done at home in California. I feared no bears, here, nor human predators, either. The water washed gently onto the shore below, and just as gently pulled back into the sea.

I lay imagining the small boats which must have traded here, men with oars, who had dropped an amphora overboard and then pushed off for some unknown destination. Had this setting out from such a tiny harbor been just a routine act for them? Had theirs been an everyday, humdrum activity? Or did every journey between ports in a lurching tiny boat constitute a wild and risky adventure, as improbable and scary as the solo journey to India still forming in my mind?

I didn't know.

I fell asleep, still not knowing how to regard the distant past, or the piece of it which had landed in my backpack. And in the morning, the triciclo driver arrived as promised to return me to civilization.

IN TOWN AGAIN, I purchased a ticket for the ferry to Thassos and sat down at the *paralia* to wait for it, laying my bulging green pack beside me on the pavement. After the weeks in Greece, the pack was once again too full. It was still dusty with the sandy soil of the land spit. The swaddled potsherd still nestled deep in its belly.

I swatted some of the dust off the pack. I lit a Greek cigarette, and winced slightly as I inhaled. Like those ancient Greek sailors, pushing out to sea, I was ready—impatient even—for the next adventure to begin; however, I still had not decided what that adventure would be. I didn't know where I was going.

The boat was not yet in sight. Watching the water sloshing against the seawall, I wondered if I should imitate those ancient sailors and toss the amphora fragment into the sea as an offering.

At a minimum, ditching it would lighten the load.

WHITE DONKEY

AND WHILE I WAS waiting, along came an American, who plopped himself down companionably beside me on the pavement. In his hands was a half-full bottle of liquor with no label on it. He offered me a slug of it.

Reader, don't get me wrong. Even back then I was not the sort of person to parade through city streets singing rowdy songs. I was more likely to dither over the correct placement of a footnote or the proper forulation of an invitation than drink in public. My undergraduate college had even had a rule against *smoking* in public, which I would probably have obeyed, had I smoked in my college days.

But this was Greece, a friendly place. Also, I had just spent several weeks immersed in another language, pretty much deprived of my own. And the overnight solo camp-out on the far side of the island had made me bolder. Here was a fellow American, proffering English language conversation along with the booze. And I was lonely. It was too good an opportunity to pass up. Stubbing out the cigarette, I took the bottle, upended it, and swallowed. The drink was a new one. It wasn't *ouzo* but *tsipouro* - yet another anise-flavored beverage I had never tried or heard of. I took another swallow.

And so I fell—not into public stupor—but into conversation. Where I came from, where I was going! These were tricky existential questions at best. I asked what an American was doing on this very out-of-the-way island. Well, said Freddy, there were a bunch of them, friends who had rented a house out in the countryside. Would I come and see it?

By now slightly tipsy, I said "Yes." There would always be another ferryboat.

We caught a taxi.

The Americans had taken over an old farmhouse. This was no ancient traditional structure like those I had visited on other islands, but rather old more in the American sense—a somewhat ramshackle sprawling dwelling sitting by some fields. They had been here awhile—weeks or months. The place looked a lot like the home I had left in East Oakland. It was friendly, cluttered, and filled with a small tribe of relaxed young people talking and cooking. It was all so familiar; I felt adopted into a new family. There seemed to be no fleas to argue about, either. Freddy passed around the *tsipouro* again, and everyone drank up.

The day wore on in pleasant conversation, smoothed by a slow unpressured intoxication. A communal dinner appeared somehow.

Later, a Greek neighbor came over. He had been here when the Nazis came, he told us, in fragmented English. The Germans, he said were bad. If the Nazis came back—*pow!*—Jorgos smacked one fist upon the other—they would kick them out again. We were all pleased. Nobody here liked Nazis. Freddy unscrewed another bottle.

The *tsipouro* was passed, and passed again. The heroic neighbor subsided into silence, and then snores. Late in the evening, a Greek man in his thirties came by leading a white mule. "*Adelphos moo?*" the man asked. Yes, his brother was here, passed out.

Together the Americans and the Greek loaded the unconscious farmer across the back of the white mule and the responsible younger brother carefully led the mule bearing the *partisan* hero away homeward.

But it was only midnight. It was too early for sleeping. Freddy and I walked the half mile to the sea and swam in the shallow waters. In the warm night water, phosphorescence lit each ripple; I could look into each small wave that rose and see tiny creatures alight within its glassy wall, like bright specks in amber. These were not fixed and fossilized, however, but moving, dancing.

We walked back to the communal farmhouse in the quiet night, and I fell asleep on a lawn chair on a screen porch, utterly at peace.

I NEVER MADE IT TO THASSOS. In the morning, when I went back to town to change my ferry ticket, I found more Americans, a father traveling with his daughter and her friend. The daughter knew my friend Jenny, a classmate from summer French classes at Georgetown. She said Jenny was working as an *au pair* in Paris. Suddenly the world seemed very compact.

I caught a boat—not the one I had planned on—but another ferry which would take me back to the mainland. We all climbed aboard still talking. When we landed, I said goodbye. I had enjoyed the gift of American company, but by now I understood I had not come on this journey to meet other Americans. And I was not going home, either. Not yet, at least.

Suddenly I felt in a hurry. I had had a good rest. The summer was advancing, and if I was serious about going east, it was time to make tracks for Istanbul. There would be no more island-hopping.

Ride-hopping followed, instead. I took no notes standing by the roadside with people I met at youth hostels. I remember climbing aboard a large truck, and later staying at a bright modern youth hostel fronting on a busy street in Thessaloniki.

Still later, as I walked through a small town between rides, on the road to the Turkish border, my nose suddenly began to bleed in the dry air. I sought out an emergency clinic where a nurse in a white uniform stuffed my nostril with gauze and bandaged up the entire nose so thoroughly I looked like a wounded war hero, or maybe the survivor of a bloody bar fight.

Once out the door, I burrowed out of the white shrouding in embarrassment. The treatment had been ridiculous and excessive, but my nose was no longer bleeding.

SOME TIME AFTERWARDS, I encountered a certain cattiness at the border, as Greek border guards commiserated that I must endure going to Turkey, and Turkish ones oozed sympathy that I had had to be in Greece.

After that, there must have been a bus ride, for I recall looking out at the dark waters of the Sea of Marmara from a right-hand window, and later still, the roar and squawk of darting vehicles, and a glimpse of a great building with minarets. I saw cobbled streets and hills, and ahead, more tossing water, with a beautiful bridge stretching over it.

Oddly, reaching this new and exotic destination felt like being back in San Francisco, although this span, which connected Istanbul's old city to the newer portions, lay much lower to the water than the Golden Gate Bridge at home. Later I would learn this bridge also crossed a Golden Gate, the original estuary mouth after which the one in San Francisco had been named.

But this was not California, and I was not going home any time soon. I found a spot to sleep in the dormitory of a cheap travelers' hotel. Then I went through the pack and pulled out the stuff I did not want to carry further. I wrapped it all up, found a post office, and mailed the parcel to the communal house in East Oakland. But like so many of the things I sent back, the package never reached its destination.

WITHOUT A FEZ

WITH $223 TUCKED AWAY for the expedition eastwards and outwardly serene, I lounged around Istanbul's ancient Sultan Ahmet neighborhood, exploring the ancient streets. Along the right-hand side of the street leading uphill from the Güngör Hotel, male tailors sat in storefronts stitching on enormous satiny bed quilts. Only steps in the other direction, the domed *Hagia Sophia*, an ancient church now turned mosque and flanked by minarets, loomed majestically.

A short walk could bring me to the Golden Horn, the estuary which divided the ancient city from its more modern half, Galata, or to Sultan Ahmet Park, an open square with a fountain at its center where young backpackers from the neighborhood's cheap hotels sometimes congregated.

Just up the street from the hotel, a low-priced restaurant dished up salads of tomato and onion, with a single hot pepper occupying the plate like a tiny ticking bomb, its stem a fuse. Proud of my ability to eat hot things, I nibbled gently at the pepper's skin, taking care not to accidentally swallow any of the seeds inside, for I had heard these could pack a fiery wallop. I went on from this appetizer to tackle the main meal of kebabs—ground meat—possibly lamb—grilled on sticks. I ate here often. Often, too, I topped off the kebabs with dessert at the Pudding Shop next door to the Güngör on my way back to the hotel.

It may have seemed that I was settling in, but appearances can be deceptive. In part I was gloating: I was celebrating. I had made it this far. I was in Istanbul, known in earlier times as Byzantium or Constantinople. I was at the gateway for the transit to India. I was eating rice pudding sprinkled with pistachio nuts, and somehow this seemed exotic and delicious, no longer the bland dessert my mother had served up in our tract home in the Washington, D.C. suburbs.

I was also stalling and trying to overcome anxiety with food. For although my habits looked orderly, my thoughts were in disarray. I had reached the end of something—the end of Europe. My voyage into the unknown was beginning.

Istanbul lay on the European continent, but I could see Asia opening. Already, aboard the minibus bringing me across European Turkey from the Greek border, I had caught glimpses of women dressed in striped baggy trousers, gathered at the ankle like those in Romantic-era harem paintings, bending over in the fields to tend crops. As the vehicle carrying me plunged—braking, honking, and veering—through the crowded streets into Istanbul's old neighborhood of Sultan Ahmet, a bustling traffic of received ideas and odd expectations pitched about and collided in my mind. This tumult had made me simultaneously seasick and hungry.

Back in childhood, I knew the city where I was now lodging as Constantinople. *Constantinople* had been a spelling word, and, a 14-letter one at that. In fourth grade, I had spelled it out correctly and won praise for mastering it. And I had marveled at the name. Like the word "Xanadu," the name "Constantinople" suggested magical worlds beyond my experience.

In college, I had studied this city by the Bosporus waters through the words of the Irish poet William Butler Yeats, who had called the place by its ancient name, Byzantium. Then much beloved by American English professors, Yeats believed that in medieval times a perfect unity existed there between the artist and the created work. This was best expressed, he thought, in Byzantine mosaics by anonymous artists and by a mechanical nightingale built to keep a sleepy—and presumably Byzantine—emperor from dozing off.

The ancient city became an icon for the poet as he struggled with the issues of aging and mortality. Late in life, Yeats elaborated a complex theory about the soul's journey after death, involving phases of the moon, purgatory, and completion of life's unfinished business. The time immediately after death, Yeats believed, would be spent "dreaming back," reliving and resolving a lifetime's discordant experiences.

Reading Yeats' poem, "Byzantium"—even after studying it many times—I still wasn't really sure what he was talking about. But each time I reached the poem's final line, "That dolphin-torn, that gong-tormented sea," the words' music and imagery gripped me strangely. I felt touched by something intense and beautiful that was now also ended and at a great distance, as if observed through wavy plate glass.

Now I had reached Byzantium, or at least Istanbul, the bustling modern city it had become, and apprehending the actual city through the veils of prior knowledge was proving tough. This city was like a multilayered and alluring pastry—its exterior colored by so much that I had read. Beneath this surface, its fillings were an enigma—some sweet, some savory, and some, perhaps, pure poison. Byzantine, in my vocabulary, referred to the sneaky and conniving inner workings of a government unresponsive to its citizens. A Richard Nixon kind of town, I suspected, full of intrigue. But James Baldwin had spent time here, too, more happily than in the United States. Was Byzantium *byzantine*? And what had led an author like Baldwin to linger here?

And where were those dolphins, anyway? When I wandered along the water's edge in Sultan Ahmet, I could see street venders hovering behind the flitting flames on their grills cooking up white-fleshed and delicious fish, which they served between thick slices of hand-cut bread to families out for an evening stroll. The families were escaping their hot apartments just as I escaped the Güngör's stifling ladies' dormitory into the Old City. But there were no dolphins visible in the waters of the Golden Horn. And the only feeding frenzy at the shoreline involved quite sedate Turkish fathers and mothers handing out fish sandwiches to their children. It didn't add up.

I saw bits of Byzantine mosaics uncovered on the walls of the *Hagia Sophia*. The fragments hinted at splendor, but even more stunning, I thought, were the massive, almost heraldic, disks bearing Arabic calligraphy, gilded arabesques in curling *kufic* script, which seemed to float above me in the *Hagia Sofia's* soaring dome. Although I could not read them, these bold graphics enthralled me, proclaiming with their existence that I stood here at the end of Europe at a crossroads where cultures had banged together and beauty had resulted.

Late at night, quite young and alive, I lay in my upper bunk in a cheap hotel, tossing in a personal purgatory. For I was doing my own dreaming back, trying to understand how I got here, what I was experiencing, and where I should go next.

If I had reached a personal crossroads, I was perfectly in harmony with the city, for Istanbul itself actually lay at a double crossroads. For ages, men on camels had trekked mountains and deserts bearing Chinese goods destined for Byzantium. Armies had marched and ridden, too, bringing slaughter and upheaval. Bus and train routes connecting Turkey to Europe still converged at Istanbul.

The second crossroads was a watery one, for on its north-south axis, the ancient city perched along a series of watercourses that connected the Mediterranean Sea to the Black Sea. Ships in the Mediterranean bound for Istanbul could enter the straits known as the Dardanelles to the south of the city and beat northwards through the tiny Sea of Marmara up to Istanbul and its fabulous harbor at the Golden Horn. North of Istanbul, the swift-flowing waters of the Bosporus linked the city to the Black Sea. All sea trade between Mediterranean nations and Russia passed through this narrow bottleneck and had done so for hundreds of years.

Legend had it that the earliest of these trading ventures was led by Jason and his Argonauts, who passed through the Dardanelles, the Sea of Marmara, and the Bosporus to the Black Sea in search of a golden fleece. These Greek voyagers are said to have located the fleece at Colchis, somewhere on the Black Sea's Eastern rim. Not very long afterwards, Greek trading colonies—Synop and Samsun and Trabzon sprang up along the Black Sea's southern shores.

The historical Jason must have been some seaborne hunter-trapper type, more like an American frontiersmen in a dugout canoe than a polished Greek hero as he charted his new route through fast-moving waters to places where barbarians might be persuaded to gather for swap meets. In California, fortune-seekers had came to the Mother Lode in 1849 to pan for gold in the Sierra streambeds. Americans called them Argonauts, after these early Black Sea explorers.

Looking beyond the mythologizing, it is easy to visualize Jason, dirty and unshaven, returning with his crew through the Bosporus bearing a load of badly-cured sheepskins and perhaps some wolf pelts to brighten Aegean cottages like ones I had seen in the Greek islands, built of sturdy poles and piled stones. Perhaps he put in to some deserted shore near the Golden Horn, dragged his overloaded vessel high on a stony beach and lighted a campfire. Or perhaps there were already settlers, even then, waiting at the water's edge to sell him grilled fish.

For it is unclear when the town later known as Byzantium came to be. Turks claim that a town existed even before Byzas, a Greek, founded a city on the present site in about 600 B.C. Greeks credit Byzas with the city's founding and named the settlement after him.

The city on the Bosporus proved an attractive prize. Phillip of Macedon, Alexander's father, winched Byzantium into his kingdom as part of a greater territory gained when he annexed Thrace, the portion of what is now Turkey that lies on the European continent. Still later in the geopolitical chess game of the ancients, Romans acquired the city. Eventually, after the original Rome was overrun by barbarians, the Emperor Constantine shifted his headquarters eastwards to Byzantium. He made it into a new Rome, after losing the original one.

People called it "Constantinople," after him. The new king in town cemented his legacy by building on seven hills in remembrance of the Eternal City he had failed to keep in his grasp. Constantine also made the Roman Empire's shift to Christianity official. From his new capital by the Bosporus, Orthodox Christianity would follow trade routes, spreading to to the Balkans and Russia as well as the Greeks of Asia Minor.

After more than a thousand years' rule by Constantine's successors—this "New Rome" too was overrun by barbarians—from Europe. Crusaders intent on rescuing the Holy Land from infidels stopped off at Constantinople on the way for some rest and relaxation. Finding the living easy and the pillage excellent, they remained, to the horror of the local community, which took many eager measures to persuade the knights of Western Christendom to pursue their quests elsewhere.

Not that the locals had been such nice guys, either: The term *Byzantine*—I knew—referred to convoluted, political scheming. This suggests assassins lurking behind the tapestries rather than harmony. The term may have been a slur, but I suspected not. Surely the emperors of Byzantium had a more lively time than simply napping with mechanical birds, particularly when faced with such unwanted lingering houseguests. Corrupt and weak officials, blinded dynastic rivals, iconoclasts intent on smashing artwork, a whore rising like an early Eva Peron to reign as empress—Constantinople had had them all.

The Crusaders' presence, defying all material realities, led to the creation of Byzantine romances. These stories were not Byzantine by virtue of being convoluted and conspiratorial, but because bards created them during the odd niche of history when cultural cross-fertilization was occurring at a fast clip. At a time when knights of Western Europe had descended on Constantinople to "save" it by thievery and rape, these stories mingled the emblematic formality of a Persian garden with Western tales of courtly love and Arthurian-style quest. In Greek! Romance, is, after all, very international.

Picture this: In a modern romance, Hollywood style, he chases her until she captures him. That's the American myth. By contrast, in a typical medieval romance, love develops wordlessly after the guy is zapped by the sight of the beloved. An amorous arrow of love shoots through his eye. The arrow plunges into his heart. (The exact biological pathway is a little uncertain here.) This embedded arrow causes him to fall ill with craving for the beloved. He seeks her through great perils, losing weight and complaining. In a Byzantine romance, the hero might also knock off a loathsome dragon, do something useful with a golden apple, and sneak out to meet the noble young lady in a really nice garden—all this in Greek, of course. (I had written a master's paper on one of these romances, when a paragraph might actually have sufficed.)

It was easy to snicker at such doings but more difficult to consider my own adventure. For an American to spend a few weeks bumming around Europe was one thing. It was merely to comply with a well-established tradition for students and artists. A grand—or in my straitened backpacker circumstances—a not-so-grand tour. But to go beyond? A man might attempt this, emulating the great explorers, but for a woman on her own—particularly one with a Catholic upbringing which had put firm limits on behavior—pressing onwards seemed like sailing off the edge of the known world. It seemed somehow forbidden.

And my attempt to secure a traveling companion had been shot down. It was too dangerous, the San Diego guy, who refused to let me travel with him, had told me. I would be a burden, he'd said.

Yet I felt also that I must go on, even if alone, or else accept a life of unacceptable limits. In an earlier time, when American men had more readily married and supported pretty, educated, more or less compliant young women, I might have turned back. Or my choice might have been framed in different terms: a choice law school vs. doctorate, perhaps. I might have joined the diplomatic corps to use my language skills. But in 1972, there was nothing to go back to—only a half-life of marginal employment and drudgery, in a country then governed by people intent on world dominance and unjust war. The journey had come as a response to all the paths that felt blocked. I was violating the rules, refusing to continue to play with a stacked deck, making a break for freedom.

I tried to pull my thoughts together. Had similar frustrations set those marauding Crusaders on the road? Maybe it wasn't all religious fervor, but rather a lust for adventure bottled up in the hearth and mead hall, where drinking, feeding, and managing the castle's accounts must have begun to seem pretty dull for men trained as warriors.

Ironically, at the same time Istanbul was occupied by scads of these restless men, and Asian-influenced romances were being created as entertainments, the absence of Crusaders who had departed for the Holy Land must have left aristocratic women of Western Europe with everything to do at home. Married off by their relatives for economic and strategic reasons, these women found themselves governing estates from under-heated castles, coping with peasant rebellions, and managing without any modern conveniences to chase out the dogs lingering under the trestle tables of the mead hall so that last year's rushes on the floor could be replaced. The medieval romances that swept Europe must have provided pretty heady stuff to ponder after sweeping up a year's bones and scouring the mead hall floor. But these women were getting a hard lesson in running the show, and it is difficult to fault them for turning to romances when they wanted to kick back and relax.

Had I finished college in the 1950s and stayed home to clean toilets and change diapers, I would have needed such an escape, as well. But one of the joys of travel was proving to be the lack of housework. No cleaning. No steam-cleaning of carpets. No flea bombs. No cooking. Perhaps I had more in common with the Crusaders than I'd thought.

My joy in such freedom had not, however, fed any impulse to trash Istanbul. I might be confused, but I was treasuring being there. And the place had been trashed enough already.

Constantinople outwaited the affliction of knightly rest-and-recreation traffic. Crusaders had debauched themselves and finally departed, leaving the city to stagger somehow on, becoming more and more depopulated and shabby, its government increasingly ineffective and enmeshed in power struggles. Finally, in 1453, all Byzantine dynastic intrigue halted abruptly. Invaders from the East conquered the capital of the once-grand Eastern Roman Empire.

Constantinople's defenders had anticipated attack. They sealed off access to the city's harbor by stringing a chain across the Golden Horn from Sultan Ahmet to the far side at Galata. But red-bearded Mehmet II, leader of the Turkish besiegers, (and a fan of Alexander the Great) ingeniously bypassed the chain. In a period of mere days, Mehmet had his troops and engineers construct a kind of skid road up and over a ridge behind the Genoese settlement at Galata. The besieging Turks then pushed and dragged 70 ships up this rugged pathway and slid them downhill into the Golden Horn.

Weary defenders watching from the city's massive walls as the small ships of the attackers plopped into the sealed-off harbor must have responded with the era's equivalent of the words, "Oh crap." For the great push-pull between Turks and Greeks over the ancient city was over: The "red apple," as Turks called Constantinople, was no longer just ripe for the taking. It was cooked. The border between West and East now shifted westwards. Constantinople's Greek-speaking Christian rulers were out. The Muslim Turks—perceived in Western eyes as savage marauders from the steppes of Asia—were running the show.

Mehmet's skid-road-facilitated conquest quickly put an end not only to the city's courtly love literature but also, during the early days of pillage, to many of the residents' lives. Chaotic rule soon gave way to Ottoman bureaucracies, however, for Mehmet and his minions instituted boring, well-organized stability. After the sacking and looting were done, Mehmet resettled the place, inviting back many of those who had fled, making amicable arrangements with traders from Italian cities, and even arranging for a Greek refugee from the sacked city to return as the new government-endorsed Patriarch of the Eastern Orthodox Church.

As before, Venetians and Genoans continued to trade. In the West, though, the Turkish conquest triggered instead a new set of fantasies. Bred perhaps of too much fireside tale-telling, these would linger well into the 20th century and permeate pulp literature, art, and early film: harems, bazaars, belly-dancing, eunuchs, selling of women as slaves. The lurid depictions fed nightmares in the West about those bad, bad people, the Turks, and their *differentness*.

These Ottoman stereotypes fed my own nightmares, as I pondered traveling onward. As with the unreliable news reports about the Vietnam War back in the United States, it was hard to sort what was defamation from what was true.

And then modern history had further confounded the issue. The Ottoman Empire founded by Mehmet II—ruled from Constantinople—endured for centuries, but eventually it, too, crumbled gradually and finally disintegrated early in the 20th century. A nationalist reformer, Mustafa Kemal Atatürk, seized power.

Blue-eyed Atatürk, though a Turk, was himself, like Alexander, a child of Macedonia. He established a new modern Turkish capital at Ankara, far from the old battle lines with Europe, where there was less historical baggage. To sanitize the old Constantinople's scandalous cosmopolitan reputation, Atatürk renamed it Istanbul.

This was another time of tumult. In a furor of nationalism, inconvenient minorities, such as Greeks and Armenians, were eliminated or expelled from Turkey, souring Greek-Turkish and Armenian-Turkish relations for generations.

I knew about this because thousands of Armenian refugees had settled in California's Central Valley. A number of descendants of these handsome people, a friend from Atwater once pointed out, had found their way to Hollywood and the television studios of the 1960s. "Armenian!" Charlie, himself half Armenian, would exclaim, pointing out the dark and winning eyes of an especially popular TV doctor. (Actually, he wasn't!) "Armenian, too!" Charlie would chuckle in satisfaction, this time indicating a handsome dark-eyed man extolling some brand of kitchen product. It was an even stranger odyssey than the journey I was contemplating.

Ruling with a heavy and very secular hand, Atatürk modernized in a hurry. He ordered the country to switch from Arabic script to the Latin alphabet. Turks were commanded to pick out last names. Women got the vote. Atatürk banned dervishes, and vigorously outlawed both the veil for women and the fez—the colorful red felt hat worn universally by men.

Knowing of the interdict on the fez, I was not expecting to see any Turks parading about as if they escaped from a Fourth of July Shriners' Parade wearing red felt hats and jeweled scimitars. Instead, the men in the neighborhood by the Güngör mostly wore flat hats like the country people of Europe or turn-of-the-century newsboys in the Bowery. Turks had turned directly from their traditional red conical hats to the modern tweedy headgear of 1920s Europe—flat hats.

Nearly 50 years after the Atatürk's order, and 34 years after his death, the flat hats remained firmly atop Istanbul's male heads.

The effect was slightly disorienting, as if I had suddenly come upon the shooting set for *How Green Was my Valley* with a Turkish cast portraying the Welsh miners in front of the Sultan's old *seraglio*. The *seraglio* itself—once the home of the royal harem under the Ottomans, was no longer even a palace. It, too, had been converted to a museum. The so-called *Sublime Port*—a term used in earlier times to describe the Ottoman government, much as Americans might refer to the White House—still stood, but now only as a fancy gateway, no longer a metaphor for enduring power over the Middle East and huge chunks of Europe.

I had arrived at a city of a multitude of names, hosting multiple nationalities, embedded if not mired in bloody history; a city whose extravagance, spiritual conflicts, sieges, sins, and structures over the millennia could easily have provided plotlines for a thousand Hollywood extravaganzas, not to mention spy stories from Mata Hari to James Bond. It was a real soap opera of a city, I decided. An Eastern Las Vegas, even if there was not a fez in sight!

But if this was romance, it was too much. Coping with it all was immobilizing me.

FEAR, LOATHING, LION'S MILK

B UT EVEN WITHOUT the fez, this old section of Istanbul retained a vestige of earlier times. For despite all the city's tangled history and upheavals, the baths at least endured. The ancient Sultan Ahmet district still maintained lavish marble baths in the Ottoman (or perhaps even Roman) style—one facility for women and one for men.

Balancing precariously on the wooden sandals provided at the baths, I entered a steamy circular room under a grand dome, rather like a formal garden without plants. Carefully removing the sandals, I sat down by a marble sink and began dipping water over myself. Then a massive woman attendant washed me thoroughly, using a cloth as coarse as sandpaper.

Steam rising from the heated marble flooring rose around us as I stared upwards into the high dome, where the vapor plumes twined and twisted like sinuous ghosts. Meanwhile, I felt a rough scrubbing like a cat's tongue on my arms and legs as the woman vigorously attacked my skin. The dirt of a month's hitch-hiking and cave-dwelling rolled off me in bits, literally a discarded skin.

A soothing rinse followed. Then I was sent to lie down and savor being clean in a little room just off the great domed hall of the bath. Like the city, I, too, had been vigorously sanitized. I felt reborn.

But my problem had not gone away. Byzantium might have figured large in Yeats' complicated theoretical universe, but I was finding neither dolphins nor gongs in the actual Istanbul. Nor golden bird, nor golden bough. But then, in Istanbul, I was not really "dreaming back" exactly as Yeats had. Rather, I was rummaging through my personal cultural ragbag for concepts to help me get a handle on a locale which had haunted Western fantasy and projections for millennia. I had retrieved a contradictory and raucous mosaic that was proving little help in the decision I needed to make. What I did have in mind terrified me.

For just as the historical hodgepodge that was now Istanbul had always been a crossroads, here, in Istanbul of 1972, I too was at a crossroads. I had reached the point where I must choose either to go forward to follow my dream or to retreat to Europe and the West. And I was scared stiff.

Before leaving home, I had toured a minesweeper tied up in the Alameda estuary not far from the house I shared with my friends in East Oakland. People we knew were attempting to convert the old World War II boat into a cruise ship. I had seen the as yet un-retrofitted Navy bunks, stacked one on top of another along the ship's hull. Now, in the cramped room jammed with metal bunks stacked three-high on an upper floor of the narrow Güngör Hotel, I felt frustrated, like someone marooned on an antiquated ship, tied up and going nowhere.

And whenever I ventured out to eat, afterwards, I left my pudding bowl to walk slowly back to the Güngör's dormitory. I was alone, scared, and still uncertain about how to go forward.

The other women sharing the room went out sightseeing. They took boat tours of the city's vaulted underground cisterns, constructed of marble in Byzantine times to assure an urban water supply. I could have joined them, but I chose not to go along. I was hiding out, fretting over the next steps in the journey.

As they came and went, I lay in my metal bunk in the women's dormitory, thumbing the guidebook. Getting to India overland involved journeying across four large countries: Turkey, Iran, Afghanistan and Pakistan. Altogether it was a distance of over 3000 miles. I envisioned something like a dead sprint through these countries which were in my way; perhaps after two to three weeks of steady travel on public transport, I could be in India.

It appeared I would have to cross Turkey—a vaster country than I had realized—to get to a city in the east of the country called Erzerum. From there, I would need to proceed past Mt. Ararat, where Noah's boat had gone aground after the Biblical Flood, to reach the Iranian border. Once in Iran, I would need to voyage halfway across it to get to the capital, Tehran; then I would need to go east a good deal more to reach its border with Afghanistan. I was still a little hazy about what would happen after I reached Afghanistan, although I knew I must pass through it and afterwards transit Pakistan as well in order to get to India.

There appeared to be two ways forward—bus and train.

To go by the bus, I would first have to catch a ferry across the Bosporus to the Asian side, then take a bus bound for Ankara, the modern capital city. At Ankara, I must change buses, and then jounce for another 710 miles to Erzerum, first by travelling northeastwards to reach the Black Sea Coast, then following along it to Trabzon. From Trabzon, the bus route veered southwards again to Erzerum. Once I reached Erzerum, I would still have to manage somehow to cross over 200 miles of rural Eastern Turkey to arrive at the border with Iran.

If I took the train, I would not have to worry about hunting for cheap hotels in strange cities at odd hours. But the train's route was even less direct. The rail route ran first southeastwards to Ankara, and then plunged even further southeastwards to Kayseri, before veering northeastwards, to Siva. After Siva, it dipped to the south again. Although my *Overland to India* book stated that the train went to Erzerum, the accompanying map illustrating the route showed the train tracks halting well short of the city. Worse yet, I could expect the train to be very crowded. I would "probably have to curl up in the aisle," my guidebook warned. Either way, the task seemed overwhelming.

It was also possible to reach India by a more southerly route, through Iraq, or by going directly from Southern Iran's deserts into Pakistan, but these routes were less well-traveled. The details of the southern route were sketchy, too. I got the general impression that I would have a harder time going that way. I felt very uneasy about how a woman would be treated.

A woman I knew who lived in a neighboring cave on Ios had gone off alone into the Middle East and led a charmed existence, camping in an Israeli *wadi* and being treated royally by Bedouins. But I was feeling frightened, not charming. There were also those tales—probably nonsense—of Caucasian women winding up in harems, of persisting slavery, kidnappings, and the like. I recalled being harassed in Paris. Although this had not been frightening, it had been annoying. How much more extreme might harassment be as I attempted to cross the countries ahead? To attempt this southern route where there were fewer Western travelers seemed beyond me.

I had seen other backpackers sitting in cafes or the Pudding Shop going over bunches of tattered papers, like ditto sheets from an impoverished elementary school: There was the *BIT Guide*, produced in London, carried by English travelers and much curled by humidity. The Danes had another, equally ragged. Everyone traded names of hotels and warnings about scams and ephemeral, sometimes frightening gossip about road hazards. Late at night, enormous sturdy Dutch or German maps would be unfolded. And then, careful to keep the map out of the juices of a final plate of *kebabs*, travelers would crane forward to look at the fine print and discuss which way to go East.

I had watched, but not joined in. Now I remained in my bunk, thumbing my *Overland to India* book, terrified of the road ahead.

It was also possible to take something called the Magic Bus all the way to India. The bus loaded up in London or Amsterdam and people rode it all the way to India. In the United States not long before, Ken Kesey and his Merry Pranksters had traveled all around the United States in a painted-up school bus. Their adventures provided fodder for a Tom Wolfe book about the early days of hippiedom and raised the question, "Are you on the bus or off the bus?" to cult status. Back in California, a San Francisco spiritual teacher had loaded his followers on aging school buses and taken them all to a commune in Tennessee.

Such bus travel didn't appeal to me. My notion of the Magic Bus—sight unseen—was that taking it would involve joining a rolling party of people preoccupied with one another, who would never even notice the countries they were passing through. Perhaps it was unfair, but I presumed the Magic Bus would be crowded and noisy and full of people taking drugs. I wouldn't be able to hear anything anyone said to me. I would be a wallflower in a crowd. It was a half-baked, socially unacceptable thought at the time, but in a barely-formulated way, I secretly wished to take a bold step—not only into my generation— but into its leadership. Ambition of this kind was not admired among tribal hippie groups in 1972, and expecially not for women. No, the Magic Bus was not the place for me.

Money, too, was a factor. I didn't have enough money to fly. Besides, this would eliminate the challenge.

The thing my mind quailed at was not the idea of being in India, but of crossing all those interim countries, about which I knew almost nothing. I re-read the information in a grim mood. Both land routes seemed really scary to attempt alone.

GLOOMILY, ONE MORNING, I put the guidebook aside and decided to go get something to eat. As I passed through Güngör's tiny lobby on my way out, I waved to Miguel at the hotel's tiny front desk. A gentle-spoken Spaniard, Miguel made the Güngör's seedy interior a safe and welcoming retreat from the noise and bustle outside the door. How he had wound up in Istanbul, I didn't know. Was he in exile? Franco still ruled in Spain, so for anyone young and rebellious, getting away from the Generalissimo would have had its advantages. I wondered if the desk clerk was on the run. There was no way to find out short of asking him, and no one had the nerve to do so. Everyone, however, knew that Miguel loved an American girl who had gone back to Kansas. It was a touching and romantic story, suitable, I thought, for a modern-day movie.

As I pushed open the hotel's front door, the Alexander coin and the tiny doll's face I had purchased in the Covered Bazaar rattled together in my pocket. Pulling out the coin, I took a good look at it. Zeus was on the back, holding a staff and a bird too tiny to identify. On the front side, Alexander was striking a dramatic pose as Heracles, his hair fluffed up in a lion's mane. The Conquerer's eyes were not so pop-eyed as on so many of the old coins, but more naturalistic. He showed a sleepy eye and a lot of chin. The face was well-proportioned, looking like a Greek god's, but with more substantial jowls, somewhat like Mussolini's. The erect lion's mane atop Alexander's head also made him look a bit like some ancient Elvis in a pompadour.

For a coin minted millennia ago, this *tetradrachm* had seemed in remarkably good shape when I bought it two days before. Now, looking very closely, I could see its bright silvery veneer was starting to crack. Already, a darker core of pot metal was visible in places where flecks of the shiny covering had flaked away. Was my adventure disintegrating too, as I dithered about what route to take?

Feeling a little like Florence Nightingale bandaging a wounded soldier, I carefully wrapped up the coin in a bit of Kleenex to protect it from being banged into by the little stone doll's face. I stuffed the wrapped coin back in my pocket, wondering if my mental image of the conqueror himself would prove as fragile.

Actually, I realized, as I stepped out onto the street, Alexander only acquired this city as part of the package he inherited from his Dad. Alexander had probably never set foot in the place, whereas I had actually made it here and knew my way around. I was one up on Alexander on that one, I thought nastily. I stalked next door and ordered pudding again.

When I had spooned up the last of the rice pudding and ordered a Greek coffee, which here had to be called a Turkish coffee, I pulled out the doll's face and examined it.

The little face did not seem a likely object to beat up on a fake Alexander *tetradrachm*, but this was a situation in which carved stone had prevailed against a hasty coating of electroplated silver. The white face was about an inch high, apparently carved in marble. The hairdo was simple, the contours of the stone cheeks, curved and smooth like the full moon. The face wore a neutral, almost preoccupied expression. To carve such a tiny face from marble must have taken great effort and the doll was undoubtedly very old. Perhaps it was not really a doll. Could this have been part of some sacred sculpture?

Now that I thought of it, most female images were either of a doll or a goddess. Goddess cults had abounded in the land that was now

Turkey. Istanbul itself, long before it was Christian or Muslim, had at one time been sacred to Artemis. Was the marble figure I bought in the bazaar not actually a doll's head, but something more? I recalled a gilded plastic statue of the Virgin Mary spotted in the gift shop of my childhood church after mass. I had coveted this little figure and had saved my allowance for weeks to buy it. Now I looked again at the enigmatic little white face in my palm. It was as mystifying to me as I was becoming to myself. Thoughtfully, I thrust it back in the pocket of my maroon jeans along with the wrapped coin.

That evening, I joined a group of Western backpackers gathering in the park. Someone passed around a bottle of *raki*—Turkey's powerful licorice-flavored answer to French Pernod. I had heard rumors—most likely untrue—that the liquor contained opium.

The drink, which Turks sometimes called Lion's Milk, certainly had a powerful effect. The crowd quickly grew merry. Some people started to sing. Soon the square by the fountain was alive with folk-singing. Turkish people in the park pressed nearer to hear the Western music. Then two English travelers started up a Donovan song I didn't know, the "Universal Soldier." It was an anti-war song. Perhaps it was not often broadcast in the United States because of the Vietnam War.

The Turkish police did not like this music much. By the time the singers reached the chorus about the soldier knowing he should not kill, uniformed men in helmets began emerging from the shadows, pulling out rubber hoses as they came. Descending on the crowd, the police started beating the Turks who had moved closer to hear the music. The impromptu concert ended abruptly. I hurried back to the Güngör.

Unable to read Turkish, I was unaware that the country's military leaders had intervened only a year earlier to force out a prime minister they disapproved of. They had executed student movement leader Deniz Gezmiş and two companions by hanging only two months before. It was no country just now for public sing-alongs.

In the night I dreamed of doll-like creatures:

We (my mother and I and perhaps some children) are in a house in my Virginia hometown discussing something ordinary, when the invasion begins. Strange vessels fly in the sky - black ships with claws like mantises. Then marionette men come to the door. They are like ventriloquist's dolls with full jointed bodies. One has a head like a waxy orange. We wait, knowing we have been conquered.

Later, a muster is held near a friend's house. Those fat enough are taken. Those not fat enough are to be fattened. I escape with others and seek refuge on a higher hill.

The scene changes, but not the sense of dread. I find jewelry, a necklace of sea green stones set in silver. Someone must have stolen a lot of things. I contemplate keeping it but then decide to call the police. I am trying without success to get through on the telephone—the classic telephone-dial-doesn't-work nightmare—when the black ships appear again in the sky.

The scene fades to a Hollywood cocktail party. I'm talking with someone who drops names. He's a director; he is making a film. I cut him off: "Tell me about your ideas, not somebody else's." He clams up, annoyed with me.

We all go into a banquet room. I'm not dressed up, but others are barefoot too. Passing down the serving line, as in a buffet, I get the wrong-sized plate. I try to cut a slice of turkey and instead get a huge chunk—too big to eat.

I woke up and lay in the metal bunk, my thoughts floating in a dozen directions, while underneath them, anxiety heaved and pulsed. Where should I go from here? How should I go? I faced the same old circle of terrifying alternatives. But something else was now entangled like flotsam in the roil of thought and dream: What was it? Byzantium, Black Ships, the tumultuous sea, biting off too much Turkey, the Bosporus, Cisterns. Boat.

Boat!

The word was like a shout. Suddenly I was wide awake. Could I go by water? Concentrating on the overland journey outlined in my guidebook, I had not considered the possibility of travelling by *boat*. Could it be done? Was there a boat?

I had been so engrossed with the chaos in my own head, I had not thought to consult the other women in the dormitory. Now I did. From the women in the adjoining bunk beds, I learned I could book passage on a Black Sea Ferry all the way to Trabzon in the east. On the *Ege* or the *Izmir* I could cruise up the Bosporus to the Black Sea and coast hundreds of miles along its southern shore for the princely sum of about $2.50. Furthermore, the two English women were planning to go East on the next boat. If I liked, they said, I could come along with them.

So the problem was solved, or should have been, but I still felt terrible. The night before I left Istanbul, I confronted my terror. This was raw terror. It didn't take any particular form, such as, "If I go, I'll run out of money." The terror just swept through me, like an icy panic. I lay in my steely bunk and shivered with it.

Finally, I had had enough. I cut my internal caterwauling off sharply, thinking: *Well, if you feel so frightened, you don't need to have this adventure. You can always just kill yourself right now.* It was harsh medicine, but looked at from that perspective, the upcoming adventure didn't seem quite so daunting.

And so I slept. And, in the morning, I got on the boat and sailed from Byzantium.

BOAT PEOPLE

I N THE MORNING AFTER the frightful night, I boarded the ferry together with Fiona and Felicity from the dormitory. As a welcome bonus, they brought a male traveling companion along with them. Julian had been on the road with the two since North Africa. However, if I had nurtured hopes that having a man along would make me feel more secure, this initial meeting quashed them. The two young Englishwomen were shorter than me, and Julian, barely taller than they were. With his sloping shoulders and narrow face, he did not look intimidating enough to discourage a mosquito.

According to the tickets, our assigned berths lay deep in the boat. Balancing our packs, we four tottered down a series of metal staircases only to discover that a great crowd was in the hold already. There were no berths left. Turkish men in country work clothes were busy staking out territory on the floor itself, planting thick bedrolls and stringing up canvas curtains to create cubicles around their families in the fast-filling hold. I briefly glimpsed children with hennaed palms and well-covered wives; then more curtains went up and walls of canvas blocked our view altogether.

Fearing there would soon be no spot anywhere aboard to lay out sleeping bags, we bolted back up the echoing steel staircases. If we had been squeezed out of steerage, we might at least snag some space on deck.

Open air space was still available. On Julian's suggestion, we stowed our packs in the shadow cast by a lifeboat hanging upside down from davits on the rear deck. Without any shade to retreat to, we would risk getting a hell of a sunburn during the three-day ride. Also, if the ferry started sinking, we would be well-positioned to be the first passengers into the lifeboat. None of us uttered this last part aloud, however.

Other Western travelers, meanwhile, were claiming places up in front of the bridge, where a breeze might reach them, if there ever was one. Like us, they were heading for India. I recognized several women from the Güngör's dormitory among the group on the forward deck.

Although there was a man in each of the deck groups, there were no couples among the Western travelers. Even if anyone among this generation made famous for free love had had the inclination, actually acting on the impulse would have required a level of privacy not possible on a boat's deck, I thought sourly. Clearly, it was to be a chaste voyage for everyone.

With a rumble, the ship backed out into the channel and pointed itself northwards. Chugging against the fast current, it pushed up through the Bosporus, passing between rows of old unpainted wooden Ottoman houses which lined the narrow strait. Some of these old-fashioned *yalis* were ornate. Yet others on the Asian side looked ramshackle and unsteady, like stacks of pies heaped too high by a careless baker. With their balconies listing and askew, the buildings appeared about to tumble board-by-weathered-board into the Bosporus, to be dragged south into the Mediterranean by the current in the strait. For a time I felt I was riding on an elevated railway observing suburbs and multistory tenements outside Chicago rather than passing between Turkish shores on the high deck of a seagoing ship. The view, like that from a commuter train as it rumbles by decaying industrial suburbs, was intimate, but hardly flattering.

Finally the big boat cleared the strait and emerged onto the vastness of the Black Sea. With a groan and a long slow pivot, the ferry swung right and headed east, hugging the coast. Ahead, I could see only calm water. To the ship's right-hand side, a ribbon of land seemed to keep pace with us. We were on course for Trabzon, 700 miles away.

IT DID NOT RAIN. (This was summer.) There was not much to do. I explored. Down a flight of stairs, on a covered deck, there was a snack bar that was sometimes open and sometimes had food. Often it had nothing and we were told to come back at another time. *Kebabs* were sometimes available, but when I sought tea, the answer from the steward was *"Chai yuk!"*

Chai was tea. *Yuk*, I soon learned, meant *there isn't any. Nope. Absolutely not!* On board, we heard it a lot. Although I saw mealtimes marked on a chalkboard, somehow I did not manage to arrive when food was actually available. I sat flat on the deck, close to the shadow of the lifeboat, with my legs out in front of me, and thought longingly of chocolate bars, bread, coffee, rice pudding, even mysterious hot peppers. But there were none. *Yuk!* I answered myself.

Hunger encourages boldness. When the boat swung into dock at one of the smaller ports, my travel foursome scurried down the gangplank to search out a marketplace. We found a food vender. But before we could finish making our purchases, in the middle of an open square in broad daylight, a man with one squinty-eye suddenly seized Felicity by the shoulder and refused to let go of her.

Short sandy-haired Julian now proved his worth. Easing slowly, never raising his voice, never seeming combative, Julian grabbed Felicity's other shoulder and tugged back just as firmly. Felicity popped like a package from the grabber's grasp. The encounter was over in seconds. Still carrying the bread we had managed to buy before the incident, we scrambled back aboard the *Ege*

I was shaken. This was exactly the kind of situation I had been most afraid of.

Julian just shrugged his sloping shoulders. "It's like a kind of judo," he explained flatly as we stepped onto the deck. "You never retaliate in kind. You don't escalate. You don't give in."

My companions had been travelling in North Africa, where precisely this kind of encounter seemed to have happened to them a lot.

"Oh, we had such an exciting time with some of those people," Felicity recalled with satisfaction, adjusting her blouse. "Do you remember that guy in Morocco? Oh, now *he* was weird!"

She shot a conspiratorial glance at Fiona. The two snickered.

This reaction seemed nuts. It was like watching women preen after being called lewd names by rowdy construction workers, but somehow much worse. The threat in the market had been serious. I now suspected my travel companions were titillated by such confrontations and sought them out. I had planned to travel all the way to India with this trio, but it was beginning to seem like a bad idea.

Later, I dragged my pack from under the lifeboat, unrolled my sleeping bag on the back deck, and lay wide awake for a long while, watching stars against a black sky, while the ship's engines thrummed through the night. I was on my way, and I was not as afraid as I had been in Istanbul. I was still wondering how I was going to get to India safely, when I fell asleep.

THE NEXT DAY, I STROLLED along the deck with an American serviceman bound for Synop. He hinted mysteriously of a secret U.S. operation that American media had just revealed. "Haven't you heard?" he whispered conspiratorially. The news exposés had compromised an important operation here in Synop, he told me. "It's in all the newspapers," he said. But the performance was lost on me. I hadn't seen any papers. The Soviet Union lay just across the sea to the north, and the Russians held the land along the Black Sea's eastern rim, too, when I thought about it. If someone wanted to do spy stuff, this was probably a fine place to set up a snooping operation.

I didn't really care. America seemed very far away from this little floating world, and this puffed-up soldier in his off-duty short-sleeved civilian sport shirt struck me as completely out-of-place among the Turks and backpackers as the ferryboat gnawed its way eastwards, pausing at intervals to release the traveling families from the hold to disembark at their home villages. I was in Asia, finally, and on my way to India. I had not come all this way to listen to some self-important Cold War junkie from home. I was glad when he got off at Synop.

In the evening, perhaps by way of apology for the scanty food, the ship's management set up a projector and screen on the front deck. Everyone trooped forward to see the free entertainment as the boat moved eastwards across a calm sea. Although the volume had been turned up to be heard over the engines, sound proved unnecessary for understanding: The movie was an Eastern, rather than a Western—an action film in what seemed to be a frontier setting: She is assaulted by bad guys and dishonored. He weeps bitter tears at her dishonor. So does she. Then they sing together. He attacks and kills the bad guys. She dies. He cries some more. Very maudlin. Very simple. Broad open spaces. Rural people. No kissing. A hit.

I gradually befriended the travelers on the forward deck. They were Eva and Michael, students from Berlin, who had met through a notice on a bulletin, and Dorrie and Melinda, Americans fresh from a six-week work stay at an Israeli *kibbutz*. But we were still separate, two bunches of Western tourists—the front deck people and the back deck people—proceeding in the same general direction. All of us being told *"Chai yuk!*

CROSSING DISPUTED TURF

O N THE THIRD night, the boat reached Trabzon, the Turkish city at the end of the line, and, as we disembarked in the darkness, the two groups of people lugging backpacks coalesced into a single cluster.

We waited in a bus station for transit onwards alongside a patient multitude of local people, under the station lights. Finally, we foreigners managed to board a minibus for Erzurum. I settled into a back seat by a partly open window. As the van started pulling from the station, a fat red-haired man approached it. Suddenly, he reached in through the vented window and savagely raked my exposed arm with his fingernails.

While the van negotiated the dark streets of Trabzon, I sat in shock, still jammed in the back seat by the window, sponging off my bleeding arm with a Kleenex. By the time we had left the town behind and were on the road to Erzurum, I was wondering whether I was going to need a booster tetanus shot.

And what was a fat red-haired man doing here, anyway? I might expect to see people of all hair colors and complexions in the melting pots of Brooklyn or San Francisco, but how did someone looking like this man come to be in Eastern Turkey? Aside from a few expensively-coifed and tinted women in the neighborhood of Istanbul's Hilton Hotel, most Turks I had seen had dark hair, dark eyes and olive skins. Was he Turkish? Some long lost descendent of Alexander's phalanx?

"Kurdish," someone in the minibus told me. "Armenian," another said. No one suggested Russian.

Here in Turkey's extreme east, the racial mix was different, reflecting the area's unsettled often deadly history. We were still in territory once occupied by Alexander's minions. Synop, where the boat had stopped, was an old Greek settlement. Trabzon where we had gotten off, had served as capital for a Greek remnant empire after Constantinople was overrun by the Turks in 1453. Erzurum itself had once been an Eastern outpost of the Roman Empire.

The local gene pool had been spiked like a science lab punch with strands and polymers from the many peoples who settled or were ousted as empires and fortunes of war scattered them across this strategic region. Armenians, who claimed the area from Biblical times, were mostly driven out and massacred in the early 20th century during the upheaval surrounding the establishment of the modern Turkish state

For a while, even in the 20th century, this region had been in Russian hands. Even now the Soviets lurked in their fortifications on the far side of Mt. Ararat, while Turks held the rest of the mountain and practiced defensive military maneuvers on its southern flank.

And my attacker: Was he a descendent of some ancient Alexandrian adventurer, an Armenian, Kurd, gypsy or Russian soldier's bastard? Or was he the grandchild of refugees, and if so, from which revolution, which culture? Was his attack on my light-skinned flesh (as pale as his) a geopolitical strike against Turkey's Western allies, or some frustrated sour grapes expression of lust? Was the attack personal or impersonal?

I had experienced very little violence. At a University of Virginia college weekend once, a boy in a taxi tore my coat because I would not make out with him in the back seat. "Look what you've done," I remember saying accusingly, holding the coat's camel hair belt under his nose to show him the stitches he had ripped. Then I had snatched up my purse, opened the cab door, and stomped up to my boarding house, abandoning the aggressor to pay the cabbie.

In graduate school, trying to cross Sproul Plaza, during the People's Park demonstrations, I had once found National Guardsmen armed with bayonets blocking my way, but no one there had actually hurt me.

This time, the situation wasn't so straightforward. I didn't deserve what had happened, but I wasn't exactly sure exactly what *had* happened, either. The nail marks on my arm told a story, but the details were tangled in a history I could not comprehend. They were as undecipherable as hieroglyphics must have been before the decoding of the Rosetta Stone.

The journey's next leg took us over the mountains to Erzurum, ancient capital of the Armenian province of Garin. I recall little more about this night ride. I had read in my guidebook bought so long ago on Telegraph Avenue that this route grew so cold in winter that truck drivers could sometimes be seen thawing their engines with blowtorches. But this was summer and there were no blizzards and blowtorches, only a rocking minibus. I brooded awhile more, and then I slept.

It was still dark when the minibus reached Erzerum. I have since read that Erzerum still retains signs of its earlier Armenian heritage—buildings which have been remodeled for Turkish purposes—but I didn't see them.

Disembarking in a glass-fronted transit station, I saw men in flat hats, as in Istanbul. Men throughout all Turkey, including those of Erzurum, had been ordered to abandon the Ottoman fez in the 1920s by Ataturk. The hat order had sparked a rebellion in Erzurum, but defiance had been firmly crushed. Permanently, it appeared: I saw the same ubiquitous flat hats in Erzerum as elsewhere.

Women were likewise freed of the veil by order of the new nationalist central government, but with veils, apparently, enforcement of the ban had been less decisive. An older woman huddled under a ragged flowing cloth in the bus station, her head definitely veiled. Sleepily, we maneuvered our luggage to a bigger bus and continued on.

By the time the sun was well up, the bus from Erzurum was winding along the southern flanks of Mt. Ararat. Noah's ark is believed by many to have made landfall on this mountain after the flood waters receded. We were not all that far here from the confluence of the Tigris and Euphrates Rivers, said to be the site of the original Eden. I had heard this called the Fertile Crescent, the birthplace of mankind, in grade school. The Arabs had called it al-Jazeera. In intervening millennia, war and mayhem and shifting borders had scattered a diversity of races in the region, just as the Scriptural elder had earlier scattered diverse species of animals from his grounded ark on Ararat across the face of the earth. Somewhere around here, the Amazons had once ruled, too, although nobody seemed exactly sure where or when.

This sweep of human history absorbed my thoughts as the bus rounded the bending curves of the foothill road. These days, Americans were barred from the mountain itself, because of constant Turkish military operations. The far side of Mt. Ararat was Soviet territory; this side belonged to Turkey, a friend to the NATO nations and host country for the spy station in Synop, or whatever it really was.

When the bus paused at a town, Turkish schoolboys, proud in their school uniforms, hair cropped close, stared at us without friendliness.

The border between Turkey and Iran lay near a place marked Bayazit on the old maps. I later identified this town in reference books as a one-time Armenian village in the Province of Garin—Garin, which once centered on Erzurum and extended from Ararat's slopes to somewhere near Trabzon. It now was no more at all.

My papers were in order. I was stamped out of Turkey at Gürbulak on July 7. It took no time at all, coming from the West in 1972 to leave Turkey behind and enter the land of the Shah.

SHOWDOWN IN MAKU

ND THEN, OUR PASSPORTS DULY stamped, we were beyond Turkey's frontier, entering Iran—the modern Persia. Not long after, the minivan brought us to Maku, the first town on the Iranian side of the border.

We stopped there for the night. By this time, after hours of being crushed together in the shared minivan, the two groups from the ferry had melded into an eight-headed entity. Together the eight of us rented an upstairs room with many small beds in a mud-fronted hotel, overlooking Maku's main street.

As we had traveled eastwards, through Turkey, time had seemed to slip a gear tooth, or two. Western Turkey, though ramshackle in places, now in retrospect seemed modern and familiar, with 20th-century inefficiencies and racing traffic. On the boat and in the country's east, we had seen hints of a more traditional culture: henna-decorated hands, a veiled woman huddled in a bus station corner.

As we looked out over Maku's main street, it was clear the clock had slowed and stuttered here much, much earlier. There's a legend that St. Thaddeus—an apostle of Jesus also known in the West as St. Jude—was martyred in Maku in the year 66 A.D. The place looked like not much had happened since. Of course, camel caravans plying their way eastwards and westwards no longer came through Maku. Instead, the town played host to truckers pausing on their highway journeys to or through the kingdom of the Shah. Ancient-looking adobe buildings still lined Maku's single business street, however. An even more ancient steep cliff loomed beyond these mud structures, seemingly composed of the same mud as the buildings.

There was no longer any sign that a Christian saint had met a dramatic end in this place. The saint probably hadn't been lucky enough to go out with a bang. Anyone obliged to stay long in this town would have suffered a martyrdom of boredom.

I wasn't bored, however. For me, reaching Maku was a high water mark, or more accurately, a milestone, or perhaps a line drawn in the dust. I had outrun my own terror and escaped from the West. I was somewhere else. I had finally gotten to the land beyond plate glass windows. Anything was possible.

And Maku definitely had possibilities. Maku looked just like a set for a Hollywood epic featuring early Christians and Romans. Viewing the scene with California eyes, I could picture a nice chariot race down the main street, with the cliff forming a dramatic backdrop. Provided, of course, that the charioteer's springs were sturdy enough.

Disorientingly, though, I began to notice that Maku also looked rather familiar. With the mud-and-wattle buildings along one side of the street nestled near the mud-colored palisade, it looked like the American West. I had seen abandoned ruins of the vanished Anasazi tribe sheltering against a cliff side on the Navajo Reservation at Canyon de Chelly. Maku's adobe structures and arid landscape called these Indian ruins to mind. The place also reminded me of the ghost towns and abandoned Western movie sets in the high desert beyond the spreading fringes of the Los Angeles suburbs. Everything there, too, was mud-colored, dusty, hot.

All that we needed to complete the fantasy, I decided, was Gary Cooper striding down a potholed Maku thoroughfare to confront his nemesis for a gun battle.

Cooper had been dead for a decade, but lacking a cowboy hero, we had the next best thing: Our hotel housed a gaggle of Australian men, loud and bawdy. They were on their way home, or to Europe, or South Africa, I forget which, but their noise was unforgettable. Evidently beer must be available somewhere in this Muslim town, or perhaps the men were hauling it secretly in their dusty Land Rover.

In the evening, we had a visitor. A local woman trooped up the hotel staircase to pay a call at the oversized bedroom where we lay chatting on our undersized cots like an affable coterie of Snow White's dwarfs. This enterprising visitor was old—at least 40—and plump. She was dressed like a gypsy fortune teller at the California state fairgrounds, glittering with bangles and sequins. Her brown hair—as a probable sop to religious sensibilities—was partially covered up with a scarf. She circled us, observing the eight dusty Westerners in dirty jeans from all angles, laughing and jingling as she went, and doing a little half-dance with her feet.

We stared back, puzzled. This dancing apparition was clearly no fairy godmother. I thought at first we were being visited by the village madwoman. Then I realized this dolled-up lady might be Maku's own edition of Miss Kitty or Miz Belle. Did she run a dance hall, I wondered? Should we point her down the hall to the Australians? Or was she merely a curious housewife, dressed up in local costume, stopping by to gape at the foreigners?

Perhaps Hollywood epics—Biblical or Western—had simply fallen out of fashion by 1972, or maybe there was not even a movie house yet in this dust-blown stop on the roadway to Asia. Or there just was not much to do in Maku. Whatever the reason, on the summer evening of our arrival, our travel-worn selves had constituted the most interesting sight in town.

In the morning, as we got up, we all noticed small blotches on our legs. These were not flea bites; I had had enough experience of fleas in East Oakland to know that much. As we lugged our packs back down the stairs to the street level, I experienced a perverse moment of exultation: Down and out in Maku, with bedbug bites to show for it! The bites might itch, but the sojourn definitely qualified as an adventure!

As I waited by the street side for the bus to Teheran, I decided that, if I ever got to direct an old-fashioned Western, I would have the good guy and the bad guy meet up at high noon in a place like this. Being

Hollywood stars, they would have the benefit of fake bullet wounds and copious flowing fake blood—not merely itchy bites—as proof of the showdown in Maku.

A COLD SHOWER IN TEHERAN

THE BUS TO TEHERAN, OPERATED by Mihantour, Iran's premier bus company, was heavily chromed and streamlined. As it pulled grandly down Maku's dusty street to pick us up, I thought again of the magnificence of the conquerors who periodically overran this sector where Armenia, Turkey, Kurdistan, and Persia bounded and blended. What would a town like Maku have made of Alexander and his trained phalanx smartly marching down its Main Street? How much pomp would it have taken to strike awe in a place now mostly infamous for its bedbugs? In 1972, an age of atomic bombs and called-in tactical strikes spilling napalm or cluster bombs from the heavens on tropical villagers, would anyone give an Alexander and his hardy band a second glance? The thought was grandiose and slightly garbled. Time had slipped again. Was I thinking about then or now or both? I dropped it.

Anyway, Alexander, had he even crossed here, might have been in a hurry, as I was, and not have given a damn what Maku's population thought. I realized I didn't either. Standing scratching by the roadside, I was hell-bent on reaching India. Iran was merely a country in the way, to be gotten through as quickly as possible. The bus stopped. In a flash, I was aboard, and Maku was disappearing in the back window.

The bus was far newer and fancier than any long distance carrier I might have taken at home. Iran's ruler, the Shah, had oil and wealth, and apparently a desire to show off his modern transit system.

I must have said something about this aloud, for Michael from Berlin shushed me. He had been to Iran before. In a lowered voice, he began explaining to us about the CIA-backed coup against a populist prime minister in 1953. Iran's oil production had been nationalized, upsetting Western companies, but the coup had quickly undone all that. The CIA's intervention had put the Shah back firmly in command. Since then, the Shah had ruled more autocratically, supported by his dreaded secret police, the SAVAK, Michael whispered. He didn't say what SAVAK stood for, but even the name sounded bad.

I knew a bit about the Shah, already. The Iranian monarch had visited the United States with his beautiful first wife in the early 1950s, on a goodwill tour, perhaps to thank America for putting him back in charge. My best friend in fourth grade was the daughter of a Farsi-speaking State Department interpreter. As his daughter, she had been allowed to go along when her father was assigned to accompany the Shah to Florida. When Katie got back to school, she brought me seashells from a distant white-sand Florida beach. These gleaming, iridescent, perfect shells were as tiny and exquisite as the details in Persian paintings.

The Shah's wife too had been gleaming and iridescent. I knew because I read about her in *Life* magazine. In the news photos at the time of their visit, the royal couple had appeared as glossy and romantic as the Kennedys later would become. America loved royalty, and even more, royal spouses. I did, too.

But now the glamorous Saroya was gone and so was some of the romantic luster. The Shah had a new wife. Wife number one, I learned, had not produced any babies. So what's a guy to do? If you're the Shah of Shahs, you gotta make the tough decisions, so he'd traded her in. Wife number two was also gleaming, iridescent, and beautiful. I could see this from color pictures of the royal couple hanging in the hotels, buses, offices. This very public upgrade of brides had been necessary to assure an heir to Iran's Peacock Throne.

The immaculate bus gleamed, like a throne room, or at least some temple to chrome. At intervals, a steward proceeded down the aisle, shaking perfume into our hands to refresh us. I tried not to be seen scratching.

The modern bus stopped at the modern bus station in Teheran, where drivers—or were they merely elderly passengers?—sat and sucked tobacco smoke through the upholstered pipes of a shared hookah.

Like Istanbul, Teheran had a cheap hotel district which catered to India travelers, but this district was much more modern. Streets were boulevards instead of cobbled lanes. There was a multi-storied Hotel Yankee, and another, the Amir Kabir, across a boulevard jammed with traffic. Our hotel was a high-rise building, not some 19th-century relic as in Istanbul. The Amir Kabir offered showers, but charged extra for hot water. Already worried about cash flow, I was hesitant to shell out the extra money. I took my showers cold and free.

I WENT OUT TO SEE THE CITY with the travelers who had been on the front deck of the Black Sea ferry. Near our hotel, we passed a modern fried chicken restaurant, with the Kentucky Colonel's headgear redrawn in neon on the sign to include a little skullcap out of deference to Muslim customers. We wandered in a modern fantastical indoor shopping mall, garnished with fairy lights, and multi-storied, like the hotel.

Crossing Teheran's streets was more treacherous than navigating inside the mall. Modern traffic lights had been introduced a few months ago by the Shah's government, but although there was heavy traffic, no one had yet learned how to obey the signals. Pedestrians were on their own in a melee of shooting vehicles.

Most women in the streets weren't veiled. Though some women wore a dark cloth over their heads and clothing, patterned or sprigged with an unobtrusive design, many others dressed as *chic* city women might in Paris, with fancy hairdos and well-cut outfits. The women who were not veiled had dark shining hair. They looked handsome, Mediterranean, modern.

The young men were less modern and Westernized, however. While local older men generally let us be, young guys were unpleasantly eager to touch the foreign women. Getting safely through the streets, even in numbers, proved difficult. We devised a hollow square formation, to protect our rear ends. Michael led the way, plowing through the crowds. Eva, Melinda, and I came after in a tight huddle behind him, while Dorrie marched a few steps behind us with a towel in her hand, poised to snap it at any passer-by who attempted to pinch or grab at us.

Many tried. The worst offender was a young man in Western dress apparently out walking with his girlfriend, who nonetheless reached out to snatch at a crotch as he passed by. In growing irritation, Eva, Melinda, and I moved warily through the busy city, following Michael and trailed by Dorrie. At times we smiled with delight to hear the whiz of the towel as Dorrie snapped it in our defense, rather as a ringmaster might hold off lions with a whip. Even if we were Western women and looked helpless, we were not wholly dependent on a man to keep us safe. After Dorrie grew tired, we took turns at the towel patrol to spell her.

Under pressure, Dorrie, Eva, Melinda, and I were turning into Amazons. "You shouldn't blame them," an American woman who lived in Isfahan lectured me, when I told her about it. "They have seen Western movies and think all women are like that." Maybe...but wasn't I human, too? It is hard to be charitable when you feel besieged.

The annoyance did not prevent us from sampling melon shakes at a corner stand. But the constant vigilance wore us down. Urban Teheran was a way station, not the destination. By the time we returned to the hotel, all of us were tired and fed up.

Back at the hotel, Fiona and Felicity and Julian—the English passengers I had traveled with from Istanbul on the ferry's back deck—still seemed uncertain about what to do next.

I showered again under cold water and thought yearningly of the luxurious Turkish baths in Istanbul, the rising steam, the hovering dome, and of the polite people in the Istanbul streets who had kept their hands to themselves. (The police with rubber hoses were forgotten.) I thought back to the episode during the ferry journey, when Fiona and Felicity had seemed to enjoy being harassed. The Amir Kabir's chilly water was bracing, and firmed up the decision I had already silently made: I didn't want to wait around and find out what these two thought of the grabby men in Iran's capital. I wanted to leave.

I pulled on my clothes and went next door to talk with the Germans and Americans I had spent the morning with. I was as ready as they were to get out of Teheran. Could I go along with them? That would be fine, they said.

As easily as that, the big travel cluster, which had formed as the boat docked at Trabzon and cohered through eastern Turkey and western Iran all the way to Teheran, now split in two. When my new travel mates—Eva and Michael from Berlin and the two Americans, Dorrie and Melinda from the kibbutz—went out to arrange for onward travel, I went along.

We were determined to sprint across the rest of Iran as fast as possible. All of us would need to get visas for India. Cleaned up, our cluster of five ventured first into Abbas Abad, the upscale neighborhood where the Indian Embassy was located. As we walked along the broad street near the embassy, it became impossible to ignore the fact that this green and gleaming suburb lacked sewers. On each side of the modern thoroughfare, a narrow cement channel carried a river of dark and apparently filthy water past the snowy facades of modern western buildings.

Next, with the Indian visas stamped in our passports, we went to the train station to reserve seats on the eastbound train. Since Michael had been this way before, we accepted his plan to team up with some other German travelers for the overnight journey to the holy city of Mashhad near Iran's eastern border. Together with the other Germans, we booked a full compartment as a precaution against unwanted attentions. It seemed unpleasantly like segregation, and I found it a shame that we needed to do this, but our treatment on the Teheran streets had provided a powerful cautionary lesson.

The next morning, as we waited at the station—a scruffy band of ill-dressed Western travelers crouched with baggage on the floor—Iranian men still tried to approach us. Station police shooed them away.

On the train itself, the presence of unveiled Western women caused a stir. As we set down our packs and seated ourselves, the window of the compartment into the train's corridor filled with the faces and gesturing hands of curious men, who pounded on the door and waggled their fingers suggestively as if grabbing at invisible female body parts.

They couldn't get in. We had firmly latched the door.

TEA AND SAVAK

I N MASHHAD, WE WERE ADOPTED as we stepped off the train by Ahmed, a friendly young man who had joined the rush of people approaching to greet new arrivals. Ahmed offered to take us on a tour of the town. He didn't ask for money. Innocents, we went with him—first to a hotel, then to a park, where we met young women our own age—students from Tehran who were in the holy city on a pilgrimage.

The women wore veils. In Mashhad, all women except ourselves were covered up under what looked like lightweight painting drop cloths. Frequently, we noticed that women held part of this cloth in place with their teeth to cover part of their faces as well. Mashhad is the site of the tomb of the Imam Reza, a martyr who is of particular holiness to Iran's Shiite Muslims. The city was very conservative. "We do not wear a veil like this when we are at home," one of the women, a Teheran graduate student, hastened to assure us, somewhat apologetically.

Melinda, Dorrie, Eva, and I paid a price for being Western women and unveiled. In a street near the shrine, small boys threw stones at us. Foreigners were not welcome at this holy site.

Untroubled by foreign jeans and tee shirts and lack of veils on the women of our group, Ahmed optimistically guided us to a carpet dealership. It seemed at first a vast grey warehouse, held up not by internal columns of steel, but by tall heaps of Persian carpets. We sat

on one beautiful rug. We drank tea and praised the handwork as a boy with a hooked implement whipped down rug after rug from the tall stacks. One by one, beautiful carpets were unfurled. One by one we commented on their beauty.

The merchant told us some were made by village or migrant women, using symbols which were traditional. One carpet featured a hookah—a Persian water pipe—in its design. Others had flowers and animals. Yet others were from the north, with different patterns and colors. In the dusty warehouse, we sat entranced, guests in an elaborate ruby-colored formal garden created by human hands, not nature. Ahmed hovered quietly by, translating as needed. Clearly, his job had been to deliver us here, and he had done it gracefully.

"Make me an offer," the merchant urged, but although all of us loved the carpets, nobody had much money. Ahmed had miscalculated. We were on our way East, not West. There was no way to carry a carpet along. Over the merchant's growing protests, we dragged ourselves, and Ahmed, away, without buying anything.

Ahmed took us next to a low budget restaurant where we were served a local soup which he claimed was a specialty of the place. The soup, which was the color of chickpeas, came with a huge oval of hot soft flatbread and a large aluminum mallet. Ahmed demonstrated how to eat the soup. Copying his gestures, I placed the metal mallet into the soup bowl and pumped it up and down, mashing together the chickpeas and the meat. Then, tearing off pieces of the soft flatbread to soak up the mush, I ate my soup.

Soon after, I needed a bathroom, and the restaurant's hostess pointed me in the right direction. I was not in modern Teheran anymore. In a row behind the building stood a line of privies with wooden seats. The experience was not new. I recalled staying in a 19th-century house on an island off the Rhode Island coast one summer as a child. That house had a hand pump at the sink in the kitchen and out back—a four-hole arrangement. *Did people chat while sitting?* I remember wondering.

Something, I told myself, *is truly international about this.*

After lunch, the ever-hopeful Ahmed made yet another suggestion. We would go and see a psychologist, he announced, "one who is interested in the West." Like docile children, once more we trooped after our volunteer guide.

The psychologist, a middle-aged balding man, welcomed us to a lovely modern apartment, furnished with exquisite carpets. Graciously, he seated us all—Michael, Dorrie, Melinda, and me, and our new pal, Ahmed—on well-made comfortable sofas. Like the carpet dealer, he served us tea. We were in a private dwelling. I had expected leisurely courteous discussion, but instead our host began—rather abruptly, I thought—to ask questions: Were we students? How did people view Iran in the West? What did...? The questions were becoming stranger and more probing. Even with differing cultural conventions, this didn't seem like a normal social encounter.

The situation was starting to feel weird and uncomfortable.

Michael grew anxious. "Let's get out of here," he hissed.

We got the message: "Uh...we have to go now," Dorrie immediately announced. We abandoned our tea and left the psychologist's apartment in a hurry. In the street outside, we thanked Ahmed and firmly dumped him.

"That was no psychologist," Michael said quietly, once we were alone. "That was one of the Shah's secret police, the SAVAK." We left the neighborhood as quickly as possible.

Once we were well away, I had time to be impressed. Here in a single day, we had chatted with mysterious veiled women, shared tea with a rug merchant, been pelted with stones by children near a mosque, and grilled by the secret police. I had witnessed a privy of massive proportions, and used it successfully.

I wondered if Alexander had passed through Mashhad. If so, I wondered if he had hurried to leave as quickly as we planned to.

In the morning, we raced to the Afghan consulate to obtain visas, and then hailed a cab for the bus station. We were running late for the bus to the border. The driver rammed down the accelerator and we sped off through traffic. When our black beetle-backed cab hit another, we scrambled into yet a third cab, leaving the drivers of the first two still arguing over the accident. We arrived at the station just in time to climb aboard the bus to the border at Taybad. This vehicle was not modern. There was no chrome in sight. Everything we owned was taken from us and strapped onto the top. As the bus lurched out of Mashhad, crammed with Western travelers headed for Afghanistan, I wondered if I would ever see my possessions again.

In the early afternoon, the bus from Mashhad rolled into the border town of Taybad. We climbed wearily down, retrieved our luggage, and handed it up to be loaded onto the roof of the bus for Afghanistan. On foot, we headed for the border crossing with our passports. Iranian border guards, however, informed us the border was already closed for the day. A crew of touts poured out of the shabby hotels which lined the town's one business street. "Hotel mister? Hotel mister?"

Although it was still broad daylight, the bus to Afghanistan would not be going anywhere. There was nothing modern about this set-up. It looked suspiciously like an old-fashioned con, orchestrated through a collusion of hotel owners and border guards: Close the border, sell more hotel rooms.

Incredulous, the Afghanistan-bound Western travelers, now swelled to a busload, declared their outrage.

"We're not such fools," someone muttered. Rebellion seethed.

"I'm not gonna be screwed into staying in any dump of a hotel," another declared. "I'd rather sleep in the desert than do that."

It sounded like a good idea. In a show of unity the entire foreign contingent retrieved our packs from the bus roof, shouldered them, and stalked around the guard post, out into the sand of the no man's land, where we sat down in protest.

Amazingly, no one stopped us. The SAVAK man had been ditched back in Mashhad and the Shah's other all-seeing minions must have been gazing elsewhere, not at the rebellious cluster of unarmed foreigners sitting so determinedly in the sand a few feet beyond his border. Perhaps bothering us might have caused an international incident. Or maybe this happened with every bus that arrived here.

All of us—European and American alike—had been brought up on

Hollywood Western movies. We knew what to do: Lacking wagons, we unrolled our bedding and laid out our sleeping bags in a circle. The day waned. Darkness came. Marko, a tall hippie from Yugoslavia, sat up, playing familiar Bob Dylan songs on his guitar and keeping watch over the rest of us protesters. It was a fine time to hear the music of wandering and restlessness and missed connections.

Then the desert wind came up. Sandy grit whipped about, smacking and scouring our faces as we lay in the sand. This was how the desert had always been for travelers.

Though only a few feet from the guard post, this camping spot was as far into the wild as I had ever been. Letting loose of the 20th century, and giving in to the necessity on which all those veiling customs in this part of the world had originally been based, I tugged a corner of scarf over my face and rolled over on my side to sleep.

It was a fitting final night at the edge of a country I hoped never to lay eyes on again.

TIME TRAVEL

IN THE MORNING, WE crossed the miles of desert no-man's-land into Afghanistan, where the calendar did not run on Western chronology. The year was no longer 1972, as indicated on my Iranian visa, but now was 1351, stamped into my passport in vibrant purple ink by an Afghan official at the Islam Qala border station.

Outside the dusty customs post awaited a bus unlike any our group of five had encountered previously on this trip across Asia. This was no Iranian Mihantour luxury cruiser with reclining seats and a fellow striding up the aisle to spray perfume onto our outstretched hands, like that we had taken on the road to Teheran. Instead, the idling bus was old, short, and hand-decorated. Idealized peaceful landscapes in restful blues and greens were painted in lozenges along the bus's flanks so that the vehicle looked like the backdrop at a carnival booth. Although the seats inside might later prove hard on our butts, we would nonetheless be traveling from the border to the ancient city of Herat within a motorized rolling billboard for an earthly paradise.

The swift passage through customs without any snarls or unreasonable searches had raised our spirits. Gamely, we handed up our backpacks to the man on the roof to be added to the unsteady heap of baggage already being strapped on top of the bus. We climbed aboard in a jolly mood. It was like getting onto a merry-go-round. Within the bus, a fringe of gilded hangings dangled along the top of the front windshield. I half expected to sit down for the ride on a lion or bear or charging horse. But I was to be disappointed: The seats were decrepit. By the standards of most amply-padded Westerners, they also looked extremely tiny.

At the front of the bus, an elderly man wearing a gold skullcap with a huge turban wound around it was already sitting in the row immediately behind the driver's seat. A huge knife, like a machete, lay in the seat beside him. A little daunted, we marched on past, squeezing into a couple of rows further to the back. After the sprint through Iran lugging our backpacks, none of us was amply-padded any more, if we ever had been. These seats might be as tiny as the ones on a school bus, but we were fit and trim now, and we managed to fit into them.

After the baggage loading finished, the driver climbed back aboard the bus, and we set off with a rattle and a roar and a belch of diesel smoke. And perhaps because this, too, reminded us of the stops and starts of childhood schoolbus excursions, we spontaneously began to sing.

When you are three Americans—two of them fresh off a *kibbutz* stay—and two Germans—who have not sung much in English since childhood—the song choices are rather limited. It was inevitable that the tunes would date from summer camp and field trips. We were not very good singers, but what we lacked in musical finesse, we made up for in volume.

The turbaned elder in the seat behind the driver swiveled his head to watch us as we sang. Clearly, he liked the music. He liked it so much he would not allow us to stop.

After a few numbers, we paused to catch our breaths, but we were not permitted to rest for long. The imposing old man gestured emphatically at us as a chorus director might. "*Brake, brake,*" he commanded, patting his knife for emphasis.

We didn't know what his words meant, but it was at least clear what he wanted. We resumed singing. However, the jolly mood had dissipated. We had, after all, slept out last night in the sand and had spent the morning in customs. We were also somewhat out of breath. And we were a little scared.

Urged on by the old man's chopping hand gestures, however, Eva, Michael, Dorrie, Melinda and I kept on singing, though a strained note had crept into our voices. All the while, we eyed the old man and his knife.

Our shared repertoire was not extensive. We all knew "Where Have All the Flowers Gone?" which is based on a Turkish poem, but somehow a protest number did not seem like a good idea just now. Finally, we managed to dredge up a few doo-dah verses of "The Camptown Races."

The bus bounced along towards Herat, accompanied by our own bouncy choruses. After the final doo-dah, still eyeing the knife warily, we rummaged even further back in childhood recollections. "Old Mac-Donald had a farm," we bellowed, thumping on the seat backs in front of us.

None of us had been raised on a farm, I realized, although the guy on the front seat with the knife undoubtedly had been. He probably really knew what farm animals should sound like. Staring at his glittering knife, like a hypnotized audience member at a magic show, I imagined our Afghan song leader could also probably gut a goat and skin it in minutes flat.

It was prudent to keep him entertained. I had earlier spent a few weeks on a Greek island. Remembering the wandering shepherds and their flocks on the hillsides in Ios, I tried to make the animal noises as realistic as possible. Surely Dorrie's and Melinda's kibbutz experiences could help out here as well! Anything to keep the peace aboard this rocking bus!

"And on his farm he had a sheep. With a ba-ha-ha-bah here and a ba-ha-ha-bah there...." I bleated, struggling to get a realistic quaver into the final "bah."

The old man did seem to like this. The fierce eyes softened a bit. "Ee-aye-ee-aye-oh!" we chorused, and stopped, exhausted. The old man picked up his knife. *Oh-oh.*

He reached for a plump yellow melon on the seat beside him and began cutting it up. He passed out slices to all of us. The performance was over, and we had really misread the man's intentions. Embarrassed, we quickly passed around the melon slices.

Eva began eating immediately.

Melinda hesitated. "I've heard that melons don't filter out amoebas," she whispered, nervously. She was a nurse, who ought to know, but under that turbaned elder's imperious eye, she ate her own portion, every bit. When we had finished, and I had spit the seeds into my last Kleenex, the old man graciously offered us seconds.

Shortly afterwards, the little bus rumbled into the outskirts of Herat. We were likely approaching Afghanistan's westernmost city using the same route taken over two thousand years ago by Alexander the Great. Although there's dispute as to whether Alexander actually conquered this city on the Silk Road or merely built it himself, it is known that when he got to this location by the Hari Rud River, Alexander had been only 26. He would have just come from Persia, where he had been making appearances in Persian costume in efforts to convince the empire he had just conquered to accept him as its new king. The conqueror had been younger than me, when he entered this area, accompanied by his phalanx of Macedonian warriors. He had made an impressive journey East.

Alexander's act was a hard one to follow, but I did have one advantage over the great conqueror. For all his achievements and costume changes, Alexander had certainly never managed to arrive in a Central Asian city sticky-handed with melon juice and sounding and feeling like a sheep.

IN THE TIME OF THE KING

THE ROAD LED PAST weather-corroded stubs of ancient monuments and mosques, among them the tomb of the Sufi poet, Ansari, then onward into the town. The bus rattled up a broad dusty street passing low buildings, well set back from the roadway. They looked like Mexican haciendas in a Zorro movie. Some of them were clearly hotels—nice ones!

We found a room for five on an upper floor at a more modest hotel fronting on the main street. Hamid, a handsome and vain young Pushtu man with slicked black hair and a full face, owned the hotel, but a pair of gentle schoolteachers, moonlighting in the tourist trade, actually ran it. Unlike Hamid, whose family came from Kandahar in the south, both Azim and Nabil were local men, not Pushtu but ethnically Persian. The two clerks looked refined, bookish, and thin. In another national setting, they might have been young professors or accountants. Hamid, on the other hand, seemed well-fed, forceful and macho. He might have been comfortable spurring a horse in a John Wayne movie, or better yet, goosing a speedy motorcycle over rough ground and flying over fences in some World War II escape film.

I ordered up a shower at the hotel. All hotels have such amenities for guests. In Teheran, I had been asked to pay extra for hot water and declined. However, I had at least been offered the possibility of entering a modern shower booth, turning on hot and cold faucets, and scrubbing away to my heart's content. A decision to shower in oil-rich Teheran had involved a modern shower stall and plumbing.

In Herat, the same decision set in motion a series of human labors. A hotel clerk called a servant and gave him orders. The servant filled up a clay pot with water and began trudging up a narrow staircase to the top of the hotel. To feed the shower, the water carrier must empty that water pot into a rooftop tank. I stood waiting, soap in hand, in a little room directly beneath the tank. Finally, gravity, rather than a pump, sent a small stream of water flowing down.

Westerners use a lot of water compared to desert people. As I soaped myself under what seemed to me little more than a trickle, I could hear the servant once again climbing the stairs and afterwards, the sloshing sound as a second potload of water tumbled into the rooftop cistern above my head. I hastened to rinse off. It was not altogether clear whether the water bearer could look down and see me in the shower, and I did not want to be putting on any cross-cultural peep show.

Another water-filled terra cotta pot stood in the hall outside the registration office. One of the clerks explained that moisture soaking through this vessel's porous sides would evaporate at a slow rate, cooling the water within. Tourists who dared drink such unpurified water could slake their thirsts using a dipper hanging beside the jar. Worried about contracting amoebic dysentery from contaminated water, I didn't dare try out the dipper.

For sundries travelers might need, a child kept shop on the steps by the hotel's doorway, spreading out coarsely-made jewelry hand-set with bright red and turquoise stones, folding knives, and other small-sized knickknacks. This was a far cry from the multi-tiered shopping mall in Teheran.

In another way, though its people were also Muslims, Afghanistan seemed utterly unlike Iran. Eva, Dorrie, Melinda and I had been harassed in contemporaryTeheran, but Iranian women themselves had appeared to walk freely in the city without veils or problems. True—in the more conservative holy city of Mashhad, small boys had pitched stones at us as we foreign women walked unveiled near the shrine of the Imam Reza. However, even in that sacred city, Iranian women's faces were not entirely covered up. They went about wearing lightweight cloths floating over their heads and clothing. Compared with Herat, even conservative Mashhad with its broad streets and sidewalks now seemed practically European.

Here in Herat, women were simply not visible. Or rather, a woman's vague outline might be glimpsed, but only as a child dressed up as a ghost is sighted on Halloween, its human form completely shrouded under draped cloth. But even children in ghost costumes still have eyeholes to peer through. In Herat, almost every woman wore an all-enveloping outer garment, which fell in tiny pleats from a cap at the top of the head almost to the ground. It obscured a woman's face completely, with a netted grillwork masking even her eyes.

Elsewhere, I would learn, the garment was also called a *burka*, but in Herat, where I initially saw this smothering costume, I heard it called a *chador*. It sounded like "shut door," and for the wearers, that's what it amounted to.

Black, brown or deep purple and usually shiny as rayon, the *chadors* eradicated women from the bustling life of the city. Were the women of Herat lean and handsome like the men? Or corpulent? I had no clue. Sometimes I caught a peek of Victorian-era pantalettes, trimmed with delicate eyelet like clothing out of *Gone with the Wind*, dangling just below the chadors' hems.

The eyelet pantalettes hinted of a private life less demure, but the women's ankles—dusty, dry, and wrinkled—testified to a hard life, made harder by the netting grillwork which restricted vision. Wearing this garment, a woman could not be seen by passers-by. From within, the door to the world and its possibilities must have seemed firmly shut. A woman could not even see to walk without tripping in the uneven street. It was as if half of Herat's population were transformed from living beings into individual walled cities, protected and imprisoned behind barriers of suffocating fabric rather than mud bricks. Literally hemmed in.

And yet, I found that as a Western woman out and about, no one bothered me. This was strange. The reaction was utterly unlike the response my mere existence in the streets had provoked in seemingly modern Teheran. My guidebook suggested that this apparent tolerance was because Afghanistan had not been a colony, under a foreign thumb. But in fact, my later reading showed Afghanistan had felt the pressures of multiple conquering thumbs: This territory had been overrun by Alexander, by Genghis Kahn, by Persian conquerors, by Tamerlane, and by the British. The guidebook acknowledged these comings and goings, but contended that only the cities had been held, and that country people could always melt back to the mountains, retaining their proud dignity and traditional ways.

It was a nice-sounding explanation, but I wasn't convinced. Here in Herat, which had been a city since ancient days, wasn't I dealing with city people, rather than country ones? The matter was surely more complex. And I couldn't see any proud dignity in hiding women so thoroughly.

Yet, as I walked along the main street, without any such veiling, no one threatened me. Eva and I entered a neighborhood teahouse, or *chaikhanna*, on the main street not far from the hotel. There tea drinkers— all men except ourselves—sat on a wide shelf, carpeted with what looked like a Mexican serape striped in alternating bands of eye-popping red and blue. At the end of this shelf, an old man sat playing an ancient stringed instrument, a rebab. The mood was very different from the razzmatazz of cassette recorders on the buses.

I sat with a short tea glass fluted like a column on a Greek temple. The tea within gleamed like an amber jewel. I listened to the instrument's plucked melody and felt soothed. I felt I could linger forever, in fact, as if I had been perched on this startlingly bright carpet sipping tea since the start of time. When I shut my eyes, the bright colors beneath me seemed to reverse and pulse and dance cartoonishly behind my eyelids, keeping time with the notes of the rebab, rather like the dancing bands of color in Walt Disney's cartoon epic, *Fantasia*.

Andy Warhol would love this, I thought, happily and somewhat giddily. I was hooked.

Eva and I finished our tea in peace. No one had denied us service. No one gave us a pinch, or even a glance. It was as if, by virtue of being foreign, we had become honorary men, immune to the social and physical pressures which forced Afghan women to shut up and cover up.

Everyone—that is, all the men, since only men could be talked to—spoke very slowly. I had thought Central Asian talk would be ornate and indirect, but the language barrier made such circumlocution impossible. In the manner of those who are first learning English, for whom circumlocutions and euphemisms are more difficult, most Afghans I talked to seemed to be saying exactly what they meant, speaking of significant matters, rather than uttering calculated patter or formulaic courtesies.

So that my own English would be understood, I, too, began speaking slowly and distinctly. I too became more direct, my language simplified. It had not occurred to me until now how much I usually softened and masked my own feelings with language, draping unpleasant truths with a flood of genteel self-abnegating prose. Now that such white lies were impossible, I was forced to speak more from the heart. My voice seemed to grow lower, clearer. I felt intensely present.

Thus unexpectedly, here in Herat, where local women were subjected and covered up, I felt both bared and safe. Even as I looked over copies of English language magazines in which the pictures of women in swimsuits had been blacked-over with a magic marker by the country's vigilant censor, I felt I had nonetheless reached someplace incredibly intimate and accepting. I found I could go where I wanted unveiled, and people spoke to me as if I were a person, not a sex object.

With Marko, the lanky taveler from Yugoslavia who had played guitar the night we all camped out in the desert no-man's-land, I crossed the street to visit a wizened old man who ran a competing hotel. Despite speaking little English, the old man held court in a small room with extraordinary charisma and charm. Was this one of those enlightened individuals I should expect to encounter along the path eastwards? I wondered, as I sat on the floor along with a half-dozen visitors in the bare, but still rather stuffy, room. Grinning and guru-like, the old man asked his grown son to translate for him. I bent forward to hear. Was a secret of life forthcoming? Would I come to understand the traditional role hashish played in this ancient culture?

The son spoke up: His father—a man who had to be at least in his seventies or eighties—was experiencing his first LSD trip, the son announced. The wrinkled oldster chuckled, and then spoke up himself.

"Girl from Tucson," he pronounced in clear English, grinning infectiously, letting us know who had provided the acid for his psychedelic experience.

I would have grinned back, but the ripe hashish smoke, which had slowly been filling the small room, was by now making me dizzy. The elder began calling on his son to bring out swords. Boxes were dragged out and opened. I was reminded of how the men in my photography class back in San Francisco had shared technical discussions, comparing the shutter speeds and spot meters on their expensive camera equipment.

I realized with a jolt that I was the only woman in the room. I got up. Marko stayed. As I left the room, the group began baring, stroking and comparing their favorite blades. I was not, after all, comfortable being one of the guys.

A DAY LATER, Michael, Dorrie, Melinda, Eva and I and trooped out to dinner at the only fancy restaurant in our part of town—an upstairs ballroom-sized establishment. The place gave new meaning to the concept of a high table, for instead of pulling chairs up to a linen-draped table, we sat on the table itself, as everyone else did, and ate from dishes set at our feet. It seemed very decadent, somehow, feasting in the air as waiters scurried along the aisles between the tables and handed up food. Social stratification here was literal: I felt like a pasha, sitting cross-legged three feet in the air, as the hustling servers raced past us, balancing platters.

Even though I was not alone, I felt a little awkward dining unveiled in a room filled with fierce-looking men. Besides us, there were almost no other women. Climbing down from the high table after dining was also an awkward experience. None of us felt any urge to repeat the adventure. It was more difficult to eat at a fancy restaurant than at a neighborhood tea house, where things were less formal.

But it was harder still to feel connected to the women of Herat. Although I have read since that in the good old days under King Zahir

Shah, who was still on his throne when I entered Herat, women were freer than they would later be under Taliban rule, I did not observe any such freedom. Somewhere, in a better part of town, there might be showers with mechanical plumbing. Somewhere, perhaps in diplomatic enclaves at consulates, women at cocktail parties might be lifting stemmed glasses in toasts alongside the visiting notables. With more money and connections, I might have joined them and my experience might have been altogether different. However, that summer in 1972, in the westernmost city in the realm of the old king, I saw only two Herati women who didn't wear the veil. One was a teller in the bank where I changed money, and the other, spotted in the fancy restaurant the night of our dinner out, was described to us later by a local man as either a belly dancer or a prostitute. All the other urban women I saw in this ancient Afghan city were thoroughly bundled under the *chador's* enveloping fabric.

Perhaps sisterhood with those veiled women I couldn't even talk to was simply too painful to contemplate. Or it is possible my surging excitement at being taken seriously came only from one chamber of the heart, while another chamber, hidden, even from me, vigorously thumped a protest I chose not to hear, or could not hear just yet. Although I was totally unexpectedly falling in love with Afghanistan, I was definitely not living like a local.

A PEARL UNSTRUNG

WANDERING IN THE CITY, I CAME upon a high ruin built of mud, undoubtedly historic. The building, at least a city block long, had rounded watchtowers at the corners of its crumbling adobe walls. I moved closer to examine the massive structure. To my amazement, soldiers issued out, violently waving their hands to chase me away. This was still a working fortress.

Although the archaeological records are fuzzy, I have since read that Alexander built (or rebuilt) this citadel before he left Herat on his way eastwards. There is a lot to be said for the written word, but where Afghanistan is concerned, not many accounts agree. Some narratives indicate the conqueror founded the town, too; others suggest Alexander simply renamed it after himself. (If so, the name didn't stick.) Indisputably, however, the actual citadel in Herat endured because it was still needed for the city's protection.

For this ancient land had a long history, and little enough of it had been peaceful. Would-be empire-builders from Alexander to Timur had come and conquered, often at heavy human cost to the local population. Timur, for example, known as Tamarlane in the West, is believed to have tied together 2,000 captives after putting down a rebellion near Herat. He then had these captive rebels—still alive—walled over to create a pillar.

Starting in the 19th century, Afghanistan faced interference from the Great Powers as the Russians and the British—jealous partners in what was diplomatically called the "Great Game"—wrangled for control of the region. Each superpower, fearful that the other might gain an advantage, had stood at or—in the British case, occasionally *within*—Afghanistan's borders, ever ready to meddle and manipulate. In the early 20th century, Germany had also joined the interested superpowers.

In addition to those who had trampled through, the region's contemporary inhabitants constituted a sometimes problematic mix of peoples. While a large nomadic population, the *kuchi*, wandered from place to place with their flocks and camels, other groups were less copacetic. In the south lived the powerful Pushtus, many of them tribal people who made claims to grandeur. Pushtus contended variously that they were either the original Aryans or else descended from the twelve lost tribes of Israel, perhaps both. In Herat, near the current border with Iran, the traditional population were not Pushtus, but ethnic Persians, the people dark-haired and fine-featured. In the central mountainous regions lived Hazara people—very Asian in appearance, and practicing a different brand of Islam. And somewhere up near the Soviet border, there were Uzbeks. While all these groups were religious Muslims, this fact did not mean that they automatically admired each other or were equal.

With the potential for disharmony seldom far off, it was no wonder that households and citadels had thick walls like those of the haciendas in the American West! Every fortified building—no matter how weather-beaten—might be needed in the future to defend against the next ambitious warlord or superpower.

Yet, despite all this and the fact the nation-state of Afghanistan had existed barely longer than the United States and thus was a mere baby in international affairs, its major cities, Herat, Kandahar, and Kabul, were venerable and famed throughout Asia.

The portion of western Afghanistan that included Herat used to be part of a region called Khorasan. This region's borders had stretched and shrunk as human migrations traversed Central Asia and empires rose and fell. In the 13th century, the poet Rumi described the world as a sea and this Khorasan region as existing like a "pearl-oyster" within that sea. Within Khorasan, Rumi affirmed, Herat was like "the pearl in the middle of the oyster."

Pearls seem to figure large in Central Asian imaginations. This may be because desert people dream of the sea. Or perhaps it is because pearls, like gems, are lustrous, rare, and shining. And lightweight: Like gems, pearls constitute highly portable wealth.

But cities are not portable. So why should the city of Herat be considered a pearl? Perhaps it was because Herat, like other Asian cities we had passed through, formed a precious bead on a string of caravan stops and oases which stretched across Asian deserts and wastelands. Along this ancient highway, actually a skein of pathways collectively known as the Silk Road, caravans bearing silk, travelers, and ideas had traveled westwards towards the barbarian marketplaces of Europe, and southwards towards India. In its heyday, made rich by trade, Herat was a very grand city, famed for its wine, its poets and scholars, and adorned by hundreds of religious colleges and thousands of shops.

In the 17th century, Herat and Khorasan still lay firmly tucked within Persia's Safavid Empire. But early in the 18th century, a Pushtu warlord from Kandahar successfully snatched Herat away from the Persians. A few years later, he lost the city to the so-called Persian "Napoleon," Nader Shah, a Persian upstart from Khorasan. Nader Shah led conquering armies all the way to India., but once he died, another Kandahari warlord, Ahmad Shah, moved in and wrested the "Pearl of Khorasan" back into Pushtu hands.

Ahmad Shah, Herat's new owner, came from the Abdali tribe of Pushtus and had a penchant for pearls. Earlier he had changed his own name and that of his tribe to "Durrani" (literally, "Pearl of the age").

Ahmad Shah Durrani must have been pleased with his acquisition of Khorasan's pearl. He must have rejoiced in the belief that his thumb was firmly planted on the lucrative silk trade and its cultural benefits. The self-made king must have felt pleasure at the prospect of rolling this shiny pearl between his fingers and watching the revenues roll into his kingly coffers.

But the Pearl of his Age had arrived a little late at the party. An era was already emerging in which caravan ground travel through desert lands would no longer constitute the preferred shipping arrangement for the world's goods. Even before Ahmad Shah mounted the throne of a unified Afghanistan in Kabul, the string on the necklace of cities binding East to West had already begun to fray.

For Herat's riches were built on the silk trade. Technological transfers had dealt this trade a series of blows. In ancient days, China held a monopoly on silk production, and all silk came from China. This Chinese monopoly was broken in 522 A.D., however, when a pair of daring monks succeeded in sneaking silkworm eggs to Byzantium hidden among their belongings. The eggs hatched. A domestic silk industry began growing up in Europe, gradually undercutting the demand for exotic Chinese imports and the need for the caravans.

Herat's fortunes fell further with the invention of better navigation instruments, for much of the laborious East-West caravan trade could shift offshore—onto ships. The deserts and mountains of what would become the contemporary landlocked Afghan state were not well-suited to developing naval power.

The coming of the industrial age completed the collapse of the caravan Silk Road with its strings of sturdy camels. The existence of planes, trains, trucks, and ships meant there were alternatives for the delivery of goods around the world. By the 20th century, in countries neighboring Afghanistan, sturdy Volvo and Mercedes trucks plied highways laid over what remained of the caravan routes; nation-spanning railroads freighted trade goods not going far enough to require hoisting aboard ocean-going vessels. And there was airfreight, too. In the age of modern shipping, a package bound from Genoa to China no longer needed to pass through Afghanistan to get there.

Deprived of the control over trade that once had made its cities wealthy, 20th-century Afghanistan had become a backwater. Borders had shifted, territory slunk away. Herat, once renowned as an international boomtown, which had hosted scholars such as Avicenna and the poet Ansari, was now hard up. Khorasan, which once included Herat and Balkh, was now a province in Iran, on the far side of the no-man's-land we had so recently crossed. Rumi's ghost, making a return visit to Herat, would have had to update his maps and his metaphor considerably, for the Pearl of Khorasan had turned out to be more of a worry bead.

In Iran, by contrast, there was trade and wealth. Oil development had fueled a great shift toward Western-style modernization, imposed outwards from Teheran to the hinterlands and downwards from an autocratic oil-rich Shah on everyone else.

But while contemporary Iran seemed to have sprinted towards a modern, if despotic statehood, Afghanistan had dawdled and grown economically shabby. Zahir Shah, Afghanistan's French-educated king was making efforts to modernize, but no legal commodity, such as oil, had emerged to buoy up Afghanistan's economy. At the time I arrived, the country's regions, though connected by age-old trade routes, were still not firmly bound together. Forbidding mountains still blocked road transport for much of the country. No railroad crossed Afghanistan. The modern highway connecting Herat to the capital at Kabul, was very recent. Built with foreign aid from Soviet Russia and the United States, it had only opened in the mid-1960s.

Afghanistan still exported sheepskins, dried fruits, and nuts. There was opium, too, I knew, but it did not grow in Herat, and I did not learn very much about it. Clearly, opium was not filling the government's coffers. And there were sweet melons; we had sampled these aboard the bus from the border. And ruddy pomegranates could be had in the market. Some of these were undoubtedly exported, but Afghans of all ethnic backgrounds, like any sensible people, probably elected to eat most of the homegrown fruit themselves.

Within Herat, the relationship between the hotel's owner and his clerks reflected the region's shifting history of conquests and migrations. Hamid, who had arrived from Kandahar with family money, seemed to occupy the top economic tier, at least for now, while the Persian-speaking hotel clerks representing the city's older local culture, were subordinated.

Like most Herat residents, both Asim and Nabil spoke *Dari*, a closer relative of the Persian language than Hamid's *Pushtu*, as their first language. This language divide was another tangible reminder that the Iran-Afghan border we had just crossed had not always stood at its 1972 location.

But speakers of Dari and speakers of Pushtu shared a common need for new economic activity. In Herat—Afghanistan's westernmost city—everyone's well-being depended on increasing trade.

ENTER THE TOURISTS, and the hope they brought. Scraggly and poor by Western standards, the overland travelers who streamed through the city on their way to India carried deutschmarks and dollars. Whether the local people approved of their customs or not, these dusty voyagers constituted the new caravan traffic, and the business community of ancient Herat was prepared to make the most of the opportunity. Were the travelers from the west interested in the culture or in drugs? Fine. Commercial opportunists were there to greet them.

Many travelers—though I was not one of these—bought hashish. However, ensnared by Herat's other commercial charms, as generations before had also been, I did go shopping. In fact, we all hit the bazaar running. West or East, the desire to shop seems to be hard-wired into the back corridors of the human brain.

Predictably, the Herat bazaar included venders of Afghan carpets, made in villages and by nomads, not in factories. The rugs' vegetable-died colors were browner and more orangey than those in Iran, the designs less polished, somehow wilder. I loved the colors, but I was going east and could not carry a heavy carpet in my pack.

Other salesmen displayed sheepskin jackets garishly embroidered with pink and blue flowers and sewn together with the thick fleece of a *karacul* sheep turned inwards for warmth. It was August and sweltering. I only glanced at the bright designs.

Shoemakers offered to measure travelers' feet for blond leather boots, made to order. But working leather into a pair of bespoke boots took time. I would not be in Herat long enough to wait ten days for boots.

I padded onwards through the bazaar in my summery Greek-bought sandals. They were of an old design. Alexander had probably also worn sandals when he trekked across Afghanistan, though his were undoubtedly not made of flexible plastic as mine were.

Yet another merchant hopefully tugged out a quilted coat made of red-and-white stripy *ikat*, a distinctive zigzag woven pattern. "From Bukhara, in the north," the shopkeeper explained to me, holding up the quilted garment to show it off. Had a camel delivered this coat? It was clearly in a very traditional style. I tried it on, but it did not fit. The coat's long sleeves extended so far they must dangle well below the knees of any man wearing it. No grown man who put his arms in such a coat would be able to use his hands unless his arms were as long as an ape's. Seeing my confusion, the merchant explained that the coat was usually worn over the shoulders, like a cape. The sleeves were purely decorative, the merchant explained.

In other words, I thought, *whoever buys this is demonstrating that he never needs to work with his hands.* But I had no use for a coat to wear and no room to carry one I couldn't wear, even if it was a precious antique. And I had a pack to carry, buses to climb on. Hands were required for this. *Ikat* was for the rich and the physically idle. (In a later century, during the U.S. occupation of Afghanistan, I would observe the country's newest elected president on television. Hamid Karzai, himself a Pushtu from the south, wearing what looked like a similar coat on his shoulders (though I couldn't see the sleeves) while addressing the U.S. Congress. But that startling event would come much later.) In 1972, knowing I could not carry much, I shrugged aside the proffered coat.

Other merchants in the bazaar hawked Afghan dresses of the style worn by the *kuchi* nomads who were camping outside of town. Each dress was of Russian cotton, printed with small flowers. Embroidery covered the chest like a breastplate. There was a slit down the front of the dress, clearly to allow the wearer to nurse a baby. Some of these bazaar dresses were genuine. Most had been run up quickly by Herat's able tailors to sell to the westerners passing through the city. But an ankle-length dress, however pretty, did not make much sense for a traveler, even without a veil. I did not want to be tripping on the hem while climbing on or off a bus. *Maybe I'll get one on the way back,* I thought.

Most Herat men wore baggy pants and over them, knee-length shirts. The typical Afghan shirt had a deep secret pocket under the right arm. This did look useful, and I wanted one. I found a tailor willing to make me such a shirt. We planned this out: The shirt would fit snugly at the shoulder. It would button over the right shoulder, with each of the small buttons secured by fabric loops. A narrow, scimitar-shaped opening, fastened together with tiny sewn straps, would stretch down from the buttons and across the top of the chest to let in air. The secret pocket under my arm would make it difficult for pickpockets to get at my passport and money. The shirt's long tail would drape loosely down over the rest of me. Wearing this flowing garment over my maroon jeans, I figured I would be very thoroughly covered.

What? Did I now want to be covered up like a lady in a *chador?* Was I perhaps giving in to a very American-style social pressure—the kind that reminds guests to show up with a bottle of wine for a potluck or be suitably— in this case—modestly—dressed for a social occasion? Was some unconscious cultural filter translating the Afghan demand for veiling into a requirement equivalent to that of wearing a hat in church? And come to think of it, hadn't I gone to church veiled myself—in white lace for my first communion as a young girl, and later in a mantilla, a Spanish veil, during my teen years? And what about Jackie Kennedy at her husband's funeral? She had been really covered up in that heavy black veil! I thought of what nuns wore before Vatican 2—how the women in religious orders in wimples and with their heads covered looked like the Biblical figures in renaissance paintings. A long, long trail of thought was opening, but I decided not to follow it just now.

For the decision to buy this particular shirt had nothing to do with a desire to cover my head. I had a far more important body part to cover. This shirt I was ordering would be longer than the mini-dresses women had been wearing back in Berkeley, and it was a good thing. I had a lengthy bus ride across the Afghan countryside coming up. The long shirttail would allow me enough privacy to squat to pee by the roadside if no toilet was available.

Tea accompanied the transaction. The tea arrived with a dish of hard sugar candies. Following the tailor's lead, I placed a candy in my mouth, then picked up the stubby tea glass and sucked in the liquid around the candy. The taste grew sweeter as I slurped. Doing this was a little noisy, but delightful.

Then the tailor helped me pick out the material—sturdy cotton in a light blue. It would wash easily in a hand basin.

Lunchtime came before our arrangements were complete. The tailor beckoned. His lunch was a floppy oval of bread about the size of a child's homemade skateboard, baked fresh that same morning with a beehive-shaped oven. Tearing his bread down the middle, he offered me half, and we chomped agreeably together, washing down the bread with more tea. Lunch over, my new friend measured me carefully and discreetly. He began swiftly cutting fabric. As I left, he was already pumping the treadle on his sewing machine.

"YOU HAVE to pay for a bride?"

"Yes, a lot." Back at the hotel in the evening, a cluster of us sat talking with the clerks in the hotel's small upstairs office, reaching into one another's worlds. Both young men were educated, but penniless. Despite the heat, Azim wore a Western outfit, well tailored and probably hard come-by in a town where most men—even the ebullient hotel owner—dressed in the local uniform of long shirt and baggy pants.

Asim told us his father was dead. This meant he was responsible for his widowed mother and sister. He was depressed because he lacked the money to pay for a bride. In fact many young men in the city would not marry at all because they could not come up with the bride price. This was clearly a matter of great sadness.

Nabil also had a sister and mother to support. Both men worked double jobs. They were schoolteachers by day and moonlighted as hotel clerks by night, but they were still poor. Among Herat's Persian population, the two men were part of an educated elite: They had been trained to speak English. And their moods, their demeanors spoke of other cultural history. They were the successors to the city's glorious heritage, which, though now dimmed, was still a matter of intense local pride.

They spoke slowly, and there was a kind of grace in their speech. We had met our counterparts, the local intelligentsia. Their courtesy revealed the social graces of an intact civilization, not a fragmented one such as the war-torn superpower I had left. They were doing all they could to get by and care for their families, yet the future did not look good for them. Both men struck me as upright in the extreme, amidst fallen times, and I was profoundly touched. We sat quietly in the tiny office, contemplating the sadness of these men being unable to marry.

"OHHHHHH," said Eva, suddenly shocked. We were walking with Asim on Herat's main street, not far from the ruined, but still occupied, citadel. A woman had stepped before us as we walked along the street. Her face was bare. She was thin, and she was begging. In her arms, a baby lay limply. The child was clearly very sick. We stopped.

In Berlin, where Eva lived, there were probably no beggars, but on Telegraph Avenue and the streets of Southside Berkeley, back in California, runaways, the indigent, and gentle people (often wildly dressed) pestered every passer-by with demands for spare change. Often I had shrugged off their requests, but this was different. Here, there was no Free Clinic to turn to. There were no food stamps.

Asim explained that the woman was one of many *kuchi* nomads driven down to an encampment outside the city by a severe drought. These nomads had once roved the northern deserts with huge flocks. Now their flocks were gone. *Kuchi* women, Asim told us, had been selling their possessions—even their ornate *chadors*—in town, to get money for food.

From conversations with the clerks we knew that in Afghanistan the web of family and clan kept hunger and illness at bay. For the *kuchi*, this web had collapsed.

Eva and I guided the mother and child into a pharmacy a few doors down the street. Asim translated. From our limited funds, we bought vitamins and medicine. Asim explained to the *kuchi* woman how to give them to the baby.

As we came out of the pharmacy, and the woman walked off with the medicine, we all knew our help was insufficient. For the *kuchi* there was no food and no government willing to help. We all knew that, too. There was no magical solution. Asim didn't need to tell us that the baby's problem was probably starvation. Despite our help, the baby would probably die. We stood sadly in the street, feeling helpless.

I had done so little. It was Eva who had leaped to intervene.

Confronted with a direct human problem, she had reacted immediately and then acted decisively, while I had fumbled, still lost inside myself, still struggling to find and name my elusive feelings. I had been a sleepwalker. I had merely joined in, helping to lead the woman with the ailing child into the pharmacy, to be looked at by the pharmacist. And I had helped to pay for the medicine.

But now Asim was looking at both of us, his handsome face alight. He cared deeply that we had cared. Eva's swift compassion, and my acquiescence, I realized, had bound the three of us together. It was my turn to be stunned. Even though I knew I didn't deserve the admiration, and even though our efforts would undoubtedly fail, and even against the backdrop of this terrible shared sadness, it felt very good to be someone's hero.

PEARLS AND SWINE

OUTSIDE AND INSIDE, HERAT WAS hot. In the summer night, the foreign guests at the adobe hotel abandoned their stifling rooms. Michael, Dorrie, Melinda, Eva and I joined the others in climbing to the hotel roof, where we slept out under the bright Afghan stars to catch any whisper of cooling breeze.

Handsome Hamid joined the travelers on the rooftop. Whispering continued late into the simmering night, as the hotel owner attempted to charm one of the women tourists.

The August days grew even hotter, but since we were leaving soon, I made an effort to see the sights. In the late afternoon, conducted by a bus driver who had befriended us, Eva and I traveled out to the tomb of the poet Ansari, some ways out of the city. Khwajah Abdullah Ansari was an 11th-century Sufi, an ecstatic, a mystic and Muslim saint, whose songs and poetry in both Persian and Arabic were still revered throughout the region. Educated in Western literature only, I had not heard of this poet before, but clearly in Herat he was much beloved, a hometown guy of epic stature.

We arrived at the tomb. There was a dome. We climbed up some steps to peep down into it. Inside was another dome, like a small pearl growing within the bigger shell. This inner edifice had been constructed soon after the mystic's death. The second dome was built over it centuries later, the bus driver told us.

No ascetic, Ansari had been passionate about his mystical yearning for union with God. "Lord, send me staggering with the wine of your love!" he had written.

I perched high on the ancient building staring down into the even more ancient tomb-within-a-tomb amid the silence of the quickly fading desert twilight. What was within this inner shell? The dome, with the smaller one within seemed somehow more pregnant than funereal. It reminded me of one of those Russian *matryoska* dolls which opens up to reveal an even smaller one nested inside its wooden belly.

Ansari had actually written about nesting. The poet wrote of nursing a drop of self in a pearl, which he described as being cradled within a shell formed by the human heart. Pearls again! Pearls and love! This was not exactly John Wayne stuff.

Love, or something feral resembling it, was in the air in the August heat. Short, blond, round and spunky, Eva was also an Afghan man's pearl, I suspected. And I should have suspected much more, a day or so later, when Hamid the hotel keeper proposed that we make a visit to a famous formal garden outside town. The bus driver went with us once again, but this time handsome Hamid drove his recent model year American car.

We drove outside of town and then onward for what seemed like miles. The sun dipped and set promptly. Finally the car stopped. We all climbed out of the comfortable American seats.

Through I anticipated a crowded tea garden, festive families, rattling glassware, and tables alight with candles or lanterns in a serene country setting, there were no pleasure-takers. No one was here except us. The garden was completely empty of visitors. In fact it was hard even to perceive the garden's features, for the light was failing.

I stood by the car, surprised. And then I stepped forward into the garden. I could make out nothing of this setting I had been told would be so fabulous.

And before my eyes had fully adjusted, the bus driver grasped my arms and began to pull me away. This small man, stronger than he looked, was dragging me down the hill, into the growing darkness. Already the others were out of sight in the dim landscape.

"*Hilfe*, Eva," I squeaked out in German, trying hard to keep the panic out of my voice, as the old man yanked me along. I must keep him from guessing how frightened I suddenly was. "*Hilfe!*" I called again, striving for a more normal tone. The effort made my voice unnaturally shrill. I hoped the bus driver didn't speak German.

There isn't an exact word for rape in German. The nearest the language gets to is "offer violence to a woman."

My German wasn't that extensive, but Eva got the idea.

"I'm coming, Shelley," Eva sang out. And come she did. I could hear her moving on the hillside, calling, "Where are you, Shelley?" And then, cheerfully and very loudly, closer by: "Oh, I see you!" I could hear her jogging down the hill towards me even as I felt the man's strong hands, wrenching me further away from the safety of Hamid's car.

Then I could see her, too, a firmer shadow on the shadowy hillside. "Oh, there you are!" Eva cried cheerily, as if nothing at all were going on.

Rape is a sneaky business, sometimes forestalled by public shame. The bus driver abruptly let go. I had been rescued by someone half my size.

I cannot remember what the garden looked like. I cannot remember how we all bundled back into Hamid's car. I cannot remember a single word that was spoken within the American sedan on the uncomfortable drive back to Herat.

Our handsome hotel keeper, Hamid, I figured later, may have wanted some time alone with Eva to try his luck. Or perhaps he had simply taken a bribe from the bus driver for conniving to let me be abducted into the darkness. Perhaps I had even been purchased. I had not been raped, but there was no doubt about what the man had intended. I was shaken and very angry. And I was also very grateful to my traveling companion. Eva may have been short, but she was as brave as any ancient warrior.

OUR DAYS IN HERAT GREW SHORT. I no longer felt like lingering. On one of the final afternoons, coming back to the hotel from the bazaar by a roundabout route, I discovered yet another market. Along the length of a city block somewhere back of the citadel were laid out what appeared to be the discards of America's garage sales and flea markets: stiff shoes with crunched down heels, mangy sweaters, crumpled cotton. Were these American charity items come astray in the marketplace? Later, I learned charity donations considered too miserable to sell in the U.S. are routinely baled and sold abroad. Thus our discarded fashions, unexpectedly, are peddled in the Afghan street market. In a trading culture, everything—valuable or not—is negotiable.

Even brides. Years later, I would find out how Asim and Nabil resolved their marriage dilemma. They traded sisters. Azim married Nabil's sister and Nabil married Asim's. No bride prices were exchanged, and both men were happier. The terrible debt of the bride price had been evaded. My friends had reached the ultimate creative solution for a society steeped in trade.

I would not get to meet the brides. Shortly after my journey across Afghanistan, the king was driven from his throne in a coup. A new government decreed that Westerners might no longer visit in Afghans' homes. However, the new government had acted too late to stem the tide of Westernization. By 1974, Asim and Nabil were entertaining new dreams, inspired by what they had learned about the prosperity of the West. Both longed to journey to Germany, where Nabil had an uncle who might help them get settled. When I finally got home myself, I sent money to help with this. But not long afterwards, the Soviets marched in, and communications broke off.

However that all comes much later. On this first journey East, I learned that in places where people of different cultures came together to trade, sometimes it was all right to let outsiders be themselves. And sometimes not. I learned that custom determined what women wore and were. I learned that hunger could mean death. I had known this intellectually before, but now the knowledge was visceral and painful.

Afghanistan was not a peaceful place. Alexander conquered and left, though a trail of occupying soldiers remained after his departure. Over millennia, new conquerors came and conquered and were routed by still other conquerors. In the nineteenth century, the British had been forced out. Did Herat's men want to veil and sequester women because of such unsettled situations, just as they maintained the mud-walled citadel?

Or did a trading culture demand the veiling because women, too, were trade goods, possessions. Did each enveloping veil serve as a mini-warehouse for negotiable property? An ugly thought.

But who was I to judge? Should I not be tolerant? My own country was in disarray and polarized: Black vs. White, Latino farm workers vs. growers, police vs. hippies, young vs. old. Abroad, America was at war with people of a small (I then supposed) Asian nation. At home, we had riots in cities on hot summer nights. Hugh Hefner was extolling the birth control pill and free love, demonstrators took over universities, and the President was haranguing about the existence of some silent majority—invisible as the Holy Ghost—that cleaved to home and hearth, law and order, and hated all these changes. No wonder I was finding multi-culturalism puzzling.

And what, in the world's crowded arena of warring cultures, was OK? Was anything intrinsically OK? Or had the question become—What was OK with *me*? I was slipping out of my American skin, like a woman discarding a veil, or perhaps really slipping more directly into my true emerging self, dithering, questioning, and brimming with a desire to remake this place I was visiting in a more just image. But my woman's skin—did I have even one? And if so, what did it consist of? Not a veil, certainly.

A DAY OR TWO BEFORE LEAVING HERAT, overcoming scruples about my tight budget, I bought a *kuchi* veil in the bazaar. This was not an entire *chador*, but rather the embroidered strip that decorates the front of a nomad veil. I had figured out how to bargain, and ultimately it did not cost very much. The veil would be a reminder of Herat.

"That's a *kuchi chador*," Asim exclaimed, approvingly, turning the decorated cloth in his delicate hands when I showed the piece to him in the hotel office. This veil's front border was made up of dark cloth, quilted and stiffened with bits of rayon, sprigged Russian cotton and other rags and remnants which had been appliquéd onto it. Then everything had been overlaid with embroidery, mostly in gold and silver thread.

Unlike the all-enveloping *chador* of the cities, a *kuchi* veil does not cover the wearer's face, but rather frames it, a little like a halo. Yet the ragbag of materials that went into this quilted border strip revealed that *kuchi chadors*–however beautiful–are literally a patchwork of the stuff of daily life.

Later, examining my purchase, I would make out an intriguing line of embroidered geometric figures lined up along its edge. Each figure is nearly identical to the others. The uniformity is remarkable, considering that all are worked by hand and not by machine.

These figures are familiar, like those that can be found in the Balkans, embroidered on the sleeves of women's blouses. Such symbols form the heritage of all of us in the West and many in Asia.

They represent women.

This veil's pattern is of a row of golden women, dancing perhaps, against a patchwork background of old silk velvet, striped rayon, printed Russian cotton, and night-black cloaking. A line of women in long skirts, side by side. Their outlines are the same as those of the barebreasted women bull dancers on a Cretan sarcophagus. Their silhouettes are pretty much the same as those of the skirted stick figures to be found on the doors of ladies' bathrooms in modern airports.

Turning the cloth strip in my own hands, I wondered: Was I somehow in that dancing line, too, though in so many ways my life was so different from the lives of women who tended camels and tents? Our paths had intersected on a street in a Silk Road city, and one of these most traditional of women, had begged from me with a starving baby in her arms. Was I at core so different?

AM I ? Pondering this today, as my son slumbers in his cousin's room in suburban Southern California, while my husband chats with his brother-in-law at the glass-topped table on the patio outside the modern kitchen with its flat-top range and double-doored refrigerator, I still question:

> *What does this mean? How much of me is just myself and how much derives from this stretching legacy of all of us, or some of us. Are we close or distant cousins of those wandering in Central Asia,*

asserting their identities with needles and with thread as gold as the stuff of Rumpelstiltskin tales.... outside of time?

Sigmund Freud got it wrong. The question is not only about what women want, but the even more fraught conundrum about what women are.

THROUGHOUT THE PERIOD IN HERAT, the Alexander coin and the tiny carved marble woman's face joggled almost forgotten in my pocket, the coin remembered only for a moment on the day the soldiers streamed from the crumbling fortress, like ants from a kicked nest. Afghanistan certainly didn't need any more conquering heroes. As to little marble doll-faced goddesses—that question was still wide open.

But I put off introspection. During the summer days in Herat, I had moved far beyond the paralysis of decision-making that had clouded my consciousness in Istanbul. *Wake up, Shelley,* I lectured myself:

> *You have new friends, too much stimulus, and too much contact with the real world to spend time hung up on symbols. That outer world can be dangerous. It requires your full attention*

However, the painful and puzzling riddle persisted: How much of what I took to be myself was actually just some artifact, no less arbitrary, bizarre, and skewed than the shrouding of women in Herat? Thinking of this, I wondered whether such sequestering was really any stranger than the contradictions in a Western culture, whose male-piloted airplanes dropped napalm on hapless women villagers in Vietnam, while at home other male managers who had avoided the draft seethed and howled about the outrage of women wearing pants to work?

I was a woman, but what did that mean?

It was a compelling question, and I knew I could not put off answering it forever. But this was not the time for in-depth consideration. The bus to Kabul would be leaving the next day. Fortunately, it would not be driven by my attacker.

I folded up the *kuchi* veil, gold thread inward and hidden, and almost reverently tucked the little bundle into my pack, next to the guidebook from Berkeley. I knew I would be journeying to India and back again with the veil and the riddle it presented. Three things were clear: It was a woman's veil. It was a woman's handwork. And third, there were no pearls on it anywhere.

The next day, wearing the new blue Afghan shirt—the first item of clothing I had ever owned that was made exactly to my own measure—I climbed on the bus and left Herat.

THE GANDHARA ROAD

THE FIVE OF US, WHO HAD BANDED together to cross Turkey and Iran, drew apart after Herat. Michael and the two *kibutzniks* wanted to see the giant Buddhas carved in the cliff side at Bamyan and visit the blue lakes at Band-e Amir, while I, soured by the prior evening's misadventure in the park with Hamid and the bus driver, was not eager to sample any more out-of-the-way places. We worked it out: All of us would take a marathon bus ride to the Afghan capital. From there, Michael, Dorrie, and Melinda would catch a second bus northwards. Eva and I would get off in Kabul, see the sights, and then continue on to Pakistan. The others could catch up with us, following their side-trip to the north.

All day and night the bus coursed through the desert over a good road that dipped first southwards to the city of Kandahar and from there ran northeast, up to the capital at Kabul. It was a new road, built with foreign aid money. The Russians had paid for the stretch from Herat to Kandahar The Americans, eager not to be outspent by the Communists in the U.S.S.R., had sprung for the costs of the second leg, from Kandahar to Kabul.

Out the window, the land looked like the American southwestern deserts, with rocks and dry ground and broad arroyos, but here there were no freeways, no intervals of sprawl, no ranch homes, used car lots or towering cities, only the one road. We crossed low bridges over wide washes. Heaps of stones and dried debris at the approaches to these bridges gave ample evidence that when major rains occurred, as happened sometimes, even in the desert, the seemingly sturdy bridge spans became useless concrete islands, outflanked and surrounded by fast-flowing floodwaters. We passed guard posts and the occasional gas station, but overall, there was plenty of nothing. It looked like the terrain of a spaghetti Western.

When at last it came time to eat, the bus pulled off the road. We all climbed out and soon found ourselves squatting on the floor amid the other passengers in a weathered mud building, spooning up our dinners. Everyone's meal was identical: the same heap of rice—*pilau*—topped with chunks of mutton in a thickened sauce. It was simple and good and came with the ubiquitous floppy Afghan flatbread. Tea to wash down the *pilau* and bread arrived in cheap, colorful Japanese-made pots.

These teapots reminded me that throughout history similar trade goods had traveled by caravan across Asia's interior deserts to the markets of the West, with much of this traffic passing through Afghanistan. With the completion of the new roads, Volvo and Mercedes trucks were replacing most of the camel traffic in this sector, but much else remained the same. Marveling that my meal came from a menu crafted in Marco Polo's time, I went outside to locate the privy. I found it out behind the ancient building. This privy, too, was not much altered, and there was no toilet paper.

Then all of us—those in turbans and those in blue jeans alike in this, Afghanistan's most modern year of 1351 (1972 to us from the West)—climbed back aboard our ornately painted diesel bus, and the vehicle roared down the road again like a mechanized dragon. Had we all been journeying by caravan a thousand years before, or even a decade ago, the drill and decorations would probably have been much the same, though loading up the camels for departure might have taken longer.

A few hours before dawn, the bus rolled into Kandahar, the only major city on the road across southern Afghanistan. Kandahar, like Herat, is believed by many to have been founded by Alexander the

Great. Some accounts say the voyaging soldier named it after himself, as he did all the cities he founded, and that the name *Alexandria* somehow got transmuted into *Kandahar* as marauders from differing language groups took over this regional trade center and struggled with the pronunciation in Turkish, Persian, and tribal dialects.

Another version of the story claims *Kandahar* is a corruption of *Gandhara*. This was an almost mythic Buddhist kingdom adjacent to Bactria. Greek and Macedonian soldiers, left in charge by Alexander when he headed back toward Persia, ruled over Bactria for generations afterwards, contributing their Greek culture and genes to this distant Asian outpost. Traces of this heritage still turn up in areas where those Greco-Bactrian kings once governed: blue-eyed, blond-haired Afghans in villages, coins pulled from archeological digs, bearing Greek inscriptions.

In the neighboring kingdom of Gandhara, this cultural *mélange* was stranger yet. In Gandhara, artistic conventions which came with Alexander's soldiers became cross-pollinated with the region's developing Buddhist art. I had heard of Gandharan Buddhist sculptures that look much more like pieces sliced off the Parthenon than traditional formal religious sculpture from southern Asia, though I had never seen any.

Not everyone believes that Kandahar was Gandhara, though. Others say Kandahar was at one time the capital of a Greek-ruled country called Arachosia, literally translated, "the land of the Aryans." They say a monarch named Demetrius once ruled there—a practicing Buddhist who struck coins with Greek lettering on them—remarkably like the coin from Istanbul with Alexander's likeness which still rode in my pocket.

Yet others maintain, based on vaguely similar place names, that the Kandahar region is the motherland of Croatia. And since all of these purportedly historical regions had borders which grew or shrank over time, there was also disagreement about where any of them had actually been located.

While the fuzziness about borders and histories might make my head spin today, in 1972, the bare thought of such cultural collisions and transformations occurring along the Silk Road thrilled me. At home, Californians were experimenting with Zen Buddhism, with meditation and Asian religions. I understood that distant antecedents of this heady mingling had bubbled and fused in Central Asia, forming odd amalgams which were then carried along caravan routes or shuffled in the wake of conquering armies. I took comfort in this. It meant somehow, that nothing was dropped or forgotten, that we all continue in some kind of enduring context, a flood and ferment of ever-reconfiguring consciousness and creativity, even if the facts get rather mixed up along the way.

What are facts, after all, if your assessment of reality is swinging like a pendulum between Buddhist austerity and the extravagantly sensual naturalism of Greek figure sculpture? There is an image, in Wikipedia, of a coin struck by Demetrius of Kandahar: It is lettered in Greek, with the king's image shown in classical profile. Above his forehead—no doubt intended as a symbol of power—extends a supple elephant's trunk. Not exactly Greek stuff.

But even Demetrius has his detractors. Still other historians don't even mention Arachosia or the Croatians. They dismiss the Gandhara-is-Kandahar thesis as total hogwash. The Gandharan kingdom lay someplace else entirely, they claim. The historical Gandhara becomes as elusive as the sequestered fictional kingdom of Shangri-La or the American Southwest's Lost Dutchman goldmine.

While I should have loved to think of Kandahar as ancient Gandhara or one of the many cities dubbed *Alexandria* along the conqueror's path, local evidence to support the claims was scanty. Recent talk among the backpacking travelers pegged contemporary Kandahar as brutal and tribal—the site of a recent execution by locals of four traveling Frenchmen who had been, the story said, so disrespectful as to speak to a veiled woman. These foreign men had been beheaded, I was told. Recalling this, I was happy that our stop would be brief and that I would not be forced to get off and stand around. As an unveiled woman stranded at this hour in a public place, I feared I would become a target for some kind of violence.

Certainly nothing ancient, romantic or particularly dreadful was evident, however, as the bus idled beneath harsh lights a few hours before dawn. Through the window, I could see we were in some kind of market, amid the stench of fermenting melons and rotting vegetables. Only men were about. There might be another side to Kandahar, some place where gentle people recited Persian love poetry to one another within walled gardens, or a hidden dig where archaeologists were even now unearthing silver coins that would clinch their case for Gandhara, Arachosia, or Croatia. Whatever the heritage, the stench in the market where the bus had paused was so strong that even Alexander would have held his nose. Fortunately, the bus plunged onward again. I slept, waking under a sky great with bright stars undimmed by city lights, then slept again.

IT WAS LATE MORNING when the bus arrived in Kabul. The touts were waiting for us even before Eva and I reclaimed our packs. "Hotel missus? Hotel missus?" Thin men in short sleeved shirts and western pants crushed around us, blocking the way. "Hotel, guest house, very clean?" A guest house business card was shoved almost into Eva's face, close under her nose. "Hotel? Missus?" Outraged, she snatched the card and tore it in half.

It was the would-be guide's only printed card. He was livid: "If you were a man, I would kill you," he told Eva.

But Eva—all five feet of her—was hot, tired, and mortally sick of being pestered.

"Well, I'm not," she snapped right back, daring the man to make good on his threat. After a brief staring contest, we grabbed our packs and walked away.

None of the men followed. Instead, we let a child guide us to a simple hotel on the far side of the Kabul River. We checked in, and, sitting in the baking hotel room, talked over our travel plans. We were just making up our minds that we would proceed onward to India as fast as possible, when there was a rap on the room's door.

I opened it to find the hotel's desk clerk, a smiling teenager, standing just outside. He entered, lugging an electric fan he had brought for our comfort. We could see there was an electrical socket in the wall. The fan, apparently a refugee from the 1930s, had an electrical cord, but the cord had no plug at the end of it. Instead, a pair of stripped wires protruded from the cord's cloth wrapping.

As we watched with languid curiosity, the clerk grasped these wires and stuck them, one by one, into the holes in the room's wall socket. I expected him to leap up with hair standing on end from an electrical shock, but nothing like that happened. Instead, the fan merely hummed to life. Its battered and dingy blade began grudgingly to rotate, and the air in the room started to stir. The desk clerk—who might have been 14—stood up with a wide smile. "There," he seemed to be saying with satisfaction. "You will be comfortable with us." He didn't actually say this, but his gestures and gracious smile left no room for misinterpretation. Having fulfilled his duty of Afghan hospitality, the youngster left. Gradually, the room grew cooler and we began to revive.

Towards dinner time, the sizzling noonday heat outside became more tolerable. We ventured out and over the bridge to Kabul's downtown. Somewhere beyond that financial district, bustling with busy moneychangers' booths, we had heard that a Western-style restaurant existed. There were no other women out. We edged past men in traditional costume, long shirts and baggy pants. They ignored us.

We made our way through the crowds, finding the place. I ate a hamburger, my first in many months. The restaurant was jammed with travelers; some of their faces were familiar from Istanbul. Others were new.

PERHAPS IT WAS AT THIS RESTAURANT that we encountered the Swedes. Their names were Sigrid and Bertil, and they were tall and thin and blond, like heroes in a fantasy epic featuring dwarves and elves, or sprung from an old Icelandic saga. But once they opened their mouths, all traces of epic origins evaporated, for the two spoke in the Oxford accents of highly-educated professionals. Sigrid was a social worker at home, Bertil, an engineer. They came from a Stockholm suburb. Clad in sensible jeans and clean cotton tee shirts, the Swedes were piloting—not some narrow lapstraked Viking ship with a dragon at its bow—but a recent-model Volkswagen bus, two-toned in blue and white. In this, they had come successfully across the desert and were now going on to India and Ceylon. And to my delight, the Swedes had room for passengers. They agreed to take Eva and me through Pakistan, for a share of the gas money.

A day later, we left in their VW bus for Jalalabad and points south.

Travel by private vehicle differed from travel by Afghan bus. At the checkpoints, men in ill-fitting Russian uniforms demanded travel documents. Gassing up involved dealing with more uniformed men in barren, sullen countryside settings, who tended gas pumps nearly as ancient as the elusive kingdom of Gandhara.

Neat and purposive, the two Swedes, with their spotless vehicle, seemed antithetical to our wild surroundings. We split the gas costs, Bertil computing our share precisely on his slide rule. But somewhere within these two sedate travelers burned a fierce sense of adventure and rebellion. It must have been there, for how else could this disparate group of people pull together so well when I pulled the stupid caper at the Khyber Pass?

And why, oh why, did I do it?

The road from Kabul to Jalalabad followed the disastrous gorge route along the Kabul River taken by Elphinstone's army as it withdrew at the end of the first Afghan War in 1842. The British had occupied several Afghan cities and unseated the country's monarch, replacing him with a man of their own choosing. But things didn't work out, and the puppet king soon faced an insurgency. Outflanked by a shrewd Afghan warlord, and unable to hang onto Kabul, the British determined to pull out of the city after a key political officer was assassinated. The warlord promised an escort and food to speed the unwanted troops, camp followers, and occupiers on their way. Short of options, the British authorities decided to take the offer and march out.

But the warlord failed to deliver this support, and the British had retreated down the road through the gorge towards Jalalabad and the Khyber Pass and India, coming under repeated attacks from tribal fighters and perhaps the warlord's own men. Of the thousands of soldiers, women, children, and camp followers who had set out on the forced march, only a sole individual reached Jalalabad alive. The rest of the ill-fated travelers, except for hostages and a prudent few who had managed to slip into the hills unnoticed, were killed or died from the cold.

The rebel warlord, I read later, had been unhappy because his own father—the deposed king—was being held hostage by the British. Perhaps he also felt his country had been occupied by British troops for far too long. The British had entered Afghanistan nearly three years before without too much difficulty, using the 19th-century geopolitical rationale that they needed to secure it in order to prevent the Russians from moving in and threatening India's borders; however, getting back out again had proved a disaster. What a mess!

My own knowledge at the time was not so specific. In childhood, I read a Classic Comic version of *King of the Khyber Rifles,* a now-forgotten adventure episode featuring an underground river, caverns, a dashing white man in a pith helmet, and, of course, guns. I could not remember who won the day in the comic book adventure, but I suspected the winners weren't the local people. As good Muslims, Afghans did not go in for graphic art depicting humans, so there were no heroic paintings in the Kabul Museum to offer the Afghans' version of events to travelers who couldn't speak the language.

The road leading to the Khyber Pass and Pakistan goes through Pushtu country. These tribal people are famous the world over as fierce, fearless, and vindictive fighters—nobody to fool around with, as the British had learned to their cost. But although we were familiar with the Pushtu tribes' reputation, none of us knew in detail about the gorge's bloody history as we passed through it. Along the roadside, on this summer day, we could see Pushtu men strolling in their long white shirts and baggy pants. They wore distinctive rolled-up camel-colored hats—a little like the black watch cap worn by my friend at the gas station in Berkeley. The caps looked warm for the day, but desert country usually grows cold at night, even in the hottest season, so perhaps the hats became more necessary in the evening.

However, the day was pleasant, and within the van, we were oblivious. The Swedes chatted in slightly lilting English as the van proceeded along this historically bloody trade route. Sweden is a long country, with lots of forests and lonely distances between towns. "A *Swedish mile* is ten kilometers," Sigrid told us. "We call them 'smiles.'" It seemed a fitting measure for the wild country outside the window—a vaster mile.

But perhaps I had ingested something of the Afghan attitude. We had noticed a level of ill-feeling between Afghans and Pakistanis. Afghans and Pakistanis were all were Islamic together. However, the distinctions between the lean and warlike hill people, who lived on both sides of the border, and southern Pakistan's farmers and city folk did not go unmarked. Afghans we talked with tended to regard their country's southern neighbors with a smirk, as if the very fact of their existence were a joke. They snickered about Pakistanis with contempt, as urbanized, citified, and soft-living incompetents. They told Pakistani jokes. Anyone who downs a beer in a country bar in the United States might recognize the attitude. Compared to Afghans, particularly Pushtus, our acquaintances implied, the Pakistanis were pretty wimpy.

So as we prepared to enter Pakistan at the Afghan-Pakistan border station before the Khyber Pass, I reacted strongly when a familiar scene unfurled.

"Border closed," we were told abruptly. As at the Iranian side of the border with Afghanistan, the touts came running, gleefully eager for potential overnight customers. "Hotel, mister? Hotel, missus?" Another business opportunity created for local hotels! Another delay. And in such an unsettled place.

No way!

And it was hot, too. I lost my temper. I grew furious. I stalked into the border office where two of these urbanized soft-appearing men were sitting near an ancient desk. "If you do not let us go through today, I must call Karachi," I imperiously lectured the border officials in the office at this dust-blown crossing.

"My father is at the American embassy in Karachi." Where this performance came from besides sheer frustration at the last-minute shakedown, I had no idea. But it was a cowboy kind of place, this flat terrain between the rock-lined gorge and the mountain pass, and, for the first time in a rather meek life, I was gambling recklessly. "My father is expecting me," I continued in an outraged theatrical voice. "What am I to tell him, if we do not arrive on the day he expects us?"

No reaction. I upped the ante.

"My father is an official of the American embassy." I repeated. "We must call him." I stabbed an angry finger at the black telephone on the more senior official's desk. "You must pay for the call."

It was a bluff. My father worked for the U.S. government all right, but at the Agriculture Department. He was at the Foreign Agriculture Division, sure enough, but not for this hemisphere. And he was in Washington, not Karachi. He might have become a foreign attaché somewhere—perhaps in the Caribbean on which he was an expert—but my mother did not want to move outside the country and we never got past talking about a foreign assignment around the dinner table. I was lying through my teeth.

My Pakistani high school classmate had been from Karachi, though, and I was under the mistaken impression that Karachi was still Pakistan's capital. In fact, it wasn't, now that Islamabad had been built, more in the middle of the country.

I had a flash memory of my homeroom classmate, suddenly. Chanda wore traditional clothing which modestly covered her legs, as was required in what was then called West Pakistan, but her father was urging her to dress in a more American style—so as to seem more like the rest of us. However, this posed a problem; although showing her legs would be unthinkable for Chanda back in Pakistan, at my high school in the Northern Virginia suburbs, as in most Virginia public schools, it was strictly forbidden for girls to show up for class in pants. She would have to wear a skirt. And because high school is in some ways the same the whole world over for girls, Chanda brought up the obvious technical question—one she felt she could not discuss with her father. "What do you do about—you know—the hair that grows on your legs?" my friend whispered to me. She raised a pantalette-like hem on the right leg of her national costume to show what she meant. Dark hairs, the same color as the thick black hair on Chanda's well-brushed head, feathered her calf. Quickly, before the ringing of the homeroom bell could cut off our conversation, I explained to her in a whisper about the American custom of shaving legs.

Chanda's father would not have approved of what I was up to. My father would be horrified, if he ever found out. But I couldn't stop. I had just exited a country where the meek got stuck under veils–no, not veils–worse–those all-encompassing *chadors* that made a woman half blind staring through a screen in an enveloping costume that made her look like a walking half-inflated parachute and tripped her as well. I had mostly been treated nicely myself, except for that one attempted rape in the garden outside Herat, but I was fed up with men telling women what to do. These Pakistani officials were just the latest offenders in what was now a long long road's procession of men giving orders and thwarting women who wanted to do something or get somewhere. Now my bottled-up fury came spewing out. It was road rage, but it was also a manifesto: "No more docile Miss Mouse for me."

"My father will be very upset to learn that I have been delayed," I now loudly reiterated, putting on as arrogant a voice as I could muster. "It is your responsibility," I told the officials. My English was growing more formal by the moment. It always does when I get mad.

The two men huddled, looking abashed and uncertain. Despite the maroon jeans and dusty hippie hairstyle, here was an obnoxious Western woman in full ire–an incomprehensible virago, someone clearly oblivious to the subtle suggestion of a bribe, someone you dared not put in jail for fear of potential unpleasant consequences.

Afghan police would either have simply flung me in jail or laughed at me.

There was a small silence, while the harassed men considered their options. Finally we were told: "You may go through the pass, but you must take a soldier with you." The Swedes cheered, betraying the fact that beneath their buttoned-down behavior they were not as tame as they seemed. Also, none of us wanted to spend the night in this godforsaken outpost.

Our passports were quickly stamped. The border barrier was pushed aside. Bertil revved the motor; Sigrid sat upright and prim at his side on the bench seat. An armed soldier–now *our* soldier–climbed into the back of the VW van joining Eva, me, the Swedes' camping accessories, and our piled packs. Thus we set off, after "official" closing hours, into the Khyber Pass. It was about three o'clock in the afternoon.

The van climbed past cemeteries with streamers flying from the graves. We passed Pushtu houses—looking like frontier fortresses in old Hollywood Westerns, their thick adobe walls pierced at intervals with loophole windows. Although our passports had been stamped and we had crossed the border between Afghanistan and Pakistan, it was hard to see much difference. Regardless of the official border line drawn by the British over this desolate landscape, we were still in the hills, still in *Pustunistan*, among the tribal people.

We passed a roadside sign indicating a separate route for caravans— a camel in silhouette on a yellow field.

And what a soldier now rode crouched beside us in the back of the powder-blue van! Unshaven and trussed in a hastily tied white turban, he bore a carbine across his back and a bandolier across his chest like a desperado out of the old American West.

Despite the short temper and bravado, I am a born coward if I stop to reflect. I began to have misgivings. But there was no way to turn back. I had gotten us all into this

The road was narrow. We climbed through desert countryside on snaking switchbacks. Mud-colored hills gave way to mud-colored stony mountains. We climbed more. Eventually we came to a town high up— Landi Kotal—famous for its gunsmiths and smugglers. Twilight seemed to be coming frightfully early. Perhaps the early border closure had been based on local conditions, and was more than just a hustle to drum up hotel business.

Landi Kotal's dusty main street was filled with tough-looking men. Women were all kept out of sight. Bertil drove cautiously through the town, with Sigrid sitting upright and dignified beside him, Eva and I sat on the floor in the back with our bodyguard, who said nothing. We passed through town quickly. All of us were holding our collective breaths.

Then there was more twisty road. The armed soldier still sat quietly in our midst, a source of growing uneasiness. *What if he's really a bandit?* I wondered as we plunged along the road, past more houses like block-houses. This looked like dangerous and desolate country. It would be so easy to take us out, with no other travelers going through. What would a working VW bus bring in this part of the world? Were our traveler's checks cashable?

Abruptly, the bodyguard raised his hand. We must stop. Bertil halted the van.

"This is it," I thought, "We're dead." The soldier climbed down from the van. *Christ, abandoned in the pass! The guide slipping away, or worse, shooting us and then dead tourists discovered....* The headline was writing itself.

But instead, our bodyguard faced West and bowed. It was time for prayer.

And then we plunged onward through the growing darkness.

IT WAS FULLY DARK as we came down out of the mountains in Pakistan's Frontier Province. Here there were still men with camel-colored hats and carbines in the streets. We set down the soldier and drove on to a Dak bungalow, outside Peshawar. This was a civil servant lodging left over from the days of the British Raj. Now it served as a government-run guesthouse.

The place reminded me vaguely of the infirmary at my college, which had been well supplied with ancient yearbooks and trash reading for the 1912 set: books of the Clara Barton, nurse and Laura-goes-to-college variety. Lady Baden-Powell or some other ofttimes Girl Scout leader could show up at any minute to lead games and find herself right at home. It felt like what summer camp should be like when it rains—old building, odd old books, and a profound aura of safety.

This was my first experience of the former British Raj. The manager, a willowy elderly man, no doubt had been on duty here since before Independence and India's rupture with Pakistan a quarter century before. He found our adventure in the wild borderlands amusing.

In 1927, he told us, hill people captured an English woman with the intention of holding her for ransom. "But instead of collecting, they returned her voluntarily within a week," he chuckled. This was some old, anti-colonial joke, a *back-at-ya* to the British! I pictured a bossy Mary Poppins type among the Khyber's brigands, sharp-tongued and complaining noisily until her kidnappers got sick of her.

Perhaps the border guards are accustomed to being bullied over the early closure of the crossing, I thought. I felt briefly ashamed of what I had done, but any shame was quickly outweighed by my relief at being secure in the Dak Bungalow instead of warding off bedbugs or worse at a slapped-together border hotel in Torkham Khyber.

And then, while I was still pondering this, the dignified manager beckoned us closer. Leaning towards his four exhausted guests and lowering his voice, the old man inquired, "Do you want *chars, chares?*"

No one said anything for about a minute. "He means hashish," somebody finally whispered. What was being proposed was most likely illegal. The old retainer got no takers. We stumbled to our beds and slept like stones.

Years later, a generation after the trip was over, I would learn that we had come down through the Khyber Pass into the ancient valley of Gandhara. But by the time we reached it, the gentle Buddhists were long gone.

SHIVERS IN PAKISTAN

IN THE MORNING, FOLLOWING a big breakfast, we heaped our packs into the two-toned camper-bus. With Bertil at the wheel, commenting on how Sweden's roads had switched from left-hand to right-hand driving in 1967, we passed out of Peshawar. Pakistan officially required left-hand driving. This hadn't mattered much in the narrow Khyber Pass, but now the road was wide enough for Bertil to drive on the left, so we were thankful he still remembered how. Actually though, it didn't really seem to make much difference. Our fellow travelers—cars, trucks, horse-drawn vehicles—seemed to be all over the road. In our minds, the road also seemed to run southwards. This too was an illusion. It ran east. We were crossing a northern flap of Pakistan in the direction of Islamabad, the recently-constructed capital city (the one I hadn't heard of a day ago). We would need to report in there to obtain the road permits that would allow us to leave Pakistan for India.

Somewhere we must have crossed the mighty Indus River, its waters as yet unthrottled by the massive Taribel Dam rising in the mountains to the north, but I never saw it. Perhaps in this post-monsoon season, the great river was merely trickling, as some rivers do in California during the dry season. Perhaps I did not notice the Indus because I was getting sick.

We stopped for the night in a small village. Local girls ambled to the well, enormous clay water pots balancing easily on their heads.

Away from all urban clatter, we seemed to have journeyed much further back in time than the British colonial-era Dak Bungalow where we had been fed the morning's western breakfast of eggs and toast. This was more like the timeless rural India as I had envisioned, tropical and archaic and suffused with tranquility.

But legally, this ancient place was not even India any longer; it was Pakistan, a new nation sculpted from the top of India only a quarter century earlier to create a homeland for Muslims. Like the separation of conjoined twins, partition of mostly Muslim Pakistan from mostly-Hindu India had been extremely messy. Partition (usually spelled with a capital P) was a time of tumult and slaughter as displaced populations scrambled to reach safety beyond borders hastily scribbled on a map by a British official who first laid eyes on the Indian Subcontinent just a few weeks prior to Independence.

Blood had flowed along the railroad lines during Partition as thousands fleeing one way or the other were slaughtered by members of opposing religious factions.

Yet this quiet village close to the country's middle seemed unaffected. We were relatively far from troubled borders, and the chaos seemed never to have touched these tranquil surroundings. Rural settings such as this one, I was beginning to understand, do not generally participate even in the modest development leaps boasted by major cities. And sometimes, though not always, they are spared the political upheavals as well.

However, I was beginning to shiver despite the heat. And shivered and shivered and shook and shook. Concerned as the quaking continued, Sigrid leaped to the rescue, tugging the blankets and covers from the camper-bus to cover me. Seeing these were not enough, she piled on wraps from our packs until there were no more to heap on me. And still I lay, palsied and quivering, on the floor of the bare room.

My fever spiked. And then, just as abruptly, it dropped again. The shaking stopped. I thrust off the blankets. Had I accidentally skipped a malaria tablet? Taken too many by accident? Was it something I ate during that nice eggy English breakfast at the Dak Bungalow? I did not find out, and the fever did not return. By the next morning, I was able to travel. But this would not be the end of shivers associated with Pakistan.

BYPASSING THE OLD CITY of Rawalpindi, Bertil and Sigrid's camper-bus proceeded onward to Islamabad, the sparkling new capital, to find the road permit office. I had been shocked after the border crossing to discover Karachi was no longer Pakistan's capital. The capital had shifted— first to Rawalpindi in 1958 and later, in 1960, to the newly-built city at Islamabad. Fortunately, the officials at the border had not been too firmly aware of this, either.

I was not completely ignorant about the local situation. Pakistan and India, I knew, generally didn't get along. There had been longstanding bad blood between Muslims and Hindus, which was complicated by mutual accusations of massacres and double dealings during Partition. The British, acknowledging that independence was inevitable, had de- camped, leaving Muslim Pakistan and predominantly-Hindu India to settle differences themselves by slugging it out in a series of regional wars, starting in 1947 with a clash over Kashmir. In the Pakistani view, India had somehow connived to cling to this desirable province despite its Muslim majority. Pakistanis felt that Kashmir should be pried loose from India's grip and joined to Pakistan instead. By 1965, Pakistan would be again at war with India over the Kashmir region, and the dispute would continue to simmer.

But in fact, Pakistan hadn't done too well with its Muslim neigh- bors, either. In the post-Partition era, Afghanistan had sought by vari- ous means to change the Durand Line, an arbitrary border drawn by the British in the 19th century to separate Afghanistan from British India. With Independence, territory to the south of the Durand Line become Pakistan. However, the Afghans contended the Durand Line split the Pushtu peoples, leaving as many as five million Pushtus stuck in Pakistan. From the Afghan viewpoint, this Pushtu-occupied chunk of Pakistan's northern provinces belonged in Afghanistan proper, or at least should become a friendly, independent Pushtu state, *Pushtuni-stan*. If the claimed territory could somehow provide a seaport for land- locked Afghanistan, so much the better, Kabul felt.

159

Pakistani authorities angrily countered that Afghanistan was out to destabilize their infant country, and the spat was on. In 1961, Pakistan barred Afghan nomads from crossing to the country without presenting visas, passports, and international health certificates. Obtaining such documents, of course, was a near impossibility for the often illiterate tribal people on caravan migrations.

Fanning the fire, Pakistan shuttered Afghanistan's consulates and ordered Afghan diplomats to leave the country. In retaliation, Afghanistan then closed off its southern border crossings, blocking traffic to and from Pakistan. Although the Shah of Iran eventually negotiated a peace between the two Islamic countries, the Afghan-Pakistan border did not reopen until 1963.

A yet more recent dispute had deprived Pakistan of its isolated eastern portion. At Partition, the British created Pakistan with East and West wings. Although governed jointly as a single nation, these territories lay a thousand miles apart and were ethnically different. Residents of the East Wing of the country—East Pakistan—were unhappy with an unequal division of representation and resources, which they believed favored the West Wing. Led by the Awami League, they sought independence.

Even KPFA, our local listener-sponsored radio station in far-off California had mentioned this latest struggle, but I didn't know the rest.

The country's military strongman, Yahya Kahn, who was in charge of Pakistan's government, himself came from the country's West Wing. In an effort to crush the independence movement and keep the East Wing from seceding, he authorized attacks on its civilians. Pakistan's troops, themselves drawn mostly from the West Wing, heartily complied.

The result was mayhem. Officials of the pro-independence Awami League, which had just won a majority in Pakistan's parliament through legal elections, were executed in their homes. The Awami League's leader was kidnapped. A university in the East Wing was attacked and a women's dormitory burned. The women students were shot as they tried to escape the flames.

Death squads roamed, killing freely.

Millions of refugees from Pakistan's East Wing had fled southwards into India. Pakistan's military, suspicious that India might be supporting the East Wing, then launched a pre-emptive air attack against Indian bases. India responded by invading the East Wing.

Days later, India prevailed, and the war was over. In the wake of the fighting, East Pakistan became the independent nation of Bangladesh, departing the East-West union with more than half the population of the formerly unified country.

Although the hot fighting was over months before, ill feeling in the war's aftermath still simmered as we drove down the road to Islamabad, for some 90,000 Pakistani soldiers remained stuck in India, held as prisoners of war.

This was perhaps not the best time for innocent tourists to come calling. While the situation wasn't quite the equivalent of touring Tokyo in 1946, the local mood in the western half of the former unified Pakistan was far from happy. In this season after the country split in two, local tourist boards, if any had existed, might truthfully have proclaimed: *Pakistan—see it while it lasts.*

"DON'T SQUEEZE YAHYA!"

G IVEN PAKISTAN'S TRACK RECORD for neighborly relations, I was lucky to have gotten across any border at all into the country. But, although I was crossing the country just a little over eight months following the ceasefire, I had only vague notions of what had taken place.

The East-West dispute seemed to have little to do with me. I had no idea back in 1972 that U.S. President Richard Nixon had been involved and favored West Pakistan over East, or that Henry Kissinger had sought to deploy an American aircraft carrier into the Bengal Sea by East Pakistan. And what a humbling irony—to learn from a Wikipedia entry, a generation after the Watergate scandal and Nixon's resignation, and after Nixon was long dead—about the ethnic cleansing that was carried out in East Pakistan, as America "tilted" its policy towards the aggressors from Pakistan's West Wing.

Atrocity claims during warfare can often be unreliable and exaggerated. However, East Pakistan had credible witnesses to the awful events—in this case—American diplomats on the scene. Archer Blood, American Counsel General in East Pakistan, had cabled Washington in alarm:

> Our government has failed to denounce the suppression of democracy.... Our government has failed to take forceful measures to protect [East Pakistan's] citizens while at the same time bending over backwards to placate the West Pak[istan] dominated

government.... [W]e have chosen not to intervene, even morally, on the grounds that the Awami conflict, in which unfortunately the overworked term genocide is applicable, is purely an internal matter of a sovereign state.

Supporting Blood's protest in a follow-up telegram, 29 fellow American Foreign Service officers cabled Washington, declaring themselves

...mute and horrified witnesses to a reign of terror by the Pak[istani] Military. Evidence continues to mount that the ... authorities have list of AWAMI League supporters whom they are systematically eliminating by seeking them out in their homes and shooting them down.

But Richard Nixon, at the time still unimpeached and President of the United States, had received an invitation to send an American envoy to China along with an American team that the Chinese had invited to come and play ping-pong there. Since the U.S. did not have diplomatic relations with Chairman Mao's mainland China, the invitation had arrived by a roundabout route. China's friend and ally, Pakistan, had been requested to forward the Chinese invitation onwards to Washington. This put Pakistan's leader, Yahya Khan, in the middle of the deal, as a kind of postman for the valued Chinese overture.

According to Christopher Hitchens, who detailed the episode in his 2001 book, *The Trial of Henry Kissinger*, Nixon's thinking ran something like this: Since India was good friends with the Soviet Union, Washington—given the chance—should respond by cozying up to the Chinese. The U.S. President did not want to do anything to mess up any diplomatic raprochement with China by putting pressure on Pakistan's leader, Yahya Khan, over human rights violations.

Joseph L. Galloway, a journalist who had personally reported on the East Wing atrocities, reported that Nixon, himself, had hand-scrawled instructions regarding Pakistan: "To all hands: DON'T squeeze Yahya at this time...." Writing in an obituary in the Knight-Ridder newspapers, following Archer Blood's death in 2004, Galloway commented: "So nobody in authority squeezed Yahya Khan, the killings continued and 20 million Bengali refugees [from East Pakistan] poured into India."

The slaughters from Partition and this recent civil war made the

British losses of around 16,000 in the gorge on the road from Kabul to Jalalabad look relatively paltry.

For his courageous act in authoring the cable protesting the atrocities, Counsel General Archer Blood was recalled to Washington. He had sacrificed his career by refusing to keep his mouth shut.

READING OF THIS, I HAVE TO WONDER: If my own father had actually been posted to Pakistan, as I had falsely claimed, what side might he have taken? Would his mother's Quaker heritage of non-violence and abolitionism have prevailed? Or would he have done what he usually did, motivated by his own Depression-era hardships and his determination to support his family and send his daughters to college: keep his head down and follow orders?

It is difficult to wish such a choice on a parent whose Agriculture Department career was spent working on drought-relief, New Deal crop subsidies, and farmer cooperatives—not intrigue, geopolitics, and civil war. For once, I am glad my father never took a foreign assignment.

But at the time, I knew nothing about Blood or his protest. In summer of 1972, the lethal ping-pong had appeared to be all of a regional kind. If Pakistan seemed to be undergoing a fever of its own—a war fever, and in this case, a chronic one—it was not American doing, or so I then thought. Back then, horrified by my country's war in Vietnam, I had desperately wanted clean hands and was willing to travel to the ends of the earth to get them.

Ironically, the name *Pakistan*, coined by Muslim Indian students in England during the 1930s, literally translated from Persian, means "land of the pure," according to Stephen Philip Cohen's thoughtful book, *The Idea of Pakistan*. In 1972, however, Pakistan was not a good place to find purity. Or perhaps the message to me should have been: *Beware of the pure at heart, for they can certainly cause a lot of misery.*

In the ceasefire that existed as I entered Pakistan, newly-formed Bangladesh, which had been East Pakistan only a year ago, was licking its wounds. Bangladeshis contended the new country's civilian casulties numbered as many as three million, a devastating price for independence. Far fewer civilians died in West Pakistan, but the thousands of prisoners of war were still being held in India. They would not see home again until 1974. People must have been experiencing a high degree of shock.

Though Blood is little known in the United States, his book on the massacre is still in print and available on Amazon. It ships from Bangladesh, where Archer Blood remains a hero of the Independence.

ROAD PERMIT

IGNORANCE ON THE PART OF THOSE just passing through a country is not bliss, though. It fosters uneasiness. And there was that other, earlier baggage that probably contributed to my feelings of unease as I crossed the country, all unknowing. It was the deadly baggage of Partition—followed by a most frantic and uncivil war as Moslems struggled to reach a Pakistan newly severed from India, and Sikhs and Hindus, caught in this now explicitly Muslim north land, struggled to get out.

The Sikhs had seen their homeland—the Punjab Province—split in two, with many of their holy places winding up in territory assigned to Muslim Pakistan. Meanwhile Amritsar, their holiest city, remained within India. In 1972, a string of Indian Army military installations, many of them manned by unhappy Sikhs, faced Pakistan along the far side of the troubled border we were about to cross.

Complicate this situation with continuing skirmishes between Pakistan and India over the Kashmir—a mostly-Muslim province still held by India—and you get a sticky visa office.

Because of the recent war, our intended border crossing at Wagha-Attari Road would be open just a couple of hours a week, on Thursday mornings. It was fortunate Eva and I had already stopped off in Teheran to get our visas to enter India, for I doubt we could have obtained any Indian visas in Pakistan. The challenge which faced us was now to obtain transit visas called road permits, which would grant us permission to leave Pakistan. Any delay in getting these essential documents might mean missing the Thursday border opening and having to wait a week in steamy Lahore until the border crossing opened again. There was no place else to cross.

Eva, Sigrid, Bertil and I arrived in Islamabad to discover a bottleneck and travelers' reunion simultaneously under way outside the road permit office. All the crew of Swedes, Germans, Danes, Americans, English, Aussies and others who had journeyed the overland route needed road permits to go onwards. While Sigrid and Bertil stood courteously like good middle-class citizens of a prosperous northern European neutral country, the rest of us, poorly dressed, travel-stained, and plopped like beggars on the floor outside the passport official's office, sat chatting in bunches.

We went in by turns. Seen through the open door, the official, a portly bureaucrat, was clearly unhappy. "You are Russian!" he exclaimed accusingly to one unfortunate applicant as she entered, plucking up her Swiss passport from the pile on his desk.

"No, not Russian," the appalled applicant could be heard replying, "Swiss!" She was more polite than I had been in dealing with bureaucrats.

"But it is a Russian passport," he responded forcefully. "See," he said, waving the passport triumphantly. "It is red." Except for a large white Swiss cross, the cover of the passport, visible even through the open door, was indeed red.

Outside in the hallway, the motley crowd of lightly washed Europeans and Americans awaiting our turns struggled to control our faces. Even an audible groan or chuckle might damage this woman's chances of getting out of the country and proceeding on her way.

We heard a thump as the visa stamp came down hard on another passport, the sound amplified as it echoed through the official's metal desk. The line was moving. Yet another victim entered the portly official's office. (My guidebook included an explicit warning not to antagonize this particular Pakistani official: "Try not to freak him out too much, because he can and does refuse.")

An hour later, still snickering, we were all back out in the parking lot. There we encountered other friends from the journey overland. Rural hippies in bib overalls from somewhere in Belgium, these travelers had slid open the side door of their delivery truck to allow the new-hatched chicks they carried with them out to scratch for seeds among the weeds poking through the tarmac. Later, in India, we would meet again, and I would learn the chicks were no more, for in that very parking lot, feral Pakistani cats had attacked and devoured them. But that at least was not the Pakistani government's doing.

THE HAUNTED HOSTEL IN LAHORE

APERS NOW IN ORDER for the border crossing, we hit the road again, aiming south now, toward Lahore and the Indian border. We passed through flat country along a broad straight road bordered by greenery. Driving in Pakistan, we could not make speed. There were careening Volvo trucks and dawdling ox-carts to avoid. Whenever we stopped by the roadside, curious country people appeared from nowhere to gaze at us. The countryside looked prosperous. This was no desert like Afghanistan, but a breadbasket—or perhaps a rice basket.

Lahore was a town without women. While Afghan women had sometimes been out and abroad in the streets in Herat and Kabul, covered in the ugly *chadors*, here in Lahore, there were simply no women to be seen, only men and boys.

People spoke English more readily here. Asking instructions of a very civil man in the street, we were told to "turn left after two furlongs." I only knew what a furlong was—an eighth of a mile—from reading Walter Farley's horse books as a child. Trotting tracks are measured in furlongs. Other instructions were in equally archaic English, and less accurate. It seemed anyone was delighted to tell us courteously where to go, but whether the instructions would actually get us there seemed of little importance.

We planned to stay at a youth hostel the Swedes had read about. The hostel, when we finally located it, turned out to be a large ivy-covered building. It resembled any college's off-campus international student center. The building was clearly a relic of colonial days, but it was decayed, and the concierge, a bent old man who spoke English, did not want to admit us. Finally, he gave in and reluctantly pried open creaky iron gates.

Once inside, I felt I had dropped into an Agatha Christie novel from the 1930s. We were the sole guests—the only ones in decades, I suspected. The building had a European feel and also felt abandoned—emptied of English youth or Anglicized local students by Independence and Partition, with its hallways and furnishings still intact. That had been a long time ago. Somehow the edifice was still funded and persisted, a fossil orphaned of its original purpose. Was the place a boys' school? An embassy? A club for English bureaucrats a long, long way from home?

The halls echoed. Our every move seemed a clatter and a desecration, for events had isolated, not destroyed this place, sequestering us temporarily in the British Raj of long ago, where none of us had ever planned to visit.

Escaping to the pavement of a busy street, I located a curry vender. The man ladled up a small serving for even smaller *paisa* coins—tiny fractions of a Pakistani rupee. The food was like fire. The curry—a chickpea concoction—was the most fiercely hot I had ever tasted. Dipping my mouth close to the cleverly folded leaf that held my meal, I found I could only snatch nips, not eat. I like spicy fare but even travels in Mexico had not prepared me for the blazing chiles in Lahore.

A few well-stewed chickpeas in the fiery sauce, singeing a pathway down my esophagus, reached my stomach. Looking into the leaf-cup, I could see how little of its contents I had successfully swallowed, but I didn't feel hungry any more. Traffic rattled noisily past as I turned back to the hostel.

The hostel formed a shadowy contrast to the bedlam and vibrant bustle of the streets beyond its heavy doors. It was a negative to the venders and traffic and brightness and heat.

As I had earlier learned in Italy while staying at Mussolini's mistress's villa, there is something uncannily ghostly and desolate about occupying a building so disruptively repurposed. Here in Lahore, it was as if with our enthusiasm and chatter and intentions, we were letting the ghost team down. Certainly the old man tending the place seemed to think so. He made it clear that the presence of hostel guests was an interruption, but of what, we could barely guess. Perhaps he only wanted his past back. Partition had been a mess. Another arbitrary line drawn by the British which had infinitely screwed up ordinary people's lives!

Perhaps our own internationalism and enthusiastic mobility—the fact that we would be crossing that forbidden border in a mere two days—stirred bitter reflections, too. If so, our host clearly wasn't about to tell us.

Or maybe he missed the Raj. But although with our light brown and blond hair and blue eyes we all looked vaguely British, none of us actually were. And in our jeans and tee shirts and backpacks, we must have looked to the old man more like bazaar venders and porters than students and professionals. We simply did not fill the bill. While Sigrid and Bertil appeared somewhat more professional, as a group we were still not respectable enough.

This non-welcome was much more subtle than simply being hated. To be hated, we must have some importance. We had none and constituted merely a distasteful distraction.

A travel writer describes places—the bulbous domes, crenellated parapets, sky-reaching minarets, thronging *souks*, and the blues of the Aegean. But aside from the ivy and the high brick walls, I can't remember what this place looked like; I remember how it felt and that this was important, although at the time I didn't understand why this was so. It is possible to sense a mood even without knowing all the details. The mood was lousy.

West Pakistan's hopes for a bright future as a Muslim state had been scuttled by the severing of East Pakistan from the nation. Despite China's support, India had handily defeated Pakistan's army; meanwhile, West Pakistan's attacks on India had done little damage. Nixon's "tilt" notwithstanding, Yahya had gone down in flames, his place as head of state now taken by the ambitious Zufilkar Ali Bhutto.

If our host knew of these things—and he must have—he probably surmised that the presence of Westerners at his hostel meant trouble. Alternatively, like many who remembered what by present standards must have seemed relative peace under the British Raj, our host may have simply wanted to crawl into his shadowy building, recreate a dream of that prior security and forget the last 25 years, particularly the most recent one. For this was now, more than ever, no country for old men.

For our parts, the border crossing coming up took up most of our attention. We were itching to be gone as vigorously as our host seemed eager to have this creepy anachronism back to himself. Eva and I were eager to press on to Delhi. Sigrid and Bertil were already talking of Ceylon. But due to the recent war, the border gates creaked open for only a few hours one day a week and that day was still two days off. We must wait. Fretting to be gone, we considered Pakistan a way station, an obligatory waiting room, a delay.

There was a certain negative balance all around: We were not our host's desired guests. His place was not our desired destination. We too were looking for more ancient and perhaps less painful, truths.

But soon it was Thursday, and we departed from Lahore and its ghostly hostel, leaving our reluctant host still snarled in contentious national history, old and recent, and circling his premises pointlessly like a demented last bee guarding an already-raided hive.

CROSSING TO INDIA

WE DID NO SINGING in Pakistan and found precious little honey during our hasty passage. When Eva and I once more were sitting with Bertil and Sigrid in the two-toned Volkswagen bus, heading from Lahore to the exit point at Wagha, I realized I was hungry. There was nothing I could do about it. We were on our way to the border, and it would soon be time to stand in line again.

Up to now there had been few choices about route. The increasingly international trickle of Westerners had swelled to include Danes, Dutch, Swiss, Germans, Swedes, Australians, Yugoslavs, and some English. The weeklong border closure had backed up this current into a swelling pool of travelers milling before the customs station—together again after being dispersed since Islamabad.

Returning from his jaunt to the north of Afghanistan, Michael now found Eva and me in this crowd as we waited by the camper-bus for our turn to cross into India. I have read that children, isolated from their families' speech in a strange land, create their own new language complete with intricacies of grammar. We people of the road were doing the same—creating a new and transnational culture as our paths diverged and reunited. These cultural fusions had taken place along the Silk Road and as we passed through the trials of getting into and out of Pakistan. We were no longer simply Germans, Danes, Dutch or Americans, English or Aussies, but were becoming people of the road together—nomads in motion with our own customs and folklore.

Now Michael added a boost to that evolving body of mythology as he joined us in the enormous line at the border. "You won't believe how I got through the Khyber Pass," he announced, obviously bursting to tell the story.

We listened as he told of catching a taxi through the Khyber Pass, of clinging to the top of the aging American Chevrolet. There were 20 other passengers riding inside and on top along with their baggage. For once, a sturdy American car had been put to full efficient use!

As we waited, Michael described the blue lakes at Band-e Amir and the giant Buddhas in their cliffside niches at Bamian. Dorrie and Melinda were to meet us in Delhi, and we would learn their adventures when we met up there.

AFTER ALL THE EFFORT TO GET VISAS, finally leaving Pakistan proved trouble-free, if slow. No one bothered much about us as we exited through the checkpoint.

Getting into India in August of 1972 was more complicated. Entering travelers were ushered for processing into a room full of turbaned men unhurriedly writing. What were we bringing into India? "Cameras? Tape recorders?"

"Rupees?" The only correct answer to this latter question was an emphatic "No!" Like many countries, India vigorously supported its official exchange rate. Bringing Indian rupees into India was forbidden, even if the currency had been obtained at a bank. The rate outside the country might go up and down, but it was always considerably better than an Indian bank would give. Many a traveler mentally patted a secret pocket or walked a little more deliberately on a shoe padded with contraband currency, and lied.

Officials pried through backpacks and bedrolls as the line of travelers snaked through a huge room furnished with rows of counters. As in Pakistan, they spoke English.

"What is this for?" a customs officer interrogated a traveler near me, holding up a medicine bottle pried from her rucksack.

"Lice," came the succinct answer.

"And this?"

"Lice, too."

"And *this*?" My own head was beginning to feel itchy as I waited, listening.

"Also for lice," came the mournful answer. "Do you know anything that works?" the young woman pleaded.

I stood as far as possible from her pack. I did not have lice, yet, and wanted to stay that way.

Sikhs in long beards and turbans marked down anything of customs interest found among our possessions. I suspected Michael was bringing in Indian rupees, but if so, his illicit currency stash was not discovered. Eva, Sigrid, Bertil and I had nothing material to hide.

As my ownership of a single reflex camera was duly recorded in my passport, I stood thinking about how hungry I was. I had not thrived on the curry in Lahore, and now that we were finally in India, it felt like lunchtime. Looking out past the customs room at the bright noonday sunlight I realized that Pakistan had left me starving.

Finally, the probing of the the backpack's contents by the elderly bearded clerk was finished. Last entries were scribbled in my passport. I swept up scattered possessions from the customs counter and tumbled them haphazardly back into the green backpack. I strapped the pack shut. Shouldering it, I stepped across the threshold of the customs building and out, into the bright sunlight.

Into India at last. I had made it.

GOING FOR THE GOLD

EMERGING FROM THE CUSTOMS building into the early afternoon sunlight I saw a line of young girls selling food along the street. Each wore her dark hair piled in a bun on top of her head. Each bun was covered with a handkerchief. *Good*, I thought. *Here even girls are involved with selling in the marketplace. No more hiding them under veils.* It was a nice change from Pakistan, where all the women had been to be so utterly missing from the public life of the street.

However, I had misread the situation: This was the Punjab—or at least the portion of Punjab that remained in India after Pakistan was split off in 1947. Punjab, at least on this side of the border, was still the homeland of the Sikhs, and male Sikhs, by religious custom, do not cut their hair. These youthful venders were not girls, after all, but Sikh boys, their uncut locks pulled up neatly out of the way.

I was disappointed, but still hungry. We had changed a little money. Now I handed over an unfamiliar coin to a juvenile salesman and was given in return a heaping portion of unfamiliar street food, wrapped up in a cone of newspaper.

I peered into the cone. Inside lay small bumpy nuggets that were clearly deep-fried. Although it was a long time since my last bucket of American fried chicken, the look and smell were instantly familiar. But India was mostly vegetarian, so this couldn't be chicken. In fact, the snack pieces in the newspaper cone were *pakoras*—bits of vegetable coated with a spicy chickpea-flour batter and then fried up to a warm gold.

I bit into one piece, and then another. The *pakoras* had all the crunch and snap of the Kentucky Colonel's specialty, but tasted lighter and spicier. Each bite was delicious. If this was typical Indian street food, I had stumbled on a treasure, for the entire coneful only cost about a nickel. I could afford to eat *pakoras* as frequently as I liked. I quickly gobbled down the rest and bought a second cone. Vegetables were healthy food and fried ones verifiably safe to eat.

But there was little time to contemplate my satisfaction. Already Michael was tugging us away. He had been in India before and was impatient to get going. We would not need any hotel that night, he declared. He knew of a better place to stay in Amritsar. We swiftly made plans. We would meet up with the Swedes the next morning for the trip to Delhi. While they headed for a campground, Eva and I scampered after Michael as he dodged through streets crammed with a tangle of motorized rickshaws, small cars, delivery trucks and horse-drawn *tongas*.

Our destination turned out to be the Golden Temple itself–the holy place of the Sikhs. Although the splitting of the Punjab Province during Partition had stranded some Sikh holy places on the Pakistani side of the border, this–the Sikh religion's most important site–had remained part of India.

The Temple had a tradition of offering hospitality to pilgrims. It welcomed even Western visitors with backpacks. I was amazed. Spiritually, this was the equivalent of getting a bed in St. Peter's while touring the Vatican. It was also free.

We plopped down our packs in a stone-floored hall in the temple compound that served as sleeping quarters for pilgrims. Our stuff would be safe under the watchful eye of a towering guard with a long spear. As we left to tour the Golden Temple itself, I glanced back at him a little anxiously, hoping that the spear was only ceremonial. Although we had breakfasted in Pakistan and it was only a little after lunchtime, already I felt a world away from the Lahore youth hostel with its dour English-speaking caretaker.

The Temple enclosure itself contained a large clean pool, and the pool area was patrolled—not by lifeguards—but by men in turbans who carried long swords. I could see an elaborate golden structure at the far side. In a gilded cupola, a very old man with a white beard sat reading from a massive book.

The idea of a pool at a place of worship was not really so strange. Didn't the Irish have sacred wells? And King Arthur had a Lady of the Lake. I knew Hindus worshiped the Ganges River. With greater experience of India, I would grow more used to the notion of worship combined with water, to seeing sacred pools in odd places: with half-drowned temples in the desert, or bathing ghats—terraced steps—in Varanasi, leading down into the Ganges River, where the faithful could descend to immerse themselves. Dating from the 1400s, Sikhism incorporated some elements of ancient Hindu water worship, just as Western Christianity—also modern when compared to 8,000-year-old Hinduism—preserved ancient Indo-European elements in ceremonies like baptism.

On the day I entered India, dusty from the border crossing, the pool seemed limitless; gazing at the the temple enclosure with the gleaming cupola and the spreading water, I felt I had wandered into a fairytale, complete with moat and golden castle. But I hadn't wandered here, of course; Michael had pushed us into coming. And it wasn't really a castle. It was a church, with real people worshipping.

But this was a church with what looked like an Olympic-sized swimming pool at its heart. Sikh pilgrims—men, women and children—slowly walked around it. The women wore long loose trousers covered with immaculate tunic tops. All the men were dressed in carefully-wrapped turbans. The effect was impressive—rather like attending services at a very fancy church on Easter Sunday. I could see that some of the pilgrims were also getting into the water.

A dignified Sikh volunteered to stroll beside us along the pool's rim. Courteously, he explained what we were seeing. This was their holiest place, he explained.

Sikhs follow a succession of gurus who have outlined a pathway of behavior, our guide went on, but the final guru is the holy book itself. Each subsequent guru elaborated the concepts further, he told us. Sikh men, to demonstrate their commitment to this religion, do not cut their hair or beards. They wear a knife and certain special clothing.

So Sikhs were not a race: They were joined in a culture, united by their beliefs and religious practice. I glanced over the water at the the old man studying the giant book before him. I visualized the gurus as a series of benevolent old bearded men, like a row of frosted antique glass ornaments trimmed with gold and intense colors. A succession of treasures themselves, the gurus had forged and refined this young religion, using bits of the old ones and their own, new insights, teaching about a single omnipresent god and the brotherhood of man.

This was a familiar creed, and was not what I expected to discover in India. I was impressed and touched by these people who believed they had found noble ideas and were sharing them with us.

But after awhile Michael grew restive: It was time to go, he urged; we must find a restaurant. And off we went—this time to a tiny eatery back of the bazaar. I sampled *lassi*—a chilled yogurt drink.

"*Lassi* also comes salted," Michael instructed. Salted *Lassi* might be a boon in a hot climate, but my tongue shriveled as I tried to imagine how *salted* yogurt would taste. Sweet *lassi*, however, was cooling and perfect. We feasted on *mutter paneer*—a hearty curry of peas made with cubes of homemade cheese. I piled it on top of a mound of rice. Thinking back to the morning's golden pakoras, I decided that Amritsar's treasures were culinary as well as spiritual.

Back at the temple guest lodge, lights-out came early. Travelers of all kinds rolled out their bedrolls on the stone floor around the perimeters of the large dark room. I lay there looking up at the daunting spear-carrying guard. He seemed like some impassive statue of Neptune transported from a Roman temple. There was no rowdiness or misbehavior. I would have liked to read, even if only by using a flashlight, but I did not dare to challenge the guard's authority. Nobody else chose to either. I dropped off to sleep, still wondering whether he was there to protect us, or to restrain us. I didn't find out which, but whenever I woke, the silent warrior was still at his post, spear in hand. He watched over us all through the night until sunlight's rays penetrated the darkened room and we rose in the golden light.

THE CIRCUS

THE FOLLOWING DAY, we rejoined Sigrid and Bertil to roll on to Delhi. Bertil drove, still keeping to the left hand side of the road. Once again, the road lay straight and fringed with green. India looked just like Pakistan. Wherever we stopped, hordes of curious children gathered. There would be no one at first—an empty landscape. And then, one, two, ten, twenty, thirty.... The crowd would continue to grow.

The Swedes intended to camp out in their vehicle on the outskirts of New Delhi. Again, they let us off. Catching a motorcycle-drawn taxi, Eva, Michael, and I entered India's capital city.

We headed for Connaught Circus. This Indian circus was not some showplace for contortionists and performing elephants, but rather a busy, broad traffic circle at the heart of India's capital. The circular island at its center was lined with small shops.

We found a place to stay at a nearby guest house operated by Mrs. Clooney, a tall Eurasian woman with graying hair, who guided us through a warren of hallways to a multi-bedded room. Tossing our packs on the cots, we headed back to the Circus, Michael once more striding ahead, while Eva and I raced to keep up.

The roundabout stank of vehicle fumes, for the circling street was choked with traffic. Taxis, overflowing buses, and motor scooters burdened with multiple passengers contended with motorcycle-driven three-wheeled rickshaws and horse-drawn *tongas* on the belching, beeping, squealing ring that surrounded the arcade of shops.

Darting into this chaos, Eva and I, still following Michael, somehow crossed to the safety of the traffic circle's center without being mowed down by buses or scooters. There, as at the eye of a hurricane, relative quiet prevailed. Shops fronting the walkway inside the roundabout offered goods difficult to obtain in rural villages: Glasses with round red frames like Mahatma Gandhi's, suits made to measure, cameras, cassette recorders and color film. Here we could browse, sit down for a cup of tea, or simply stroll the sidewalk.

Dorrie and Melinda had arrived in Delhi before us. As agreed in Afghanistan, we met up with them at the Madras Coffee House, a large restaurant on the Circus rim. Within the large cafe, sheltered from the noise of the ring of speeding traffic, we felt we had reached the city's less frenetic heart! Waiters in stiff-starched turbans served up soft-boiled eggs with buttered toast and vegetarian sandwiches stuffed with watercress. Compared to our street-food snacking over the recent days, and the delicious curry in Amritsar, this seemed sickroom food—soft, bland, and British.

Perhaps this was just as well. Melinda was sick. She had caught amoebic dysentery somewhere on her journey and now looked frail.

Businessmen in white shirts and dark pants packed the cafe, sipping sweetened milky *chai* or cracking eggs boiled English-style in the restaurant's shady interior as a fierce sun broiled everyone outside. In this artificial twilight, members of our reunited group traded stories of our adventures while traveling apart. Dorrie had bought a beautiful peasant shirt, embroidered in red and blue, but after she laundered it in a guestroom sink, the colors had run together, creating a blotchy mess of the original needlework.

Our impressions similarly ran together and overlapped: money-changing stories, crowded transit, nights spent sprawled on hard floors in teahouses on the road to Marzar-i-Sharif, Eva's feisty confrontation with the hotel tout in Kabul, and my own outburst at the border station which led to our journey through the Khyber Pass with the armed soldier. Michael's passage through that same pass clinging to the roof of the overloaded Chevy was recounted for the entire group.

Only Melinda said little. She didn't need to. She looked pale and fragile, no longer the hardy Amazon who had set out for India after weeks on an Israeli farming *kibbutz*. Though less seriously ill, the rest of us had a good idea what her experiences had been. We sipped our tea, heavy with milk and sugar as outside the afternoon sun traveled into the West. We had become old hands at something, but couldn't quite put our fingers at what. Maybe just travel. Although traveling by a colorful variety of means, we had all made it to India. We had survived the journey. So now what?

Scanning the menu, I ordered vegetable cutlets. Although meat was missing from this small deep-fried entree, once again, the saffrony gold-brown color and texture were familiar. This was a meal to make a Kentucky colonel proud!

We called for more *chai* and sat drinking it in the semi-darkness. We planned our trip onward. We chatted. No one wanted to go out into that hot sun.

But we had to, eventually.

It was a little cooler when we finally emerged. After the vast stretches of Afghan desert, and even after the busier green-fringed highway through Pakistan and Northern India, the motor noise from real city streets was overpowering. We five wandered part way around the ring of shops, still talking eagerly. Tempting tri-colored Neapolitan ice cream, sliced in a brick, could be savored at one of places, but after a glance at Melinda, we all trooped by. No one dared try it. Melinda and Dorrie had chosen to fly rather than crossing the Khyber Pass, and now Melinda was sick. The suspicion hung in the air that Western food, in the tropical heat, might be even more risky than the eating Eva and I had done at street stands.

Some of the group needed rupees. India's official exchange rate of seven rupees to the dollar was unrealistic; violations of the country's currency laws were flagrant. Western travelers, having traversed what seemed like a few thousand years in human history in the short weeks of crossing to India, knew how how to take advantage of a city when one was available. The best black market rates would be here in Delhi, not in some village later on. This, too, was business which could be conducted in the vicinity of Connaught Circus.

It was not difficult. A likely looking man soon approached. "Follow me, mister," he said to Michael. Then he led the way to a taxi, and we all packed into it. The taxi took us—not to a knife in a blind alley—but to a modern commercial building, where civilized transactions took place in an upstairs office.

Exchange rates were haggled down to the last decimal place. Careful to make handwriten signatures legible, dusty travelers signed over slightly bent American Express checks to the black marketeers and received in return small heaps of well-worn bills.

After the wrinkled and fading rupees were fingered to locate the metal threads that indicated the banknotes were genuine, and the bills were tucked away in wallets and money belts, the entire group headed back to the Circus.

Still hurrying after Michael, who seemed to have some way of simply shoving his way through the human jams without causing offense, we went shopping. We needed to buy clothing. Everything which had come with us from Istanbul was worn or ripped or dirty. Plus it was hotter here. Still feeling like children playing follow-the-leader, we rounded the Circus, in search of lightweight clothing.

I didn't question why I followed Michael so passively. I was overwhelmed with heat and noise and crowds. I had used up my urges for adventure at the Khyber pass and now didn't care who went first. Michael plunged happily ahead, diving into crowds, and if he was willing to be the point man on this, I was content to merely paddle along in his wake, taking advantage of any openings he created which would get us closer to getting out of Delhi as soon as possible.

If this was India, Michael decided, we must all get shirts of *khadi* cloth. Gandhi, with his famous spinning wheel, had turned this domestic homespun cotton into a statement of political correctness during the Independence movement. India could make its own cloth at the village level, foregoing the British mills and factories, Gandhi had declared. Young and old, activists of the Independence movement declared their political rejection of the colonial mercantile system which fed the British cotton factories by spinning their own.

Decades after Independence, political figures with the Indian Congress party, which had agitated for independence, still could be picked out of a crowd by their *khadi* garments. At a small shop on the Circus, all of us dutifully bought homespun sleeveless shirts.

We bought white drawstring pants of ordinary machine-made cotton. If not as politically significant, the pants were at least more comfortable than my maroon jeans. Soon, all of us were out on the Circus again, transformed into the very images of nonviolent Western truth-seekers. *Satyagraha*, my friend! It was Gandhi's term, and it meant "Soul Power!"

A river of busy Delhians in their dark pants and white business shirts, streamed around both sides of the roadblock formed by our cluster of Westerners standing outside the shop in our new white cotton pants. They were used to such transformations.

But any search for spiritual truth amid Gandhi's teachings would have to wait. We needed to secure reservations for an outbound train. We speed-walked the Circus perimeter, forming a short parade of white-clad legs racing after Michael as he stalked a taxi, rather like a band of enthusiastic tropical missionaries pursuing a convert.

Further along the curving sidewalk, a nightclub advertised buffalo burgers, since cows were sacred and therefore off-limits as burger material. As we examined the posted menu, the club's bouncer turned away a man dressed up in eye makeup and a sari, who had sought to enter. The doorman's refusal sparked a loud and acrimonious shouting match in the street, halting foot traffic. Momentarily, we were stuck behind the disputants.

Back home in San Francisco, a cabaret-style revue featuring female impersonators was winning a loyal audience for campy showmanship, but I was surprised to encounter a transvestite in India, wearing nine yards of sari and a short-sleeved *choli* blouse.

I had been reasonably clear, although unhappy, about where the Afghans stood on the roles of the sexes. In Pakistan, the roles of men and women had likewise seemed pretty clear-cut. Now, for the second time in a trio of days, India was utterly confusing me. Who would covet a woman's life here?

Perhaps Alexander would have taken this more in stride. After all, hadn't the Conqueror himself occasionally dressed up as the goddess Artemis? But Alexander, stalled by the problem of elephants deployed against his troops, never made it as far as Delhi. I was on my own with this one, or rather halted in foot traffic while following in the footsteps of a German student from Berlin.

Still unable to move, I began thinking about hamburgers, wondering whether water buffalo tasted like they looked. Actually cows didn't look that tasty either, I decided. How much was the cover charge at this club? Who went to it? Did people in India, land of arranged marriages, actually *date*? Hearing a shout in slightly-accented English, I looked up. Michael had found another gap and was forging through it. We pushed after him, leaving the nightclub doorway and its disputants behind.

Finally latching onto a taxi, we crammed in and headed for the train station, hoping the reservation window would still be open.

THIRD CLASS HARD

W HEN WE MET UP WITH Sigrid and Bertil at the Madras Coffee House, a day after our assault on the railway reservation office, none of us still resembled the bedraggled Westerners who had arrived at Delhi in the couple's two-toned Volkswagen bus.

We were all—even Dorrie and Melinda—now dressed in lightweight clothing for India. I wore my new shirt of homespun *khadi*. The sleeveless shirt's loose weave was proving very comfortable in Delhi's roasting heat. I had on my new loose drawstring cotton pants. They covered my legs modestly, but they also allowed for lots of air.

Looking up at the slowly revolving ceiling fan, which reminded me of the set of some Humphrey Bogart World War II-era movie, I realized that keeping cool would henceforth become a personal quest, no longer a matter to be left to building managers and air-conditioning technicians.

Strapped on my feet were the soft plastic sandals I had bought on the Greek island. They too allowed for plenty of air, if there was any moving air to be found. Meanwhile the hiking boots I had carried from California still dangled from the front of the green backpack, their leather laces knotted to a ring on the pack's front. Leaving the guesthouse that morning, I had propped the pack upright against my cot and thought about the boots. I wouldn't throw them away. The boots were too hot to wear here in India, but I might need them later in Nepal, where the deep tread of their lugged Vibram soles might help me cling to rocks on mountain trails.

Or something.

Nepal was our goal; that was decided. But what I would do in that Himalayan country was still too nebulous to imagine. I knew I wanted to visit the Monkey Temple to see if it indeed resembled the Mormon Temple in the Oakland Hills. Perhaps I could strap myself into the heavy boots and climb it. I wondered if I still had any heavy socks.

We five who had met on the Black Sea Ferry were going east and north. Bertil and Sigrid were going south. Over *chai* and watercress sandwiches and boiled eggs in tiny eggcups, Eva, Michael, and I settled up with Bertil and Sigrid for our last leg of the ride in the VW bus.

Using the back of a spoon, I battered an egg open. A bright orange yoke spilled out onto my plate. As I mopped it up with a *chapati*, Bertil pulled out his slide rule and for the final time calculated each rider's share of the gasoline charges. Eva and I counted out newly-acquired rupees and *paisa* for the transit from Kabul to Delhi, and Michael did so for his share of the ride from the Pakistan border.

In the street outside, we waved as the Swedes headed back to their campground outside the city. Their journey would take them to an uninhabited atoll in the Maldives Islands. Sitting in their Stockholm apartment when we next met, Bertil told me wistfully about how the fisherman's boat had dropped them off and the two had spent eight days swimming and grilling seafood on the isolated beach.

Getting back to his engineering job had been tough, Bertil confided, as he clicked the slide projector, bringing up further images of tides lapping and fish being raised joyfully from an abundant ocean. I sat watching, disloyally thinking about how much one beach resembles another, but I kept quiet, realizing that I was merely jealous. I could not know, as I do now, that rising waters caused by global warming are drowning the atolls of the Maldive group and that Bertil's loss of a paradise has become the world's problem, not merely his own.

The rest of us were setting out for Kathmandu. We would still see plenty of India as we crossed it by train. Was this wise? Eva and Dorrie seemed hardy enough. Melinda, though game for travel, still looked unhealthy. I, too, was thin, though fully recovered from the fever in Pakistan. We were wiser, more experienced travelers now. Slowly, and of necessity, we had all learned the word for *toilet* in a handful of languages. And to look where we stepped.

Michael, for his part, looked even sturdier than before. He seemed to be shedding his European student persona and emerging, thriving, in a more ancient role—that of a goatherd mustering a shambling flock, a comic and solid Virgil to our collective weak-stomached Aeneases. Unperturbed, he had guided us through the complexities of train reservations at a window where no one believed in waiting in line. Would-be train travelers had pushed and shouted, but somehow, amid a competing sea of waving arms, Michael pressed the right amount of rupees into the proper hands and arrangements were completed. The train was very inexpensive. Somehow, at the Delhi consulate, visas for Nepal got duly stamped into our passports.

Wise or not, we were ready. We could go. *Farewell Mrs. Clooney. We're bound for Kathmandu.*

ON THE DAY OF DEPARTURE, somehow, after dashing in Michael's wake past the Second Class Ladies Waiting Room, the First Class Ladies' Waiting Room, and the people who were no longer waiting but merely living on the station floor, we located a train car displaying our very own names, spelled out correctly on a typed list. We all bundled in. We sat down in the compartment and thumped our backpacks onto the floor. Then with grinding sounds and whistling, the train lurched, and we were off, bound for Varanasi by *third class hard.*

Hard class is a literal term. Our reservations were for a compartment with unpadded wooden benches. When night came, sets of hinged wooden shelves, which folded flat against the compartment walls in the daytime, were opened to create two tiers of additional sleeping platforms above the seats.

As the steam train rolled toward the holy city of Varanasi on the first leg of the trip, I settled myself on my side on a topmost narrow bunk, covering my face entirely with a scarf to keep my eyes and mouth free of cinders from the locomotive. A conductor had warned us that sparks might blow in through the open window and I had no desire to become an accidental fire-eater.

In the morning, and throughout the next day—for we were not on an express train—food venders raced up to the car at the frequent stops. Hands reached up to our window, proffering sweetened milky tea in rough clay cups: "*Chai*, Missus?" They held out curried potatoes or spicy chickpeas, each portion spooned onto its own large leaf. Still others thrust up twists of newspaper, filled with fried *pakoras* as delightful as those I had first sampled at the India border.

It was all delicious. I could pick and choose for *paisa*—for pennies. In California, it was usually necessary to drive a car to get to a fast food restaurant; here the fast food came directly to us. Everything did. There was no need to worry about going hungry. The train stopped every few minutes.

Children bustled through the car selling newspapers and *paan*—betel leaf—accompanied by dabs of various condiments. *Paan* is said to be a stimulant and to cure worms, but chewing betel stains the teeth and leaves the mouth looking bloody. None of us was tempted to try this.

Between such distractions, we talked, or dozed as the train bounced onward. Idly, I dealt out cards in the Tarot deck I had brought from California. It seemed to be a peaceable, health-food-style Tarot, featuring vegetables instead of swords and pentacles and hanged men. My own fortunes frequently involved eggplant, which was fine with me. I was happy to be eating food I didn't have to prepare.

There is little housework on a train. There were no dishes for me to wash, no autopsies to type up. Despite the hard bench, I was in heaven. Less celestial, at the end of the car, a toilet which was essentially a hole in the floor to squat over, awaited my every urge.

WE GOT OFF IN VARANASI–"BENARES" to the English. There were no more nightclubs with buffalo burgers. Instead, what we thought of as the real India was before us.

Off the train and up the street, we all trudged after Michael. Michael, meanwhile, followed after a German communist and the two men the communist had hired to carry his luggage. We Americans sneered at the idea of a man hiring servants, but Michael patiently explained that the young communist was creating jobs.

I stared at the German and his porters, realizing I had never seen a communist before. On TV, yes: Kruschev thumping his shoe on a desk at the United Nations, Fidel Castro in military fatigues with his Jesus beard, and the dashing Che Guevara, every New Left woman's fantasy of a Latin lover. But this German looked ordinary. He wore his dark hair cut shorter than Michael's. His clothes were a little bit cleaner. So this was a communist on vacation busy creating jobs! Thinking about my own slim resources, I wondered how he could afford to do this. I realized I didn't know very much about Germany. My own pack felt very heavy, but Michael's logic still didn't budge me.

Street signs were in Hindi only. We were all progressing in *where-are-we* disorientation, walking up a long gentle slope. We coped by trooping after Michael, who in turn followed the German communist, whose porters knew the way. Eventually, we all reached a government tourist bungalow. In its dormitory, a line of wooden *charpoys*–bed frames cross-strapped with ropes–filled a long room. There were no mattresses. Ceiling fans lazily stirred the air above our heads. This was someplace Little Orphan Annie might have been sent to for fresh air and a cure, or Oliver Twist remanded to as a punishment for requesting a second bowl of soup. I dug out the padlock purchased in Greece and chained my backpack to the leg of this minimal bed. This was exactly the situation I had bought the padlock for a continent ago.

Like so many buildings we had seen along the way to India, the tourist bungalow vaguely resembled one of California's Spanish missions. It had an arcade and courtyard. We sat outdoors at rickety tea tables and ordered Eagle brand beer in tall brown bottles–an extravagant treat, after India's hopscotch of dry provinces. Travelers shared tales–of the people who went mad from culture shock, of the German communist and his baggage carriers, of Tibetan medicine made from ground-up precious stones. We whetted our whistles until we were perhaps as high and screechy as eagles hiding out in a cozy nest.

Outside the tourist bungalow lay a land without labels in any Western language, confusing and hot. Eventually, we had to go and see it.

191

Michael and Dorrie and Melinda went off somewhere. Eva and I ventured out

Men at a silk factory beckoned as we walked down the street

"Come in misses. Come in misses," the workers called. They seated Eva at the broad silk loom and showed her how to pass the shuttle through the strung warp. They laughed as she complied adding a few more lines of brilliant silk thread to the sari under way. Then they asked for money.

"No," Eva laughed right back. "I've been doing your work."

We sought refuge from the sun at a tiny restaurant, a cement hole with Indian movie posters plastered on the walls. A little homesick, Eva tried to get tea fixed the way that Germans drink it.

"*Chai* without any milk or sugar," she mimed, striving to put the request into some kind of mutually comprehensible sign language. The proprietor, a friendly guy, was convulsed with laughter by such a silly outlandish desire. Giggling, he fed us curried spinach and rice, and still chuckling, plucked a calendar bearing a lady movie star's photo off his wall and presented it to her. The tea arrived sweetened and milky, as usual. We left, Eva carrying the movie star calendar.

Outdoors we found no street signs to help us find our way back. We wandered the wide dusty streets, pretending to be trekking in the countryside, hoping our feet might recognize clues to a route back which escaped our conscious minds.

Eventually we found ourselves trudging up a hill, and then the tourist bungalow with its courtyard and spindly chairs emerged, just where we had left them.

Varanasi is a holy city. For Hindus, this city by the Ganges River is the place to come to die. The river is said to be pure, to cleanse all. Ashes of bodies burned by its side are tipped into the river. Another day, Eva and I took a boat out. The oarsman pulled up-river, past *ghats*, broad cement staircases at the side of the river. We saw crowds and giant parasols. Some of the faithful had climbed down the steep steps. People were dipping themselves in the holy Ganges. We passed pyres—places where bodies were being consumed by flames.

"Ooooh," exclaimed Eva, suddenly in real pain, for a baby's body was floating downstream, face downwards, head bobbing.

On land again: "See the sexy temple sculptures," a tout demanded, snickering slightly. Forming a frieze around the small temple, the sexy sculptures were hard to miss. Bulbous boobs. Hands everywhere. Did the gods have more hands for better sex?

LATER, ON MY OWN AND LOST again, I was caught up in a crowd passing down to the river. Drawn along, I came to a red-painted shrine in the street. It was a shrine to Ganesh, the elephant god who brings good luck. At least I think it was. The red sculpture on a building's outer wall seemed the right color for Ganesh. What was it? This surely was something important—something ultimate.

I pressed closer to the shrine, but I still couldn't make out what it was. Some women were ardently pressing their hands onto the rosy surface. Others were smearing it with something oily. Flowers lay in little piles on the ground. But centuries of such reverent touching had obliterated all details of the sculpture. It was no longer possible to make out what this shape, polished and eroded by human hands, even represented. It was now a blob, a formless blood-red blob.

I started back in confusion and sudden nausea. I had moved closer, emotionally prepared to view a carved and explicit deity, not this red-daubed undulating surface. Yet people were worshiping it.

Suddenly I felt a terrible long way from home. What people were doing in this street seemed to have so little to do with the tidy lectures and structured meditations at the sedate and ascetic Hindu *ashram* I stayed at once in the California foothills. I reeled away.

I thought of Dante's *Inferno*, or of all those crowds hustling along in Eliot's *Waste Land*, so many creatures: poor, dusty, dying, undone. Yet these women were bearing flowers, worshipping a thing whose meaning had been obliterated by stroking hands.

The city by the Ganges was proving upsettingly beyond my understanding. Or rather, I was taking in too much, far too fast. I understood that I was overstimulated and in trouble, but I had no comfortable way to process that understanding either.

Too much, I kept repeating to myself, as if articulating the thought would help. *I am understanding too much. I can't contain it or digest it.* And there was no way to turn it off. I ached for the quiet of the California hills, but there was no way of going back.

And it was very hot. The welcoming overhead fan in the tourist bungalow seemed now ordinary and familiar and Western. the spartan dormitory, a refuge. I lay on my *charpoy*, wishing not to see or hear or smell anything at all.

THE TOURIST BUNGALOW MANAGER INVITED me to tea. We sat at one of the battered courtyard tables in rickety chairs. *Clap clap.* He called a servant to bring tea. But no tea came. At the shaky table in the bungalow garden, the manager told me of his master's degree in history and explained his theory of how Chile and thence the Western Hemisphere were settled by voyagers from India in Vedic times, long ago. It was India, he said, that carried civilization to the rest of the world. He clapped again. But the tea still failed to show up.

I didn't believe that sailors from India discovered South America. I put his theory in a mental file alongside claims of levitation by American Transcendental meditators and the miraculous cures achieved by Lydia Pinkham's cure-all ointment.

Going out again, I found there were *saddhus* in the streets. *Saddhus* are pilgrims who have voluntarily given up everything, families, possessions, even clothes, to wander. Many were stoned. Some had painted faces. Some carried spears. Some of them were naked. I passed a *saddhu* as I hurried down the street in confusion and rising panic. The *saddhu* looked straight at me, his expression full of infinite love, like a blast of brightness. This man with nothing had nothing but compassion and love for me. His gaze jolted me from my growing rage brought on by heat and disorientation.

Another day rain came, offering relief from the heat but none from Varanasi's strangeness. A naked man in glasses pedaled down the wet street, his clothes neatly piled on his head.

Once again I hiked back towards the tourist bungalow, seeking the familiar wide street and the gentle hill, letting my feet find the way and pretending I was on some mountain trail and not in a crowded ancient city without street signs in English.

Two skinny boys caught up to me, and began harassing. "Money missus? Money!" I was American, fed from infancy with vitamins, homogenized milk, and lots of meat. This conveyed some advantage: I was taller.

Swelling with sudden fury, I took firm hold of their bicycle's front wheel. "Leave me alone, or I will break your bike," I told them, meaning business. They believed me and left off. I reached the courtyard and its familiar disorder with relief.

Clearly, I was unraveling. It was all too much, much too much. I had wanted this, but now I didn't.

IT WAS WELL PAST TIME TO LEAVE the bodies, the burning, the holy men with wild faces, the tea which didn't arrive, the Eagle beer and the wistful manager. Michael was willing to push on, and the rest of us, by this time, eager to follow the leader. And so the five voyagers fell into line again, Michael leading onward, as before. Back on the train we climbed, bound this time for Raxaul, where we could cross the border and take a bus up the mountains to Kathmandu in Nepal.

It costs almost nothing, we again congratulated ourselves, when we were once more aboard the train. *Only $20 to cross the country.* But we sounded a little hollow.

And Melinda, by this time, was not the only one fleeing frequently to the bathroom at the end of the car. We were all peeing and shitting into the squatting hole while the train bumped over tracks. There was no need to linger in the reeking toilet, for diarrhea flowed from our bodies almost instantly. More cinders from the locomotive bounced into the compartment. Veils have another purpose—to protect the face, protect the eyes. In parts of the Indian countryside men as well as women partially cover their faces—not to avoid prying eyes, but to ward against flying sand. But in hard class we were dodging industrial grit. Hot grit!

"Excuse me," said the male passengers. "From which country are you coming? Are you married? How many children? Where is your husband?"

The train clattered on. I drank *chai* from more pottery cups, ate curry or potatoes from more folded leaves at stations. Outside along the track, the *paan* man sold his betel with areca nut. Inside the car, the chewers looked hydrophobic, their teeth as crimson as fangs of feasting vampires.

BEFORE COMING TO INDIA, I did not understand much about hunger. I knew lack of food led to death, but what I didn't get was that death wasn't instant. I know now that hunger can lead to slow decay and increased vulnerability to other diseases. A reason for death may not be listed as starvation-related, if anyone keeps records, even though starvation is the true cause.

In India of the 1970s, alongside the tracks at the outskirts of cities, child beggars screamed up at passing trains, their swelled bellies—usually typical of toddler physique—not signs of health, but of undernourishment.

In Turkey, red hair might signify a differing ethnic background, perhaps Armenian or Kurd. Red hair on a street child in India often meant *kwashiorkor*—a starvation-related disease. Starvation, even when survived, contributes to retardation. Its results were visible in the gaping, vacant faces among the adult poor, particularly in cities, where bodies, but not brains, had survived the stresses of childhood.

I understand this more clearly now. On the train, I mostly felt it. It felt like a wall of pain.

This was no longer a paradise. I had sought India, and now I was seeing it. Like Scrooge on Christmas Eve, I was being shown the world, unmerciful and unmercifully. But I no longer wanted to be back in California. I would rather be here than anywhere else.

And yet, part of me was looking forward to the border crossing. There would be no more hard class travel for us in Nepal. No train lines at all went to Kathmandu.

INCHING TOWARD KATHMANDU

AT LAST, WE STUMBLED wearily off the train, in dusty Raxaul—a town much smaller than Berkeley—at the foot of the Himalayas. Michael, Eva, Dorrie, Melinda and I, who had ridden the Black Sea Ferry, crossed together into Iran and Afghanistan, and reunited in Delhi for this train ride halfway across India, were again a traveling unit. At the hotel we found five pint-sized beds clustered close together in a small room, threw down our packs, and slept. It was our last night in India.

Marshaling in front of the hotel in the bright morning, lugging our packs and packages, we surely did not resemble Alexander's disciplined phalanx breaking camp. Out early, I had watched as a local man brushed his teeth, using the fibrous end of a twig plucked fresh from a green tree instead of a toothbrush. The twig-scrub must have worked well, for as the others joined me, he flashed us all a wondrous white-toothed smile. Then, plucking up our packs and spirits like seasoned gypsies, we five clumped to the roadside. Michael snagged a conveyance—taxi or horse-drawn *tonga*—I can't remember which. We all boarded and bumped along to another unmemorable border.

All unmemorable border crossings are by definition good ones. They are the uneventful international transactions where no one questions your papers, where your camera and tape recorder are not described in your passport with odd-colored indelible ink, where no one demands *baksheesh* and where no travel-group member is body-searched or left behind in custody.

Having arrived safely in Nepal, we five climbed onto a bus bound for Kathmandu, the capital. And after a bit, the bus itself began to climb.

The bus had the usual odd-shaped mysterious baggage piled high on top. This time, however, there were no melons and no fierce old man in a turban commanding us to sing. I would like to say that this was just as well, for with all the vehicle's gyrations, we could not have managed a single verse between the sickening slumps to one side or the other. I would like to say that after each dramatic yaw, the bus somehow recovered itself before reaching the point of capsizing. But that would not be true. The bus to Kathmandu had neither shot springs, nor rocking shocks.

I would like to say that the ride was a wheezing mechanical workout for a middle-aged and poorly maintained vehicle as it faced the challenges of unimaginably steep grades, hairpin turns, gasping drop-offs, and that defying logic and gravity, the bus reeled onward and upward through curves and switchbacks. That too would not be exactly true, although there were drop-offs and hairpin turns in abundance.

We were indeed inching upwards—were inching up the Curia Range in fact—but the bus was a good one. It neither pitched nor leaned excessively as it ascended the narrow road etched into the flanks of the mountains. And the road was relatively new. The Churias are mere baby mountains compared to the snow-crowned Himalayas that lie off beyond Kathmandu, but to the five of us—after the hot flat spaces of the Indian subcontinent—they seemed gigantic. Creeping up such mountains in a bus was more akin to flying than driving.

In northern Mexico's mountains, I once rode a bus beside a woman who pointed out to me each place where a truck or car had failed to negotiate a sudden turn. At each spot where a vehicle built for crawling along land's horizontal byways had rebelled at the steep grades, taken flight, and then, like Icarus scorched in the white solar light, plunged down, and now lay broken and clasped fatally to the warm earth's breast in the undying grasp of gravity at the bottom of a gorge, my seatmate crossed herself. Often flowers or a handmade cross marked the site of such disasters. My seatmate on that journey made sure I did not miss out on any of these memorials, either.

But there is no need to attempt a flight to the heavens when a perfectly good, if narrow, road will take you to an earthly paradise for less than a fistful of Nepali rupees. Inspired by Michael's thrifty traveling skills, we had all become extreme low-budget soarers. The twists and turns and stops were just part of the economy package.

Our bus clung to the road. No goats boarded. No helpless squirming feet of unidentified fowls protruded from paper bags and baskets. It was a bus full of men. I remember the bus chiefly because it had no toilet. And because Melinda had dysentery, she had to stop a lot.

At each sign of impending emergency, we begged the driver to halt. The driver braked; the door squealed open. Melinda got off quickly. The male passengers snickered. As Melinda raced to the rear, seeking minimal shelter behind the vehicle, the men began enthusiastically trooping down the steps and out the door. They were following her.

This, I thought privately, *is the awfulest*. But Melinda, ill as she was, moved faster than her followers. In a flash she was emptied and back, bounding up the bus steps. The men reboarded the bus enthusiastically. The gearbox ground a bit, and we resumed our progress upwards. Until she had to stop again.

At bends in the road, streams poured down the cliffs above us, passed under the road, and joined leaping whitewater torrents headed downhill. Peering down into one ravine, as the bus skated successfully around a jaw-droppingly tight curve, I could see women among a crew of workers armed with mallets perched among the boulders in midstream. They were cracking open smaller rocks in search of rubies. Amid the rushing waters coursing through the flinty Himalayan landscape, the women's mallets crashed down on hard rock like the sledges of Alabama chain gang prisoners. But this harsh labor was wetter and even more precarious. I had never considered before that rubies glinting in a red-jeweled crown might have resulted from such backbreaking labor in a foaming river. Or that women broke rocks in mountain streams for a living.

Continuing, the bus forged upwards past steep mountains terraced with rice paddies. Each earth-ribbed terrace held in place a chunk of mountainside already covered in brilliant green shoots. Such mountains may have grunted barrenly up from the earth's core in tectonic halts and jerks, but human labor here transformed them into something infinitely more bountiful, for this rice land was Edenic, fertile. It looked like the green morning of the world, if the world were a nice place. Seeing the terraces, I felt my heart expanding in the thinning air.

Then, as the bus paused at another bend in this twisty road, I glimpsed an ancient woman under a green tree with huge leaves which grew from a pile of mossy rocks. She was leaning slightly over a stick jutting from the hillside. A light beam etched a straight white line along the the stick. The stick must have been hollow and carried water from a spring, for the figure was taking a mouthful. Water droplets tumbled like diamonds from her hand and arm.

In the foreground, nearer the paused bus, a young mother stood beside an open-topped 50-gallon drum, smoothing her daughter's hair. Sunlight feathered the lichened boulders, stroked highlights on the daughter's arm, bounced glistening on the mother's oiled hair, and tweaked the rim of the water drum with a ring of white light.

A ruined doorpost near them spoke of long human habitation, but I felt like a birdwatcher. I had sighted a rare nest of humans, thriving in a green wrinkle of mountainside.

As I raised my camera, the daughter turned slightly, peering toward my world, the dusty bus windows, the heaped backpacks and mysterious bundles, as I peered into hers. It was a brief and intimate exchange.

Halfway round the world and over forty years later, I wonder, did the daughter's feet follow her glance? Were the trees cut down? Is she old, now, too? Further, I wonder today, can I scan this mysterious picture for my computer? Can my software bring to light details in the photo that my human memory no longer contains? Will I see the snake?

Or was the road itself the snake, bringing the outside world like a great red tempting apple to a place that needed nothing?

Why was this bend in the road so important? Journey is sensation, perception. I had felt—sweated, smelled, shopped, eaten, and eyed—my way through Asia. While some memories thankfully vanish, others remain as brilliant as light on leaf. Writing, I seek meaning. I scrabble raw experience into a thing. I snatch at it on film, tweak time's nose, seize the moment, grasp at experience, tease out ideas, delve. But why dig here? What rubies am I seeking?

There must be some inference here: Old woman at the well, mother tending her daughter. Did I never see such things? Why was this so important? Somehow I had arrived starving at a place noted for starvation and was unexpectedly fed.

In the months before I left California, as the Vietnam War dragged on and protests against it mounted, I had a recurring dream: A baby, fat and round like the Buddha, sat injured and wailing among the wreckage of civilization. I recalled seeing a historic photograph of the aftermath of a Japanese attack on Manchuria in the thirties. In that photo, the baby sits weeping before the smoking wreckage of a bombed railway bridge. In my dream, as I moved closer, the weeping dream-baby became smaller and smaller, until, like an ant, it crawled, ever-dwindling, away into the lawn. Receding among the grass blades, as in a palm forest, the baby became so tiny that like a grain of sand, it was lost in the lawn, and though I searched, I could no longer find it.

I didn't have a lawn. I didn't want a pregnancy. But this diminishing creature haunted my dreams. Always it evaded me. Always, perhaps, I evaded it too.

Months before leaving home, I attended a local clinic to receive an intra-uterine device to prevent pregnancy. No one ever told me much about childbirth. My mother had been doped asleep when she gave birth and could not tell me. But in the clinic, as the nurse dilated my cervix to place the little fishhook in my womb, I experienced for the first time an unfamiliar and terrible pain and I knew that childbirth must be like that.

One more strike against the idea of procreating.

Yet here, on this cleft in the mountain on the road to Kathmandu was another understanding—a mother and daughter in an affectionate moment, generations, the flow of water and gentle sunlight. Without fakery. No Madison Avenue trumpery.

Was it a baby I wanted? A family life? The thought threw me back in my seat. I was stunned that a desire so simple and primitive could be a piece of the confusing mosaic that was my life. Was my journey East after my heart's desire reaching a turning point of some kind?

I jammed the thought away.

The journey resumed. The bus rumbled around the next bend into the next new valley, leaving behind the primal farmyard scene with the woman and child. And I went with it.

A look at Google Earth today does not reveal exactly where that miniature valley lay hidden. The computer screen shows a rather straight highway leading North from Birganj; then the road begins to twist and twine upon itself, snaking in ever tightening coils to what must be a high pass in the Churias. Ultimately the roadway pivots eastwards and plunges giddily downhill toward the city marked with a star in the Valley of Kathmandu. It is a seasick-making road.

In 1972, my bus arrived safely. Later, my friend Adam's bus would not. Adam and his wife ran a small graphics business out of a modernist house high in the hills east of the San Francisco Bay. I did not know they had set out for Kathmandu. I learned of their journey only after their deaths, when I saw a wire photo in the *San Francisco Chronicle* showing flaming pyres looking like the aftermaths of monks' self-immolations in Vietnam. These were the funeral pyres for Adam and his wife. After their bus plunged from the road to Kathmandu, their families opted not to fly the bodies home. Years after my journey, Adam and his wife died by the road on which I felt I had been born.

In the Indian cities, the human encounters had been often overwhelming and often beyond comprehension, but through the bus window on the upward ascent, Asia emerged a little at a time at a pace I could deal with. The need to slow things down is cultural, perhaps. I heard a secondhand tale, of an Indian man going somewhere by train, who experienced the opposite problem when he found himself all alone in a train compartment. Physically alone for the first time in his life, he became terrified.

My problem was the reverse. I did fine on stony heights, stringing baggage on a bus, or taking tea in a desert caravanserai. But in Varanasi watching dozens of hands caressing and anointing a shapeless red blob, I had become disoriented. Like an early movie in which the spaces between the stills could be perceived but flickered by too fast to be absorbed, travel was too often a flickering alternation of dark and light, with little scenes and epic ones mixed up, where I became the unwilling audience, and the director was either mad or absent. The only defining order I could bring to such floods of experience came from an inadequate Western mindset, a budding feminism, some slim notions about eastern religions, and an obsession with a sea-green globe. Often these were not enough to make sense of my surroundings.

But in quieter moments, there were also intimate spells like this one, gazing into the green world, when my faltering and overwhelmed perception became sharply focused, precise, when I saw and felt and also often photographed across a temporal and cultural abyss. And this time someone stared back!

Just before this journey, my therapist instructed me to just receive experience. I rejected this. Since childhood, I had framed sentences in my mind to describe all I saw. "I experience and then create," I remember rebuking him. I was not cut out to feel without responding using the structuring props of language. Sometimes in India, there had simply been no sentences big enough to do the job.

Did Adam die here at this curve, I now wonder, *or somewhere up the road?* Had Adam and his wife, both artists, been overwhelmed in India too? And did my friends experience the same completeness as I did in the Himalayan brightness before their bus plunged off the narrow road?

AT MY KITCHEN TABLE IN CALIFORNIA, a clicking sound disturbs this writing. *It's a mouse,* I think, at first, but actually it is a spider with a huge task, subduing a struggling insect bigger than itself. The victim insect somehow makes a clicking noise as it is rotated by the busy spider, like a pot on a wheel.

I could shut down this scenario. I could perform an ordinary household task, say, seize a dust mop and deal death to spider and prey together. I have that power over life and death. I could shutter and dismiss this roadside vision on the way to Kathmandu as well. But long ago instead I took a photo in a narrow valley at a crook in the road, and I must deal with it, though the subject, which appears so simple, is bigger than myself.

In some ways, I am like the spider, for I turn this seeming trifle from my journey East, examining it from all sides, probing, sucking the meaning, swallowing, digesting and being nourished by this encounter on the narrow road where others close to me met death. I try to understand what made that single encounter so important. I am still trying. My prey is narrative.

MONKEY TEMPLE

ATE IN THE AFTERNOON, when we rolled into Kathmandu—it proved as dirty and wonderful a city as I was ever to see. From my hotel room three floors up with a rainbow painted on its wall by a former occupant, I could peer down into a courtyard piled high with refuse and excrement. Ducks foraged amid the mess.

When I lived in the East Oakland flatlands in a post-earthquake bungalow with a Morris chair and aging lace at the front window, my housemate Theo sometimes compared the vista of the gilded steeples of the Mormon Temple in the Oakland Hills to the Monkey Temple in Kathmandu.

Now in Kathmandu, faced with the genuine Monkey Temple, I discovered there was a big difference, for the Mormon Temple in Oakland did not possess a pair of eyes on the top, looking back.

The genuine Monkey Temple does. Its painted eyes perch above a nose shaped like a question mark and somewhat resemble the single all-seeing eyeball engraved on the backside of the dollar bill. These are not the unwinking eyes of sleeplessness, or the prying ones of some puritan deity, snooping out sins, or pissed-off and full of aggressive attitude, like the sharp eye of the eagle also on the U.S. dollar! The eyes on the hilltop stupa outside of Kathmandu are painted in bold sweeps like the exaggerated makeup on a Balinese dancer; the rims too are ornamented in strong lines. The eyes—meant to depict the Buddha's—are open, but disengaged, calmly accepting the surrounding lively world with all its ups and downs.

This is a good thing, for Kathmandu was—and probably still is—lively. The city has a broad river, a massive bas-relief of the mother goddess Kali, dancing and waving her many arms amid the towering tiered pagodas at Durbar Square.

It has a Temple of the Living Goddess. The Living Goddess job is an appointive position. A girl is selected for the goddess post at around age 14, serves for awhile, and then, like Miss America, gets to step down without being sacrificed.

Walking back to our hotel one night after drinking a considerable amount of *chhaang*, the powerful local rice wine, Michael, Eva and I fell in with a joyful parade, including two trumpeters, coming from the Living Goddess's temple. Swept up in the procession, we found ourselves leading the parade down a main street, trailed by the jolly bandsmen in the brass section.

For awhile, I marched beside Michael with a scarf stretched out between us like a union banner at a Labor Day parade back home. Over and beyond the band's honking and tooting, the night was filled with vibrant voices and merriment. Invisible beings hidden and bumptious seemed to wheel and cavort in the whirling air directly above the parade despite my best efforts to not believe in them.

I decided I approved of the Living Goddess. Her followers did seem to enjoy a grand sense of fun. *Maybe women do figure in the equation, here,* I thought

Boisterous after the parade, Eva, Michael, and I trooped into a tiny restaurant for *chai*, and perhaps more *chhaang*. Eva's blond head bobbed as she exclaimed excitedly about the procession Michael and I had inadvertently spearheaded. As we sat talking, a man from an adjoining table, middle-aged, well-dressed, and rather plump, addressed us. Eyeing Eva's rounded figure approvingly, the man made Michael an offer.

Four cows.

By now, we must have had too much to drink, for Michael, instead of shooing the suitor away, immediately responded to the offer.

"No, no, not enough."

The man upped his bid. Again, Michael countered. It was becoming awkwardly clear that the would-be buyer was entirely serious. By the time the offer reached nine cows, our *chhaang* was done. We rose and trooped out, leaving behind a thoroughly crestfallen Nepali who thought he had a done deal.

Michael only laughed, and Eva and I laughed to keep him company, but it wasn't funny, really, not at all. Once more, as a woman, I was tossing in the no-man's-land between cultures.

The no-woman's-land

THE FELLOWSHIP IS BROKEN

THE UNEXPECTED BUS STOPS caused by Melinda's diarrhea on the way to Kathmandu proved a literal watershed—last straw—last gasp—a final hurrah for the two American travelers from the kibbutz. Melinda had become more chipper once the bus ride with the harrowing poo stops was over. Instead it was now Dorrie, who had seemed so unflappable during the journey, whose resolve now faltered. Dorrie, who had snapped a towel so successfully to protect our rear ends as we foraged for visas and smoothies in the streets of Teheran, now summarily declared that she had had enough

Enough of what? She couldn't precisely say. Just too much of everything: heat, illness, overstimulation, exhaustion, challenge to her beliefs, unceasing scramble, hassles, hurrying pace, street food, culture shock.

I could understand her viewpoint. Dorrie's work-stay on the *kibbutz* would have involved living in a small community out in nature, with a clear plan of what to do and lots of hard work. It would have been orderly.

Our final travel days had been a rush with a single imperative: *Get to Kathmandu.* Michael had set us a fast pace. The pace had created order. Now that we had arrived in Kathmandu, the stabilizing influence of being in transit was gone.

We all faced new streets, different foods, another language and currency, a new religion (or several, much mingled) to comprehend. Coping was more hard work, and Dorrie was burnt out.

The two women agreed to start heading home. They would fly back to Delhi at once. We all went to the airport. We waved, and Dorrie and Melinda flew off.

Eva and Michael and I planned to go trekking. I went with them to the government permit office. I was astounded to find that autumn was prime time for going climbing. I got a permit for Pokhara, on the road to Mt. Annapurna. We wouldn't actually climb, but instead would walk the lower elevations to see the countryside and villages. Our plan was to fly to Pokhara and then hit the trail.

Now the next step was in place. The permit was tucked in my passport. Thumping the passport, I felt like an adventurer. But when I thought about it, I didn't really feel like climbing even in the foothills. Besides, I liked Kathmandu. The city was less crowded than cities in India. The pace was slower. There were Buddhists and Tibetans here, and I wanted to know more about them. I hesitated.

But sometimes, what is important is not the planned, but the un-planned. In this case, it was a theft. Someone stole some raingear from Eva's and Michael's room.

They went to the police to report the loss. As an American from Berkeley in the wake of the People's Park demonstrations, I was more cynical than my German companions about police effectiveness. I figured that the only thing that would come of reporting the missing umbrellas would be lost time. But I waited for my companions anyway, not wanting to go back to my solo hotel room.

And while I was waiting at the side of a Kathmandu street, a man hurried up to me. A stranger, not tall, and probably a tradesman, by his look, he seemed a nice enough person. He asked if I would teach his family to speak English.

The man gestured up at the building across the street. I could see lively children at a pair of upper windows. Two girls in the left-hand window were jumping and smirking and leaning out, making faces. A little boy leaned perilously out of the adjoining window, while a more solemn little girl stared at him. *His kids,* I thought.

At a third window, I could see a beautiful glossy-haired woman dandling a baby. *His family. I could be living there, part of that world, teaching those children.*

An old woman leaned at another window, one floor up. She leaned on her arms, the arms crushing her breasts. She looked tired, resigned, imprisoned.

Pointing the camera upwards, I captured them all—the two windows brimming with lively children, the mother, the old woman—in a series of quick snapshots. They formed a triptych of set pieces on the stages of life.

Language lessons might free this family from some of this inexorable traditional progress from cradle to pyre. In particular, the women in the family might be released by learning English. The children might discover modern opportunities, new roles. The father—good for him—clearly realized this.

The offer tempted me. Teaching offered an opportunity to become immersed in the culture, to become a part of it. However, I would have to join a family and perhaps live by its standards, unless I was independent enough to maintain my freedom. But while I had managed to break away from 20th-century America, at least temporarily, I knew I was not strong enough to prevail as an independent woman in an even more rigid traditional culture. Not in Afghanistan and not here.

I realized sadly that although I had the language skills, I could not stay to teach these people English.

Somehow I knew also that my next steps could not involve pattering along a mountain path after Michael's bobbing red backpack. I had followed Michael's energetic lead during the sprint across India. I was grateful for the assistance in getting to Kathmandu. It had been an amazing journey, but I was a little tired of always racing.

Eva and Michael came back excited from the visit to the chief of police. They had had an adventure, and they had gotten their umbrellas back.

Excitedly they packed for Pokara and two weeks of trekking. "Come to see me in Berlin," Eva urged, as I watched her put her things into her pack. "My father has built a bathtub in my apartment. You can take a real bath." I went with them to the airport and watched their plane take off for Pokara. Then I went back to my hotel room at the city's center.

Taking the now-unneeded trekking permit out of my passport, I stowed it in a deep pocket in my backpack. Paper was lightweight. I could carry the permit home as a souvenir. I cleaned out my pockets, washed some underpants in the sink, and wrung the water out by twisting, as Eva had taught me. I spread the wet laundry out on the bed to dry.

And then, with this chore completed, I sat down next to the underwear on the narrow bed in the narrow hotel room and stared for a long while at the shining rainbow painted on one of its cement walls by a former occupant. I got up and looked out the small window. Below, in the back courtyard a pair of white ducks were wandering amid piles of garbage thrown down from the windows above; they were trolling for snacks. Would these ducks themselves become the snacks by dinnertime? Actually, maybe eating meat might not be such a great idea.

Idly, I dealt out my tarot cards with the eggplants and peppers, but I could make no sense of the results. Carefully avoiding the drying underwear, I lay down on the bed and studied the *Overland to India* guidebook. I had no clue where to go next.

I was alone and on my own in Kathmandu.

I WAS NOT REALLY ALONE, OF COURSE. The city teemed with hippies. And the local people were jolly and hospitable. But after being shielded by the company of a small crowd for so long, I felt naked. Michael was no longer around to drag me into action. When I went out, Eva was not there to join me on my walk.

In the street, I bumped into the man from San Diego I had met in Istanbul—the one who had refused to travel with me to India. Gerald was large in a particularly American way—tall and wide like a football player without being fat. He would have towered over any of our traveling fivesome, even Michael, our scrappy group leader.

Gerald seemed genuinely pleased to see me again. We sat down to a game of chess at one of the cafes. I am not usually competitive at chess, but this time I played with great attention. I refused to let my mind wander back to the insulting rejection, my raw fear in Istanbul, the sleeping-out in the no-man's land, the attack on me in Herat, or any other adventure of the journey. I concentrated on the moves on the board between us.

I was determined to win. I had succeeded despite his refusal to help. I had made it all the way to Kathmandu. I had already won. It really shouldn't matter any more, but I was still angry at him for telling me he didn't want to travel with a woman. I beat him at chess, too.

It should have been enough, but there was a problem. I was being hassled, just as the San Diego man had predicted back in Istanbul. A Nepali man was following me around. When I slid into a booth at the Tibetan cafe to eat corn fritters alongside the Australia-bound English travelers, he showed up, pushing into the booth beside me, asking questions, and spoiling my enjoyment of the fritters in sweetened syrup. His questions were the normal questions: Where was I going? Where was I from? Although he seemed very ordinary, this man frightened me, and I was alone.

I ran into him on the street. Actually, I didn't run into him; he ran into *me*. I was being stalked.

Was this man in a suit with his prosperous belly a policeman, or a government spy, or a white slave trader? Or was he merely seeking a mistress without having to pay for me in cows as Eva's suitor had proposed? Or all of these? He gave me the creeps.

The city, which had seemed so small and safe, now appeared menacing. As I passed the shrine to the Goddess Kali among the tiered pagodas on Durbar Square, it was no longer just a piece of brightly-colored statuary. I noticed the skulls set like jewels in the Goddess's crown, the red around her mouth like blood, the raised sword in one of her right hands, her hula skirt of severed heads. Would a life of limitations, of fitting oneself into a narrow woman's role with no options, give rise to the worship of a goddess of destruction? I noticed the additional fistful of severed heads dangling from one of the Goddess's left hands. She had her victims all by the hair - the way my often-angry sister sometimes grabbed me when we fought as children.

Kathmandu—or something—was getting to me. Suddenly I wanted desperately to leave!

Eva and Michael were not due back for two weeks. I decided not to wait for them.

THE ONE-WAY AIR TICKET TO DELHI was easy to arrange. Perhaps I was one of a wave of travelers who reached their high-water point in Kathmandu and made this choice as the surge retreated. I boarded the plane and entered a known world of seatbelts and scratched plastic windows. I took a window seat. The airplane taxied and lifted into the thin air.

When we reached cruising altitude, I shot off the expensive color film I had carried so carefully over sea and land since Greece. Pressing the lens against the humid dual-pane airplane window, I photographed the receding snowy bulk of Mt. Everest, up by the Tibetan border. For generations, Tibetans knew this mountain as "Holy Mother," but Andrew Waugh, a British surveyor general, had renamed it after his former boss, Sir George Everest. Even the world's tallest mountain was colonized!

From the air, the mountain appeared as neither mother nor surveyor, only a snowy distant image in my viewfinder. I shot them all—the whole diminishing lineup of knife-edged peaks. But it was I who was receding in the distance, bouncing through the cold heavens in a fragile sheetmetal coracle on my way back to Delhi. I had gotten further than Alexander, before he turned for home. I hoped that, unlike Alexander, I would survive the trip back.

We had left Mrs. Clooney's guesthouse in August. Now it was September. I was back in Delhi in a matter of hours. And then it was: *Hello Mrs. Clooney;* the snug cot in the multi-bedded room; the safe cradle of a big city where many people spoke English. All now seemed very Western. Mrs. Clooney expressed no surprise at seeing me again so soon. She seemed a bit motherly, in fact. Mrs. C., I decided, knew how to manage living in two cultures simultaneously. Maybe it took a lifetime to learn how to cope.

I decided to take things slower. For a day or two, I lay on my cot, pondering. I had left behind the women and children on the upper floors and a chance to make a life in Kathmandu. Their images would haunt me clear across the world—when I printed them later in Berlin, when I mounted them in the south of Germany, where I was teaching, when I put the pictures up on the wall much later back in California. When I see them, I recall that other life that leaned out towards me, which I did not choose to join. Already in Delhi I understood it was no longer all right with me just to stand by, observing. Yet I was not ready to do much else. I was not ready either for the perilous trip back across Asia.

And I was not done with India, either.

But I had had enough of big cities. And it was still hot in Delhi.

I lay on my cot and dithered. Finally, I decided to go to Dharamsala, in the Himalayan foothills of India's Himachal Pradesh Province. Tibetans and their leader, the Dalai Lama, had settled there after fleeing the Chinese in 1950s. Visiting the Tibetan refugee community, I figured I could see Tibetans and learn more about Buddhists.

I am not tall by Amertican standards, but, once out on the road again in India, I found I was taller than most people I met—women or men. I was no longer afraid.

A GAME OF CHESS

MCLEODGANJ WAS NOT IN my guidebook. It took me two days' travel by train and bus from Delhi, and finally a twisty climb in a taxi from the town of Dharamsala to get to this out-of-the-way sanctuary, where Buddhist refugees from Tibet had settled. The Tibetan refugee village clung to the side of a Himalayan-sized mountain and looked out over the Kangra Valley and the town of Dharamsala, below. Behind the village, and up a pine-clad trail, hulked the rest of the mountain, Hanuman Ka Tibba, part of the Dhauladhar Range. The geography reminded me of a hill house in North Berkeley, a high setting with a broad vista of a green world below. A good lookout point for a writer or observer. But the looming presence of the mountain's 18,500-foot peak just behind the town was a strong reminder I wasn't in the Bay Area any more. Part way up this mountain, I had heard, there was a waterfall worth hiking to.

Other Western travelers were here, too, but not a throng of them. Things were quiet in this almost-Himalayan village where Tibet's ruler and religious leader, the Dalai Lama, had taken refuge after trekking in from Tibet in 1959. I sat reverently outside the temple listening as aging monks chanted.

Back at the friendly guest house on the main street, a group of us Westerners curiously examined round pellets of Tibetan medicine from the Dalai Lama's doctor. The pellets, large as horse pills, were said to contain ground-up turquoise and precious metals. Rolling a pill in my palm, I marveled that the doctor in this traditional culture was a woman.

In the evening, we travelers crammed into a booth in a cafe beyond the public prayer wheels at the end the town's single horizontal street. The cafe's interior felt more like a simple ski lodge than a restaurant in India. The Tibetan woman who ran this tiny eatery served us hot *momos*—dumplings like giant matzoh balls. We sat around talking, feeling almost part of the family as the proprietor handed over her baby to its father. He sat down near us, dandling and bouncing it. Later, a local teenager wandered in carrying a guitar, sat down, and began plucking out his own riff on a Crosby, Stills & Nash tune. The song, one of my favorites, was about being on the road and having values and becoming yourself. Cultures were meeting and blending in this cheery cafe, and I was finding the mixture comfortable, even sweet, after the stress and jangle of the journey to get here.

During a stop on the bus ride up, a leper had reached through an open window and touched me. I hoped this didn't mean I would get sick. Antibiotics are supposed to cure and eliminate Hansen's disease, but these life-saving medicines appeared not to have reached the North Indian village where the leper begged. And, come to think of it, I was allergic to penicillin. I looked at the skin on my arm. It looked normal. So far, I saw no ill effects.

At the guest house, such worries evaporated amid the chuckling humor of the Tibetan landlords. Bunches of small beds were stuffed into rooms pretty much the same way they had been at other small town stop offs. Here, though, much else was different. A few steps beyond the front door led to a tiny plaza. At the village center stood a bank of large bronze prayer wheels, each bearing in raised Tibetan letters the sacred words: *Om Mane Padme Hum*—"Give me the jewel in the heart of the lotus." Devout Tibetans passing by could stop to push the heavy cylinders into motion, much as I had shoved my family's globe into spinning as a child. Tibetans believed that once revolving, the bronze wheels were released prayers into the thin mountain air.

In the evenings, talk continued among the travelers. One of them, a bearded youngster from Toronto not yet twenty, told of his intention to hike further into the mountains. His plan was simple: He would buy twenty pounds of rice, and some wheat and sugar, and follow the hill paths, trading these commodities in the places he visited. As always, I was envious. It seemed no matter how far I got, there was somewhere farther to be explored. Unlike Alexander, this Canadian was planning to engage with the culture, not conquer it.

Another voyager, who claimed he had been in South America, played small tunes by blowing into a tiny pottery ocariña. He told us of children raised in caverns who were fed on nothing but *coca* leaves. They formed a secret underground culture somewhere there. Colombia, perhaps, he thought. I listened politely, but thought this guy had possibly been on the road a little too long.

I sat in the guest house room drinking rice wine with a Swedish traveler and an American economic development worker. The American had come up from the flatlands to help the Tibetans stage a traditional opera. I had no idea what staging an opera involved. Who would the audience be for such a performance? But I wasn't really listening.

Another audience was figuring foremost in my mind, for a very important appointment was coming up. We were going to be allowed to meet with the Dalai Lama.

I felt like I had an appointment to meet the pope. It was very special, and I felt honored. This was one of the attractions of being in this particular town. In California, I was nobody, a starving former student with long brown hair, parted in the middle, one of many. Here in India, I was about to meet a God king.

"What are you going to say?" the Swede asked me in very proper Oxford English, accented just noticeably with a lilt that kept the tail-ends of words bobbing unexpectedly up and down. "We have a chance to ask a world leader something really important."

I pondered the question, momentarily. I sat on one of the four cots in our room, attempting again to fold my knees into a Zen meditation position. The cot sagged a bit, and I noticed that the maroon jeans I had bought in Berkeley six months ago were nearly kneed out. Fortunately, I wore a pair of drawstring Indian pants underneath. They were once the white pants I had bought in Delhi. Somewhere along the way, I had dyed them navy blue. The effect was of dark wrinkled underwear peeking through the holes in the jeans. I didn't care how I looked. It was chilly in McLeodganj, at nearly seven thousand feet.

The Zen position was growing uncomfortable. "I can't think of anything, really," I said finally. It was gratifying enough to be granted the audience at all.

"Well, I can," said the American economic development worker. Pete usually had something to say, I was noticing. But my attention drifted. I stared inward, reviewing a kaleidoscope of images: Sikhs with spears at the Golden Temple, Saddhus naked in the streets, men in red-rimmed round Gandhi glasses pedaling brakeless bicycles along rutted roads. I thought of the ageing women with hair tied up in braids I had seen trudging along the bank of huge bronze prayer wheels outside, pushing and turning the bronze cylinders. The women pushing the wheels reminded me of factory workers, their symbolic actions weirdly mimicking industrial ones. The slow-moving prayer wheels had creaked like millwheels as they carried prayers to heaven. Maybe the women's prayers were keeping the world on its axis.

Pete enjoyed talking contemporary matters. How to deal with farmers who didn't understand machines need oil. What the Peace Corps ought to be doing about animal husbandry. How Chandigahr, down in the flatlands, was a city built entirely by a Western architect in the International Style. While I drifted in timelessness, he worked out his agenda.

"I'm going to ask him about the arms race," Pete finally announced. *Ahhh, that!*

Well, the arms race was still with us. Like the terror when the siren went off accidentally outside my high school classroom four miles from the Pentagon in suburban Virginia, or later of exploded missiles which didn't make it to Kwajalein Atoll near Guam, leaving a streaky stain on the California night sky during my Berkeley days. I used to call in to the rock radio station to ask; they would call to the Vandenberg base, and then we would hear the latest lie over the air about how a missile went off course and of course was blown up before it could damage anything *If* you believed it.

"Everywhere you go down a trail like this in America, there seems to be a Nike missile base," an American student announced once as we hiked a trail in Europe. Now here I was in India on a journey to dip myself in healing transcendence, and that old mushroom cloud was popping up again: The indescribable final Armageddon. Another dizzying assault of the horror linked with America's wars, real or perceived.

Ignoring Pete's continuing discourse, I sought ground. I thought about sewing up my pants again, before the drawstring trousers also ripped. If I didn't do something soon, my knees might get scabby and infected.

This contemplated gesture was to be a very tiny one in favor of order in a world riven with apocalyptic peril, but I could at least keep myself warm and healthy. The needle was in my pack, along with a spool of black thread I'd bought in Athens. I had only to reach in and flip open the metal Band-Aid case I kept it in. Amid the valley of death this discussion was aiming towards, this path at least lay open to me. A path away from this terrifying talk.

But Pete was nowise done. "The Dalai Lama is a very modern guy," he went on. "I want to get a picture of what he understands."

I reviewed a handful of mental pictures: the Dalai Lama walking across the snow, through mountain passes; the portraits in the photographer's shop down the street showing Tibetan women with hairdos like Hopi Indians; mud-and-wattle structures with tapering walls; long-necked horns and rosaries carved out of human thighbones. At the photographer's shop, I had bought a photo printed from a damaged negative showing wide-mouthed silver dishes laid out on an altar, probably taken somewhere in Lhasa, Tibet's capital city, before the snowy trek over the mountains to India.

I recalled the old women with weathered faces who sat in the small plaza, behind goods spread out for sale. They sold *dorjes*–sacred objects made of brass that were also called *thunderbolts*. They sold small hand-held prayer wheels, bearing the same holy words as the plaza's bigger ones. The women sold swags of beads too—made of amber and plastic crafted to look like amber. They sold strings of red coral. They sold bits of Tibetan clothing. These vendors had probably all made the same terrible journey.

I knew a little about refugees. My aunt, a WAC during World War Two, came home after the war with a doll she had bought from a Frenchwoman while visiting liberated Paris, shortly after the German army had been driven out. The doll and its clothing were sewn from scraps of the woman's own clothing. It was gone now. When my parents retired to Florida, my mother emptied the childhood home of such superfluous possessions. But in my childhood, the brightly-dressed doll had seemed to speak to me of the unknown Frenchwoman's resourcefulness and my aunt's pity.

The French doll's arrival and eventual disappearance had been miniature close-at-hand events, not cosmic ones. Here in McLeodganj, nestled in the mountain's side, I wasn't sure I wanted to think about what kind of events the Dalai Lama understood. My context wasn't big enough.

But Björn, the Swede, felt differently: "That's a good idea," he told Pete, judiciously, adjusting his long legs. The cot in the guest house room creaked like a prayer wheel under him as he shifted position. "You should ask him how to solve the world's problems." He said it in such a low-key way, I wasn't sure at first if he was being sarcastic. But he meant it.

Swedes liked neat solutions, I was noticing. They seemed to have fixed up their own country tidily enough, and gave nice prizes to international problem-solvers. They didn't seem to think there was anything which couldn't be fixed. I wasn't so sure.

Try Kent State, where Ohio National Guardsmen shot at those anti-war protesters, I thought bitterly. *Try My Lai where those Vietnamese villagers were slaughtered*

The trial of these multi-bedded dorm rooms was that you could not avoid hearing a conversation you didn't want to be part of. Glancing floorwards, I noticed once again that my maroon jeans were gaping at the knees. I got out the thread and a large-eyed steel needle. I would stitch up whatever I could to be slightly more presentable for the audience.

Earlier, we had descended on the town. Literally descended. The main town of Dharamsala, with its Tourist Bungalow and banks, lay more than two thousand feet below McCleodganj, where the Tibetans lived. I saw soldiers along the road, uniformed and armed, many with fierce mustachios.

After seeing them, I could not easily forget—even while seeking out the elusive modern bank that could miraculously change traveler's checks into rupees—that the Great Game initiated by the British and Russians volleying over Central Asia was still being played out, even though some of the players were new.

The province of Himachal Pradesh, where we were, adjoined Kashmir—that mystery province of lakes and lovely gardens, which was nominally Indian, but whose mostly-Muslim population seethed with rebellion. We were astoundingly close to Pakistan, too. Further to the north a road strung across rocky abysses, built by the Chinese in an outlying remote area, had broached Indian borders a few years back, but the road was not even discovered in its frozen fastness for years. Once discovered, that border violation sparked a brief war between India and China. The soldiers in the town below McLeodganj had a tense alertness which spoke of the expectation of further combat.

So what was I, a spiritual refugee from my own nation's combat, doing among them? Well, I was after weather cooler than Delhi's and solace spiritual, financial, and physical, if I could find it. I was near the end of my journey and perhaps the end of my rope. I had little privacy and no solutions. But, like an Afghan nomad woman, I still had thread and needle. With sudden determination, I finally threaded the needle, bunched up the fabric, and finally began stitching up the holes in my jeans, without even taking them off first.

THE AUDIENCE WAS TO TAKE PLACE on an outdoor terrace in McLeodganj, near the Dalai Lama's residence. Six or seven of us Westerners stood waiting expectantly. Then, flanked by alert bodyguards and an interpreter, the Dalai Lama entered. I had been hearing of this God King since the 1950s. I had supposed we would meet an old man, but this one was a young man, and a man of action. He wore a red robe with his arms bared. He stood on the terrace before us, full of energy and rocking a bit on the balls of his feet, like a basketball player eager for the first ball to be thrown to him. A kind of intelligent merry expectation emanated from him. He was thoroughly in command of the situation and seemed amused by us. I suspected His Holiness didn't really need any interpreter, either.

Pete was ready, too. First pausing to get his breath, he popped out his question. I can't remember Pete's exact words, but they went something like this: "Do you realize," he asked His Holiness, "that with the push of a button, a nuclear war can be unleashed that will threaten the entire world?"

The Dalai Lama answered immediately and briefly. Then, while His Holiness stood quietly waiting, the interpreter spoke to us, relaying the message in English. It was a single syllable. "Yes," he said simply.

I found I had no question, or at least none I could ask out loud.

SOMETIME DURING MY STAY in McCleodganj, I climbed part way up the mountain behind the town, as far as the waterfall. The falls roared down beside the trail, glistening braids of white water tumbling from high on the mountain. And in the roar, somehow, I could feel the roar of life, or a roar under life, that would go on whether I was there or not. Nothing mattered, except the great white plunge of water. It seemed to me that this water was life, that it was all of us, that it flowed and fell and was under us all. Nothing mattered, although I could fool myself that this little twitching creature on its surface that was me sometimes convinced itself to the contrary. I was part of this all, a twig bumping around in this tumbling roar, and it would go on forever. And it was a great comfort to know that.

My own agenda was complete. I had found Gandhara or something like it. It would always be there, but because I had to live in this squeaking daily world, I would not always be there with it. And even that didn't matter, either.

KHYBER SYNDROME

"RIDE WANTED WEST." I sat at the India-Pakistan border on October 19 with the sign propped against the front of my knees. The night before, using a cheap ballpoint pen and a discarded piece of scrap cardboard from the end of a carton, I had laboriously drawn out the largest balloon letters I could manage, filling them in with crosshatching to make the ink look solid. I hoped the sign would be visible to approaching drivers from a distance.

I sat waiting in the dust by the roadside, wearing a sleeveless homespun *khadi* shirt and drawstring cotton pants, the big green backpack beside me. What was I thinking? This was an insane way to try to get back to Europe. It was dangerous. But I was very short of money. I had to get home, somehow, even if I was no longer sure where home was. I swallowed my fear in a choking gulp

The Land Rover that pulled over already had a Dutch passenger, a thin teenager curled up in the back seat. The driver was an Afghan. "Karim," he introduced himself in good English. Karim came from Herat, near the Iranian border. He had been in Kashmir. Now he was going home. For $10, he said he would take me all the way to Herat. Karim was stocky and prosperous-looking, with a head of thick shiny black hair, worn long. He had on traditional Afghan clothes, but a golfer's windbreaker was draped on the seatback behind him.

A Land Rover is the Cadillac of back-country driving. This Land

Rover was new and appeared carefully washed. Karim himself looked freshly-scrubbed and amiable. The Dutch passenger was scruffier and said nothing, but he looked amiable, too. I consulted my heart and stomach and found no surge of fear. I fingered the marble doll's head in my pocket and felt the fake Alexander coin for reassurance.

And after all, what other choices did I have? Grabbing up my pack and slapping away the worst of the dust, I shoved it in back next to the Dutchman. I climbed up and sat down in the passenger seat. The Rover shot off immediately, dodging around carts and pedestrians. We cleared customs in a few minutes and entered Pakistan.

Karim talked as he drove. He had fallen in love with an American woman from Los Angeles as she traveled through Herat. He told me how he left the family business and followed Suzie all the way to Kashmir. Ultimately, the romance didn't work out. Now he was going home. Home was a hotel in Herat that his family owned, one of those hacienda-style compounds set well back from the highway on the outskirts of the city, with its own road leading up to it. I had probably ridden right past it when coming into Herat for the first time.

Karim's place sounded a good deal more luxurious than the dusty place on the main street where I had stayed.

Karim's family had a political history. He spoke exuberantly of his brother's participation in a violent student uprising, as if the rebellion had been a great frolic at a carnival. (Hearing this, I suspected he was Pushtu, not Persian, but it didn't seem smart at the moment to get into a discussion about race or politics.)

Karim had been away from his duties at the hotel for months pursuing the American girl. He said he would be in trouble when he got home. "My mother is really going to beat me," he laughed, taking one hand off the wheel and jerking it up and down to demonstrate just how she would apply the stick to his back. An ox cart was coming up. Karim swooped around it and kept on talking.

I thought about the women in heavy *chadors* I had seen in the the streets of Herat. Somehow the images of these restricted women didn't square with the kind of matriarch Kasim was describing.

"*My* mother is liberated," Kasim explained, as if sensing my confusion. "You know that *chador* that all the women wear? Well, she doesn't wear it when she goes abroad. When she goes to Syria, she just puts a little scarf around her shoulders. She has been to Syria four times, all by herself, shopping."

I was in luck. On my way to India, I had crossed much of Afghanistan by public bus, and Pakistan in a VW bus, cautiously driven. Now on the way back, I was speeding across the Punjabi flatlands, leaving India's dust and crowds far behind as we chatted cozily about family life in Herat. We had common ground, for I too was going home. More or less.

The Rover made good time. By October 21, we were threading up through the Khyber Pass, approaching the crest before beginning the descent to the border crossing at Torkham. Karim was still driving fast.

Maybe too fast. To our left, the roadway fell away into a stony abyss. A rocky mountain cliff erupted at the road's edge to our right. There was no shoulder. It was no longer necessary here to drive to the left, as in the flatlands, for the road was barely wider than a single vehicle. *How much traffic is there up here, anyway?* I wondered, as we spun through yet another blind hairpin turn. Glancing behind us, I could see a cloud of dust. Pebbles kicked up by the tires were rolling toward the drop-off at the road's edge. I began to feel like a ball-bearing spinning in a roulette wheel.

A great belch of fear started to inflate in my stomach. What if we met something coming the other way?

And then, of course, we did. It was a bus descending steeply towards us from around the curve just ahead. The dusty emblem set between its pair of unlit headlamps caught the light for a second before the heavy vehicle, reeking of diesel fumes, thundered down towards us on a head-on collision course.

Time must have warped a bit then, for as I stared at those blind headlights, I was able to remember my housemate Stephanie's tale of a lurid car crash in the much milder Pacheco Pass back home in California, as she was heading to Tennessee to live on a communal farm. She told how the white car that passed the revamped school bus she was riding in smashed into a black one heading the other way. The occupants of both vehicles perished in a tower of fire and steam, and the eastbound school bus Stephanie was on, one of a small caravan, inched past this primal and final encounter and went on to Tennessee.

Stephanie led encounter groups, considered herself a Jungian. At this point she did not know yet that the Tennessee commune would be only a way station and that she was already embarked on the long pathway to a doctorate in psychology. On that narrow stretch in the windswept California pass, as she saw it, soul had met shadow. I had been very impressed.

Now Karim's foot smashed down on the Land Rover's brake pedal. I could hear the bus brakes screaming. Dust exploded in great powdery billows engulfing both vehicles. When it died down enough for us to see anything, we were all stopped. We were still alive. Karim gingerly backed up the Land Rover. The bus began inching by. I had experienced restraint, Afghan-style.

My fury exploded.

Here, in the middle of the Khyber Pass, in a vehicle still backing away from a nearly lethal collision, and barely considering what I was saying, I berated Karim. "You were going too fast," I shrieked at him. "You have to slow down."

I had yelled from the gut, not considering consequences. "If you don't slow down, I am going to get out and walk," I raged on. I had not paused to consider the prospect of actually trudging up this stony road below Landi Kotal, where the men crafted homemade rifles and smuggled for a living. We were in a remote area of scattered mud fortresses with rifle-slot windows, which housed tribal people the British had never been able to subdue. I had heard hands and noses were routinely sliced off as punishments. I was not even carrying water.

You belong in the funny farm, my interior voice spat at me. I shrank back and sat very still and small in the passenger seat, wondering how I was going to back down, or if Karim would merely put me out as I had demanded.

This was another attack of Khyber Syndrome: another terrifying episode of the Pass turning me into a madwoman. I sat in horror, awaiting my fate.

When Karim finally spoke, he was calm. "OK," he said, contritely. "I won't do more than 50 the rest of the way to Herat."

And he didn't.

We reached the border crossing alive. Karim fanned through a handful of passports and selected the one he believed would be most benign to exhibit to border officials. We were practically waved through.

Proceeding at a sedate 50 kilometers per hour, we got to Jalalabad in time for a late lunch. It was Ramadan, and observant Muslims were not supposed to eat at midday; however, there is an exemption for travelers, and the restaurant seemed untroubled at the prospect of feeding foreigners. The Dutch passenger and I both ordered. The waiter brought me a vast platter of something with raisins and carrots and I ate like a Death Row prisoner. Then we drove on, still doing 50. It would probably take an extra day to reach Herat, but peace reigned inside the Land Rover.

When we reached Kabul, Karim dropped me at the Green Hotel for the night and went off to visit friends. As I checked in, the desk clerk reminded me it was impolite to wear shoes indoors. "Leave your shoes here," he instructed, pointing to the threshold by the lobby desk. So I unstrapped the clear plastic sandals which had traveled with me all the way from Greece and left them them on the floor beside the other shoes.

In the morning, the sandals were gone. I knew that items left unsupervised in Afghanistan are usually considered to be up for grabs, but I had put the sandals there to comply with local customs.

I was broke, and I was pissed off. I didn't want to clump around in my worn hiking boots for the next two thousand miles.

"I need those shoes. I left them where you told me, and now they are stolen," I told the desk clerk. When he didn't respond, I didn't quit. "You will have to pay for the shoes," I persisted.

This got a response: The clerk, a tall, thin, starved-looking man, turned on me in fury. "Be quiet about the shoes," he hissed, "or I will kill you."

I shut up for a moment. It was the first time I had been threatened with death in a country where people usually meant it.

It was time to back off. "But without my shoes, how can I go out and buy more?" I temporized. "How can I even walk in the street?"

Shucking his own well-worn flip-flops off his feet, the clerk handed them to me. "You can borrow these." I thanked him, put them on, and went out to shop for replacement sandals.

Karim was a man of his word. Back under way, we proceeded at a snail's pace along the road that dipped south towards Kandahar and then headed northwards again to Herat. In the Land Rover's front passenger seat, looking at the empty road ahead, I began to fret about what I would find in Herat. I worried about the sleazy bus driver who had attacked me. How big was Herat anyway? Would I run into him again? What would I do?

It never occurred to me to go to the police. I wasn't even certain if there were police in Herat. I thought about Karim and his family and wondered if they would be important enough to protect me. But to my acute disappointment, when we arrived in Herat's dusty main street, Karim set me firmly down at my former hotel.

The ride was over.

I paid, said good-bye and thank you, and Karim drove off. I shouldered my pack. Passing by the child selling knickknacks at the entrance, I lugged my belongings up the familiar steps, wondering if Karim's mother would really beat him.

I WAS GLAD TO FIND MY OLD FRIENDS Asim and Nabil still presiding in the tiny hotel office. I was gladder still that Hamid, the owner, appeared not to be in town. And gladdest of all that there was no sign of the bus driver. I had not told my friends about the attack or their boss's possible complicity in it.

Winter was on its way now. I needed to prepare for cold weather as I crossed Iran and Turkey. Already, I regretted the peacoat I had discarded in Paris. Passing by the child on the steps, I went out to the bazaar. There, over companionable tea, I bargained successfuly for an Afghan coat with embroidered flowers outside and warm fleece inside.

As an afterthought, stopping to survey the crude jewelry offered by the child at the hotel's entrance, I also bought a folding knife for a few afghanis. The knife had a wooden handle, which appeared hand-carved. Opened up, it was a little bigger than a dinner knife, and its blade was marked with the name "Yousaf Rogers & Sons" and "No. 0 England." I doubted this item had ever been near England. It would be a good souvenir of Afghanistan, something to cut bread or cheese with on the road.

"My Afghan knife," I would remark casually, once back in California. People would look at me with respect, thinking of my farflung adventures. Tossing the knife into the pocket of my maroon jeans, along with the Alexander coin and the marble doll face, I climbed the stairs, happily heading for the hotel office to show off the new coat to my friends.

When I entered the office, the bus driver was there with them. He started towards me, reaching out to put his hand on my arm.

I didn't wait. I took out the knife and opened it. "Tell him," I asked my friends, speaking slowly and deliberately, "if he touches me, I will kill him."

I had not been in a physical fight since my last big squabble with my sister during our teens, and I had never before threatened anyone with a weapon. But I had some experience with knives. Hadn't I watched *West Side Story* on a fifth grade field trip? Hadn't I cut up chicken and diced onions and peppers on nights when it was my turn to cook at the house in East Oakland? I supposed I could do something with the knife if I had to. I just hoped the bus driver didn't have a knife too. Even more, I hoped that the presence of my gentle friends as witnesses would intimidate him.

Asim and Nabil didn't know about the attempted rape in the garden. I couldn't read my friends' faces, for most of my attention was on the bus driver. Asim translated.

There were a few awful seconds. Then the bus driver dropped his hand and backed away from me with a cowed look. It wasn't exactly shame, but he at least backed off.

A lifelong pacifist, I don't know what I really would have done if he had not stopped coming towards me. But I had taken decisive action. I had saved my own skin. There was some satisfaction in that.However, I still felt horrible. Although I loved Herat, staying there any longer was now impossible. My threat had worked for the present. But would the man try again?

I was worried too that by defending myself I had created a risk for my gentle friends. As a traveler, I could leave town, but they would have to remain in Herat, now with a new enemy I had made for them. There was no way out, I thought bitterly. My very existence as a woman posed a hazard to the people I cared about.

The bus driver was a scumbag—clearly not only a would-be rapist, but also a sniveling coward. I hoped he stayed frightened. I hoped he had very few friends to help him with his grudge. With me gone, the danger for my gentle friends might fade. At least I hoped so.

I fled Herat with the first bunch of travelers who would take me along. By now, I had become terrified of crossing Iran on my own. Like them or not, I would be much safer traveling in a group. Even if I were to be stuck with these people until Istanbul, anything was better than remaining in Herat and causing trouble for my friends.

We left the next day. Before I knew it, I was at the Iranian border.

QUARANTINE

MY NEW TRAVEL GROUP was an international cluster—English and Canadian and Australian young people—all traveling westwards. Our game plan was simple. After crossing to Iran, we would travel to Mashhad, and from there take the train all the way to Istanbul. I was greatly relieved not to have to attempt the journey alone.

We left Afghanistan together, but as I went through customs to enter Iran, things went awry. An official stopped me. Holding up my well-thumbed yellow vaccination certificate, he pointed to an entry. My cholera immunization, good for only six months, had run out, and with it, my luck. I must go to the hospital and get a new one, he said. In fact, the official indicated, I was to be taken there, right now!

It was a terrible moment. My companions exited the border station without me, and I was led away to a small room where there was a woman in a white uniform. I stood filled with fury and anxiety, while the nurse prepared the vaccine. She looked competent and the needle seemed clean. I was not squeamish about shots, even with big needles, but I was worried about being left behind. How would I get across Iran by myself if the rest of the group left Mashhad without me? I had only just met them and did not know if they would wait.

The nurse injected the vaccine in my right arm. Then she gave me the bad news. I must remain until it took effect. The authorities would keep me in quarantine for 48 hours.

The hospital turned out to be really only a clinic. It had a small ward with just three beds. Other hapless travelers already occupied two of the beds. One was Henrik, a young German, also on his way home. On the second bed sat a tall Pushtu tribesman with a long beard, long shirt, baggy pants and one of the camel-colored knit caps I remembered coveting when passing through the Khyber Pass. There was no mutual language to enable me to determine what he was doing so far from home.

Though they lacked a language in common, Henrik and the Push-tu hit it off. They were lively together, gesturing, clowning, and even hugging. I was the odd one out—female, grouchy, and a prisoner on the ward, serving my 48 hours of preventive isolation in the Shah's hospitality. The ward was as clean and modern as any luxury hotel; food was provided, but I took no pleasure in these amenities.

By the time we were set free, Henrik had acquired the Pushtu's undying friendship and his camel-colored borderlands tam-o-shanter. I had a new red bump on my arm.

GOING FIRST CLASS

I

T'S A BLUR HOW I GOT TO MASHHAD, once I was set free again, but when I found the hotel we had all expected to stay at, my travel companions were still there. We hastened out to buy train tickets and food for the journey.

Once again, I had to dodge the kids throwing stones, but at least, I would not be traveling alone across Iran.

We arranged for what some would call a special deal. Using our student cards, for everyone—Australian, English, and even I, the American—had one of these, we snagged first class tickets all the way from Mashhad to Istanbul. For the journey of some 1,841 miles, each of us would pay only $20. It was a terrific deal, except for one fact; although the journey would take at least three days, the train had no dining car. We must carry all our own food. Hastily, I left our hotel with Dee Anne, an Australian member of our travel group, to hit the market and stock up on things to eat.

At the market, old men sat behind bins and sacks of trail food, dried fruit, and hazelnuts—all foodstuffs that are light and easily carried. These men had plenty of experience. A generation ago the same supplies would have been carried on camel caravans. The men seemed old enough to have sold the same supplies even back then. I walked down the street, eyeing the other bazaar goods—baby cradles with side bars of turned wood, swinging beneath tall, stable frames, kerosene heaters with isinglass doors.

I felt I was experiencing frontier days, but after Afghanistan, Mashhad seemed like the frontier of civilization, not the reverse. The streets were paved. There were even concrete sidewalks. I had returned to the start of the West.

All of us were pretty broke. From the group's pooled food money, Dee Anne and I bought what the budget would stretch to. We purchased dried dates, canned food, and cheese, nuts, bread. We trusted that the cheese would keep without refrigeration for the three days of the train trip. We trusted the food would suffice for the five of us. There was a lot of trust in the arrangement: We trusted too that the train would run on time; we trusted that we would be able to share without squabbling. We trusted that we were going West. Everyone, we were sure, would be tired and crabby.

AND EVERYONE, ONCE ON THE TRAIN, was indeed tired and crabby. Everyone but Berry. At least that's what I'll call him. Berry hadn't boarded as part of our party. He had bought his own reserved ticket separately from us, and he had landed in our compartment. Slight and spacey, with an almost weightless elfin appearance, Berry seemed the very incarnation of a stoned-out, blissed-out hippie just wandered in off the Mendocino commune I used to visit. He looked like a dandelion. It was hard to imagine him as the product of a highly organized Social Democratic Scandinavian country, but he told us he was from Sweden.

Ordinarily, I should have been happy to have him in the compartment. Berry didn't take up much room, but the stoned part worried me. I had just been released from confinement in the Iranian hospital. I didn't want to visit any of the country's jails.

To our horror, it soon became apparent that this angelic apparition was also a drug smuggler. In Kathmandu, Michael had told us that as he made his way back to Europe he was planning to visit fellow Germans, still in jail after being caught with drugs while crossing Iran. Now we were crossing Iran with an actual dealer sharing the compartment, and short of turning Berry over to an unforgiving regime, we were stuck with him for the next 1,800 miles.

Thus, when we should have been assured of an easy journey and a soothing taste of first class, we experienced the train trip in concentrated doses, by turns, of terror, and hunger.

There were at least some comforts. By day I sat on upholstered seats, not boards. Each evening the conductor did come by to make up beds with fluffy white, wrinkle-free sheets. My nerves were shredded, but somehow—even though I was terrified—I managed to sleep well.

In fact, there was little else to do. Each day we dipped deeper into the paper bags holding the dried food, pulled sticky dates loose from one another, and eyed the shrinking wedge of cheese. Cooped-up passengers turned shrewish, carping and attacking one another, as Berry slumped serenely in his corner amid a fog of ganja smoke. Everyone was hungry.

The train rolled toward Lake Van, and we waited while it was loaded on a ferryboat. Then we crossed the sea-sized lake on a ship, train cars and all. Later, I noticed log cabins with peaked roofs standing in the Turkish mountain valleys, the gaps between their hand-hewn logs chinked with clay. Abe Lincoln could have been born in any one of them.

Cabins like these still stood in rural Virginia while I was growing up outside Washington D.C. Many were on the farms of former slaves freed after the Civil War. One such land holding was sold off while I was in high school, to create the area's first shopping mall. There was no interim development, no gradual transition. The freedman's cabin quite suddenly gave way to Northern Virginia mall and sprawl at the end of the 1950s, shortly before the first MacDonald's arrived.

I understood development could take place in an eyeblink. But passing through these barren Turkish highlands, witnessing the small holdings and high-set cabins in the wintry light, I nonetheless felt at the end of everything. The scenery seemed even more desolate than Afghanistan's. This Wild East had an untamed, lonely quality that mirrored the Wild West I read of during childhood in *Little House* books. It was far from urban amenities—Asian or Western—and probably, like the American frontier, bedeviled with blizzards and peopled with miserable homesteaders. Or so it seemed, from the padded seats of a first-class compartment filled with miserable hungry travelers.

Somewhere around here, not far to the north, the Amazons once ruled. There is even a scoffed-at legend in the classics that an Amazon queen got herself pregnant by Alexander, no doubt another tall tale from an earlier cowboy age!

I was as sour as the others. On that grim October day, passing through on the train, this didn't look like land anyone would want to conquer or settle on.

The train was late; the food ran out. The mood in the first class compartment worsened. When at last—after four days, not three—the train pulled in to the Hyderapasa Station, I staggered off, dragging the pack, and hauled myself onto the ferry for the short ride across the Bosporus to the European side.

After leaving that train, I never again saw Dee Anne or Berry or any of my other fellow travelers from that hungry journey. It was as if I had dreamed them all up in a dark nightmare.

AN HOUR LATER, I WAS AT THE GÜNGÖR, greeting Miguel, who still tended the front desk. His girlfriend Jeanette was back from the U.S. The two were clearly crazy in love, like doves. Miguel introduced me, and Jeannette nodded shyly. A glow of happiness seemed to envelop them both, but I barely paused to greet them. I was starving. I flung myself into the cafe down in the street and ordered kebabs. By the time the kebabs arrived, I had gobbled the sliced red onion and the fiery-looking pepper on the appetizer plate. Who cared if it burned? Who cared if I don't much like kebabs? I was back from India and I was starving.

Afterwards, I went next door to the Pudding Shop and stuffed myself with rice pudding.

THE NEXT DAY at the Grand Baths, skin and dirt peeled off me in sheets. Baked and scrubbed, I went to lie down in a cubicle to rest, but I could not rest. Racing to the toilet, I vomited up the misery of over 1800 miles cooped up with Berry and the others.

And then, I lay back weakly, and rested.

Cleaned up, I headed to the American Express office to pick up my mail. I found another cautiously-worded letter from my parents. An old friend who had planned to rendezvous with me in Athens, after all couldn't make it. None of it mattered: I had pulled off the trip.

BUT I DID NOT KNOW who had come back from India in my body. Europe was strange. I too was strange, different. I wandered to Crete and fell in with a group of Americans, French, and Germans camping by a potato field at the water's edge. I played tunes on my wooden recorder. I met a wandering flute man, selling his handmade pan-pipes along the beaches. We drank cloudy ouzo together. And I sang.

I sang the American songs which had echoed in my head during the travels: about the Tambourine Man, and love in the morning, and trying to be free. I sang "Where Have All the Flowers Gone" (By now I had mastered it in German). I sang about Suzanne and her place by the water. And hadn't I too gone down to a place by the water? And didn't I now see the world in a new way?

The other travelers, who sat with me around the campfire on the Greek beach, facing Africa, had not left Europe themselves. They loved my singing, and perhaps my bravery, too. And why not? I was putting my heart into it, belting the songs out of my belly. The songs spoke a new language I had not yet learned to form for myself.

But it was December now, and growing colder. It was time to find someplace to hole up for winter I thought about going back to California. It would be interesting to see Sweden, too, I thought. Eva had invited me to Berlin. Maybe I would go there. We all boarded the ferry to the mainland.

It was cold, colder now because I was so thin. After Athens, I drifted North, crossing into Yugoslavia, clutching the embroidered Afghan coat closed across my chest. Who was this assertive stranger in loose maroon jeans who now inhabited my timid 92-pound frame? Who was this intrepid world traveler? I had no idea.

237

STONES

THE GROUND BENEATH OUR HIKING boots felt gritty. Judy and I, thumbs out, stood beside some kind of unexpected Yugoslavian autobahn—four lanes, center divider, whizzing recent-make cars. It was December, with a bite in the air. I was on my way to Western Europe. I wasn't sure quite where I was going, but I knew Eva would be already back from Nepal. She had offered a place to stay temporarily. I thought about the real bathtub that her father had constructed in her apartment.

Among the travelers on Crete, I had experienced real joy, after the difficult journey back across Asia. Chest and inhibitions loosened by shots of *ouzo,* I had managed to put some passion into singing, and even to stretch to the the high notes in Gershwin's "Summertime."

But it wasn't summertime any longer and the living wasn't so easy. Our scene had dissolved into ever-splintering clusters. First a few of us traveled to Athens, pausing briefly at a cramped rooming house near Syntagma Square. True loves among us with separate return flight bookings sought individual paths northwards to their respective international airports. Lacking a return ticket, I thumbed northwards, still undecided about my destination.

To get from Greece to Germany involved passing through Yugoslavia. Other than changing dollars for Yugoslavian *dinar,* which, regrettably, could never be changed back, I recall little about the border crossing. My hitching partner, a friend from the beach, was not heading in the same direction. We hastily exchanged addresses and caught separate rides.

I soon found myself dropped off and alone in Skopje. At the youth hostel, a fresh group of young travelers were planning their own next steps northwards. I joined them. We were five—too many to hitch together—so somehow Judy, an English dancer who had been working in an Austrian ski resort, was delegated by her companions to hitchhike with me. I was happy not to have to attempt the journey alone, but she was furious at being dumped on a stranger by her companions. Scowling, she stood by the roadside as we thumbed at the city's outskirts.

Many cars passed. They always do, when you stand at the verge of a new stretch of road. Each hitch, particularly in a new country, is a world to itself, once it starts. Initially, you wait, forcing yourself to seem hopeful, trying to believe someone will eventually stop, even though that doesn't always happen. Then you stomp around a bit on the gravel or asphalt, or, if you're unlucky, in the roadside dust. You remind yourself mentally of the chocolate bar or miniature of brandy tucked away in the backpack against the ultimate emergency of being stranded. You regard the sky filling with lowering clouds, then look quickly away into the oncoming traffic, as if to turn aside the evil eye of an approaching storm. You conjure a ride.

Hitchhiking requires such magical thinking. You must somehow manage to be pure and keep faith in the goodness of strangers. Hang onto that optimism and the most dazzling encounters can occur. Lose it, even for an instant, and all hell ensues. Women who hitchhike together double that intuition, but also watch each other's backs, whether they like each other or not.

Non-hitchhikers believe that thumbing is a way to get where you are going, but this is only a portion of the truth. Serious travelers know that being on the way is the real adventure, that museums, cathedrals, fleabite *pensions* and guest house cots are merely shadowy way stations between those brilliant cusps where a new world opens, the road lies ahead, and the weather, if you are fortunate, exceeds the freezing point.

On this December day, the wind was cold, but I was outfitted for the occasion. I tugged the flaps of my Afghan coat close around me. Made of sheepskin and worn with the skin-side outwards, the coat was covered with stylized pink and blue embroidered flowers. The coat's exterior proclaimed *traveler* to the world, while the thick silvery fleece on the inside warmed my body. The coat was an inspired $11-dollar purchase. I wore my hiking boots with Vibram soles. My maroon jeans—bought in California on the other side of the world—were by now thoroughly gaping at the knees, in spite of my efforts to sew them up. Beneath them, I wore the blue cotton drawstring pants I had bought in Delhi. This blue lining peeked out at the kneecaps, but kept me comfortable in the drizzly morning. In my pack, a striped shawl, which had covered me on wooden sleeper shelves of Indian steam trains to keep the cinders off my face, now lay folded and ready for duty as European hostel bedding. Altogether, in various currencies which now included Yugoslavian *dinar*, I had about $50 left, not counting the spurious Alexander coin.

Watching my breath emerge as white puffs into the morning air, I performed the hitchhiker's shuffle, taking small steps to keep warm while keeping the backpack steadied upright against my leg so as to be ready to pound after a stopping vehicle, the second its brake lights showed.

Thus poised, I noticed that the fleece coat from the Herat bazaar, cured with an Afghan process I have since heard criticized, had a strong animal smell as it warmed around me, like some kind of clan talisman or fetish. *Sheep-clan girl?* Reaching into the pocket, I fingered a Tibetan coin with a hole in the middle I had discovered in a Himalayan village while ducking behind a bush to find a place to pee. I could feel, too, clicking against the coin, the cool surface of the tiny carved marble doll-face, bought in the Istanbul bazaar. I fished it out and examined it again: a female visage white and calm and moonfaced, perhaps that of a doll, or perhaps a goddess, emblematic of a serenity I was not feeling at the moment.

Judy shifted from foot to foot, still scowling, as the morning brightened slightly and drivers played their usual tricks.

We heard brakes. A driver pulled off a hundred yards up the road.

"A ride!" Snatching our heavy packs, we dashed up the road. As we neared, the driver peeled off, making a universal obscene gesture we could just see through the car's teensy back window. Deflated, we put down the packs again on the road's shoulder. It was not turning out to be a good day for magic.

I don't recall how long I and my unwilling companion stood breathing out white puffs into the morning air while the children of Marshal Tito's economic miracle flashed past us down the parkway. Judy was thawing a bit. She told of the soups she learned to make from the Austrian housewife she worked for at the ski resort. A little of this, a little of that and the result was amazing. Delicious. We stood on the shoulder talking of hot soup. We had no food.

And then, miraculously, two boys in an improbable red sports car stopped for us. They were cheerful. They were going our way. Judy and I looked at each other, and with intuition born of total dependence, we both *knew* that they were totally on the level, as we say now, *good people*. Surprised and gratified, we crammed ourselves and the packs into the car behind the front passenger seats. It was a tight squeeze—more of a luggage boot than an actual back seat, but we were on our way.

Heading northeastwards from Skopje, the highway curved inland, as if bracing for a run up the long flat center of the Yugoslavian heartland. Judy and I, having first peered at the country from the roadside, as supplicants, were now sailing along its main artery. The low clouds lifted a bit, and as the last suburbs gave way to open countryside, I began to think we might have a bright day, after all.

I had expected to catch a ride from old men in a truck carrying pitchforks. These boys in their snappy sports car didn't fit the Dogpatch image I had of Yugoslavia. But then, the four-lane freeway was a surprise, too. The boys seemed confident and hospitable. Both were almost preppy, their well-cut dark hair set off by soft vee-neck wool sweaters in gentle primary colors. The south of this country must be booming if locals drove this kind of car and dressed this way.

English Judy knew some German from her work in Austria and I had picked up a little from other student travelers. So we could talk with our benefactors. We stumbled along in German, augmenting it with gestures and a word or two of English.

We were in their neck of the woods now, guests so-to-speak, in their country. By word and gesture the boys conveyed that they wanted to share it with us. Would we like to stop and sample local cooking? They knew a restaurant. It was not to be a free meal, but at least a chance to experience something special at a modest price in their hometown. The town lay just up the road.

I had never been in Yugoslavia before, and my knowledge of the country was sketchy. I knew that World War I began here after an Austrian archduke's assassination, that Marshal Tito, now in charge, had been a partisan in World War II and didn't follow the Moscow line. I knew that Yugoslavians drank apricot brandy called *slivovitz*. *What did they eat?*

Frankly, I was hungry. Travel with the scrap of chocolate and maybe some *feta* cheese and bread tucked away with an Afghan knife to cut it might sound romantic, but after days on the road, it was all gone. After the wait in the drizzle and chill by the roadside, the idea of a cheap restaurant meal sounded wonderful.

Food hadn't been a high point of the journey back from Kathmandu. After a diet of *kebabs*, *pilaf*, and mystery meat scraps in Afghanistan, I had crossed to Iran. In Mashhad, the holy town of Shiite Islam, where the children threw stones at us, I had booked a train ticket westward, and eaten *kebabs* again, grilled ground meat on a stick.

I recalled how before boarding in Masshad, the group of us had pooled funds to purchase caravan food at the bazaar for the train journey to Istanbul—dried mulberries, filberts and other desiccated substances in a primordial Silk Road trail mix. A vendor in a long beard had weighed it out into a scale dangling from a chain, and poured it into a bag. I remembered how the bearded provisioner shoveled heavy black dates out of a barrel for us—all we could afford. But these supplies had turned out to be insufficient. When mealtime came on the train, the results of our bazaar foraging seemed like a scanty handful of seeds.

When we finally pulled into the Istanbul station on the Asian side of the Bosporus, I was starving. But I was so broke, dinner had been *kebabs*, again. It seemed as if a single specialty had dominated all Eastern kitchens since the India border. This inevitable dish, either grilled or patted into narrow greasy loaves, was the one food I had not learned to like.

I joyfully remembered other foods sampled along the way: delicate puddings in Istanbul, mutton chunks heaped on rice in an Afghan eatery, deep-fried surgary desserts whose names changed slightly from country to country, tea slurped with sugar or candy lumps, mushy soup pounded with a mallet in Iran, flattened bread hot from beehive ovens, *dahl*, *chai*, curries with homemade cheese. There had been vegetable sandwiches in New Delhi; sweetened yogurt *lassi* near the Golden Temple in Amritsar and Tibetan *momos*, like giant *matzoh* balls, in the Himalayan foothills.

Too often, though, all I could get was *kebabs*. Unhappily, I recalled the variants: *kebabs* with mint, *kebabs* garnished with a piquant pointy green pepper which looked like a *jalapeño*, *kebabs* on the ferry boat along the Black Sea from Istanbul to Trabzon, *kebabs* with *pilaf*. Like green eggs and ham in the children's book, these meaty oblongs were repeatedly offered and seldom welcome. They had come to represent the hardships of travel. *Kebabs* were the tradeoffs for mobility, the fast food of Asia. And no, I did not like them.

After weeks of such limited fare, a national specialty sounded like a real treat. With happy gestures, we signaled to the boys: *Yes, of course we will stop.*

And stop we did. But while Skopje was a buzzing city of factory workers with small cars scooting along its freeway, the young men's hometown was very different. The village had no railyards, factories, or four-lane throughways. Its streets were steep and the buildings built of stones. These were not masked under whitewashed facades as in the Greek Islands. Instead individual stones appeared to be piled one atop another in precarious balance. What should have been solid structural walls in the village reminded me instead of those heaped-rock fences which partition one hardscrabble New England farm from another. In New England, glacier-battered rocks are pried up from flinty fields like teeth from a crocodile's jaws, and stone walls are said to make good neighbors, but don't. Here, it appeared that inhabitants had heaved up stones over centuries until a town emerged, and perhaps they had done this not once, but many times over. It was as if the rocks themselves resisted joining into stable units. I felt unnerved by all that balanced mineral weight. I began to have misgivings about stopping.

Unlike the bustling and assertive Greek housewives, the townswomen moved leadenly along the cobbles, for the road in the village was also built of stones. The women walked with heads down and backs bent. They wore black like the Greek village women, but here I heard no spirited conversations. Street life included no bickering out of windows and doorways as in Iran. No women mobbed me in the street, begging for news of the West. No one even demanded how many babies I had. We travelers seemed invisible, ghosts in a ghostly place.

Is this because I have reached Europe? I wondered. Then, unexpectedly, we passed a mosque, and I was again disoriented. This *was* Europe, wasn't it?

The town felt ancient, mossy, drab, constricted. Entering the restaurant involved even more constriction. We climbed down uneven steps to a place which seemed to be sinking below street level beneath the weight of piled stones.

This subterranean restaurant was tiny. A small oilcloth covered a small table. There was not enough room for all our post-adolescent legs. The place was formal compared to the restaurants I had encountered in Asia and in Greece. That is, we were not allowed to go into the kitchen to see the food cooking and choose what we wanted. Instead, our hosts ordered, in a language I couldn't understand. Then, we four sat at the small table and struggled to recall enough German words to make small talk.

And we waited. During the wait, the length of the journey ahead of me into the deepening winter seemed, too, to sink in, and I was impatient, daunted.

It was a long wait. Did the young men's cheery talk peter out? Eventually someone emerged from the kitchen carrying loaded dishes. Glancing hopefully at my steaming plate, I glimpsed two long, brown, greasy turd-like objects, recognizable to any traveler as the generic food of Middle Eastern hard-time hamlets.

More *kebabs!*

I COULD TELL you a lot more about that journey into Europe, about the icy windswept plain to the North and the two jolly-seeming fat men who wouldn't let Judy and me out of their car until the Afghan knife was produced and shown, about the communist architect who took us to a communist canteen where the cheer was good and the food international, about walking through most of Belgrade, packs on our backs, cursing the bus conductor who would not tell us the right stop to get off the bus.

I could tell about the extremely proper evening with students in the Maribor, who took us in as night fell in a town where no one, no one at all, would give us a lift: How we all bumbled and giggled in broken German and afterwards I fell asleep musing about 19th-century student penury on a narrow couch straight out of a Dostoyevsky novel. Or about walking to the edge of Maribor in the morning, where Judy and I stationed ourselves beside the road to catch a ride into Austria. Where there was little traffic and no one stopped.

Finally, giving up all hope of a ride, we began to walk up the road, with our packs on our backs, climbing the Alpine pass on foot, until a driver ashamed to pass us by pulled over and took us.

In a warm car at last, I sank in silence. I was headed north, although I didn't really know where I was going. I had no airplane ticket home. I thought about Sweden, but that still seemed impossible. Berlin then? The car sped on into Austria.

I remember hot tea with brandy at a rural *gasthaus,* while a Father Christmas accompanied by a deformed *grampus* worked the block outside, the two carrying treats and coals respectively for local children.

In Vienna, Judy and I were denied refuge at the former bomb shelter which doubled as a youth hostel. The police refused us lodging at the jail, so we slept in the train station until a fierce old woman—probably one of those who had been carted off by the Russians to shovel coal after World War II—rousted us with curses from the hard station benches in the morning. I remember steamy milk in a German train station, after a night in the station's mission for wayfaring transients.

I could tell such stories, but the heart of this final leg of that hungry journey—seen across the intervening decades—lies in the village where we stopped to eat the local specialty with the boys driving home to their birthplace—a village then in Yugoslavia. My mind goes back again and again to that tiny place with its Ottoman past and plastered mosque, where buildings seemed made of wayward stones like those left tumbled haphazardly around a wintry beach after an unusually vigorous tide.

Like a tide too, Islam had run up onto continental Europe, arriving by the same route I had traveled. Later it receded, leaving pools of faith in places like this village.

The cheerful boys had offered us a taste of their town and, like good Muslims, the hospitality of their castle, a red sports car. I had to feel the goodwill of these kind companions as they offered familiar food in hospitality and the kinship of a communal meal. I might not like the taste of *kebabs*, but I was moved.

And I was also hungry. Of course I ate them.

And unbeknownst to any of us, this menu gave foreboding of the contradictions, rifts and ruin soon to come into this no-man's-land of piled stones. For Christians and Muslims were to struggle again, and soon, over the broken-up remainders of empires established here by conquerers from West and East.

Villages survive empires. Although Yugoslavia, the nation, exists no more, the village I stopped in might remain. Or if destroyed, it might have been rebuilt—the stones piled up again. I would like to think that.

THE SILK ROAD was never a single thoroughfare leading East or West, but rather a skein of trade routes. Sometimes the routes spawned great cities at the hubs where dusty trails converged. More often places along the way were merely pausing spots, where, as later on the American frontier, campfires might be lit and livestock bedded down. I had traveled pieces of the Road and longed to see the others. But it was in this stony village that I truly reached the Silk Road's end. At least for me back then it was the end.

Judy and I would become friends. Later she would hitch back to England and eventually manage to cross Asia overland herself to settle in Australia. The last I heard, she was studying *Tae Kwan Do* in Perth.

Eventually, still carrying my own pack and the Alexander coin, I would make my way back to California. The oversized Afghan jackknife would have to fly separately in the plane's cargo belly. Blades that size had no business in an aircraft cabin, airline officials would scold me at the check-in counter as the knife, rattling in the two-by-three foot carton they provided, disappeared up the conveyor belt. Later, at home in California, I would use it for spreading peanut butter. The long steel blade, as I expected, reaches well into deep jars. Its presence in my kitchen reminds me that the world has gotten smaller.

Kebabs are a reminder of this too. Like me, they traveled along the Silk Road, crossing cultural and ethnic lines. *Kebabs* are now found in so many places it is hard to tell where they originated. Perhaps they were invented on the road itself, as a make-do recipe fixed over a frugal campfire. They reached Europe, as I had, or perhaps originated there, like my own ancestors. It's possible *kebabs* even migrated onward to America as hamburgers, losing their sticks in transit.

I'd like to think that too.

A NEW ADVENTURE

BUT I DID NOT GO HOME just yet. A few days after leaving Yugoslavia, I stood outside the door of Eva's fourth-floor walkup in Kreutzberg near the Berlin Wall. Eva opened the door. Quickly, my friend poured water into the kettle. She put coffee beans in her electric grinder and a filter in her Melitta. She set out cups.

There was a lot to tell her about.

But before I could begin, and because she had just completed a similar journey, and knew of my likely hunger, Eva said something truly marvelous: "There's a bakery downstairs."

We tromped down the four flights to get pastries to go with our coffee. At the street-level *bäckerei*, we picked out glazed bars with apricot and cranberry, Viennese pastries I had learned to call Danish in California, jam-filled doughnuts topped with confectioners sugar known as *Berliners* elsewhere but not here in Berlin, and other sweets that I had no names for yet in any language. The lady behind the counter assembled our choices into a package that immediately began to give off the scent of sugar and fruit. Sniffing the air, I realized my European adventure was already under way.

We started back up the stairs to Eva's *wohnung*. On the first landing, carefully shifting the brimming package, Eva pointed out a bulky 19th-century electrical switch. The hall lights were all on timers, she explained, and each landing had a switch just like this one. In the evening, I must hit the switch at every landing, or the lights would go out, leaving me to stumble up the stairs in the dark.

It wasn't dark yet, but I banged on the massive light switch anyway to try it out. Somewhere above, the hall lights came on. They weren't exactly bright ones, but in my delight at mastering this small survival skill, I forgot to ask Eva about the bathtub.

A TIME FOR THANKS

ALTHOUGH THIS ADVENTURE began as a woman's solo journey, East, the account of that journey, could not have come to be without the help of a multitude. Thank you all, especially fellow members of the Rich and Famous Writing Group: Margaret Murray, Shirley Barger, Daniel Cetinich, and Nancy Webb. Thanks also to Judith Pierce Rosenberg, Paula Swenson, Nancy Pringle, Mary White, Cindy Sloan, Mary and Eddie Fitzgerald, and Kay Swendseid who read, listened, or offered encouragement along the way. I am particularly grateful to Margaret C. Murray at WriteWords Press, who has addressed this project throughout with a most nurturing vision of her role as publisher.

My books have long developing times, and this one's was unusually long. Thanks to the late Vilem Kriz, whose photography lessons inspired me, and who told us that even my photographic idol, Dorothea Lange, who looked into the souls of ordinary people, produced negatives that were faint and needed long developing times.

Thanks also to Ruth Buck Lorenzen, my late aunt, who set an example by joyfully leading the way West. Thanks to other travelers, past and present, especially to Eva Renckly, who not only saved my life, but also shared memories, as well as to Linda Wharton, and to the many other companions on the road whose names I no longer possess or cannot include, but who are nonetheless riveted in my memory.

Grateful appreciation is due also to all the travel writers who forged pathways to far-off places and impossible journeys, especially to the late Patrick Leigh Fermor and as the still very alive and kicking Mary Morris, Brad Newsham, Tim Cahill, Jeff Greenwald, Jonathan Raban, and Paul Theroux. Your writing has schooled me about the close connections between physical adventure and literature.

Special thanks to Douglas Brown, wherever you are now. You wrote the book that got me going and kept me safer on the road. Thanks also to Katherine Pennavaria and CuChullaine O'Reilly for rediscovering Overland to India.

Thanks to Joel Friedlander, Pete Masterson, and Don Monkerud for valuable wisdom on the craft of putting books together.

Thanks to the McHenry Library at the University of California, at Santa Cruz, whose shelves provided Babur's autobiography, a treasure in the history of Afghanistan. Thanks also to the Santa Cruz County Public Library, as well as numerous online resources which make modern fact-checking less of a nightmare. Since the Buck always stops here, I claim for my own any errors that remain.

Finally, thanks to my husband, Lee, who cheerfully (again!) shared our kitchen with the growing manuscript, offered unswerving loyalty throughout a multi-year writing project, and made astute comments which contributed to the final version.

It's one thing to set out to make a journey by yourself, another to tally up those who helped you build the book afterwards. Thank you. You are all my heros.

ABOUT THE AUTHOR

Following her return to California, Shelley Buck became a founding editor of the feminist news syndicate, Her Say, now archived at Harvard University. She has taught writing at colleges in the San Francisco Bay Area and currently edits ePícaro.com—an online journal of travel narratives. Her first book, *Floating Point*, chronicles life aboard a boat in the San Francisco Bay. When not breakfasting with white-faced monkeys in Costa Rica, or hitchiking through the Khyber Pass, she lives with her family in California's Santa Cruz Mountains. You can connect to Shelley at www.ShelleyBuck.com

CPSIA information can be obtained
at www.ICGtesting.com
Printed in the USA
FSOW01n1123220615
8141FS